D1070567

WITHDRAWN

Berlin 2000

The Center of Europe

David Tieman Doud

University Press of America, Inc.
Lanham • New York • London

Copyright © 1995 by
University Press of America,® Inc.
4720 Boston Way
Lanham, Maryland 20706

3 Henrietta Street
London, WC2E 8LU England

All rights reserved
Printed in the United States of America
British Cataloging in Publication Information Available

Library of Congress Cataloging-in-Publication Data

Doud, David Tieman.
Berlin 2000 : the center of Europe / David Tieman Doud.
        p.   cm.
        Includes index.
1. Berlin (Germany)--Politics and government--1990-. 2. Social
integration--Germany--Berlin. 3. Berlin (Germany)--Ethnic relations.
4. Berlin (Germany)--Economic conditions. 5. Europe--Economic
                integrations.   I. Title.
DD881.D68   1995   943.1'550879--dc20   95-31747 CIP

ISBN 0-7618-0067-0 (cloth: alk ppr.)

⊖™The paper used in this publication meets the minimum
requirements of American National Standard for Information
Sciences—Permanence of Paper for Printed Library Materials,
ANSI Z39.48—1984

DD
881
.D68
1995

071196-4356H

To my great, great, great Grandparents:
Herman Imanuel Volcmar Schultz
(born June, 1821, in Berlin, Prussia)
and Antonia Frederike Henning
(born May 19, 1831, in Stettin, Prussia)
who were married in 1856
and immigrated to the United States in June, 1857
and adopted the name Adolphus Jackson

Christo and Jeanne-Claude: Wrapped Reichstag, Berlin, 1971-95
© Christo, Photo: Wolfgang Volz

Contents

Contents

Illustrations and Maps

Illustrations

Maps

Preface

"We stand together where Europe's heart was cut in half and celebrate unity," said President Clinton on July 11, 1994, at Europe's symbol of unity, the Brandenburg Gate, "Nichts wird uns aufhalten, alles ist moeglich, Berlin ist frei" (Nothing will stop us, everything is possible, Berlin is free). Clinton was the first American President to come to the German capital since the fall of the Berlin Wall.

In 1945, Harry Truman toured the rubble of bombed-out Berlin and vowed to rebuild Europe. John Kennedy came in 1967 to reaffirm American resolve to keep Berlin free, and later, in 1987, Ronald Reagan commanded Gorbachev to "tear down the Wall." Like those who came before him, Clinton's visit also ushered in a new era. In a deeply symbolic sign of the times and, by no coincidence, on the same day that President Clinton was making his historic speech at the gate, Germany's Constitutional Court ruled that German troops could join in military missions outside the NATO area. Previously, the West German Constitution had barred the Army from operating beyond the country's borders, except when acting in defense of NATO.

Clinton was delighted to hear of the German Court's decision. At a joint press conference in Berlin with Chancellor Kohl, Clinton stated: "I am completely comfortable with the decision because the leadership of Germany, the conduct of Germany, because of the role Germany has played in the creation of Europe. Germany does not merely have the largest population in Europe, it was the leader in pushing for the integration of Europe." This decision opens the door for Germans to play a global role for the first time since World War II.

What is the post-Cold War, reunited Germany like? With whom is the United States forming, in Clinton's words, a "unique partnership" in Europe? What is the meaning of the resurgence of anti-Semitism and violence against foreigners? This book will address these questions and then attempt to address another: What will Berlin be like in the 21st Century?

The historic decision by Germany's Constitutional Court was only one symbolic sign of the times. There were also other forces at work. For instance, before President Clinton and Chancellor Kohl walked through the Brandenburg Gate, they met with European Union President Jacques Delors in Germany's future national parliament, the Reichstag. The theme of their discussion was the "deepening and widening of the transatlantic community," according to Chancellor Kohl. The three politicians believe that this must involve a strong bilateral relationship between the U.S. and the E.U., expanding eastward under German leadership. Germany, with Berlin as its locomotive, is the center of Europe. Germany is also the most powerful and influential European Union member, actively lobbying for an expanded, pan-European E.U. Therefore, Clinton, like his predecessors, chooses Germany to be the United States' partner in Europe. Clinton emphasized this choice in Berlin, the largest urban center between Paris and Moscow.

One theme of this book is that the German government's move back to its traditional center in Berlin is symbolic of a return to the country's Prussian roots. Germany was united under Prussian leadership in 1871; the country fought its wars and built its economy from Berlin. Only because of the artificial division of Germany during the Cold War did this center of activity cease to develop. Now it is the biggest construction site on the continent. It will be interesting to explore the ways in which the Germans are preparing themselves for a resurgence of their Prussian regional tradition in Northern Europe as the European Union expands to the East.

President Clinton didn't just come to Berlin to lobby for stronger German leadership. His visit marked the end of an era for other reasons too. Earlier in the day, on July 11, 1994, Clinton presided over the ceremony deactivating the U.S. Army's Berlin brigade, which was organized in 1945 to oversee the U.S. military mission in Berlin. With the brigade's lowered American flag in hand, Clinton bade farewell to the last thousand troops. "We are marking the end of a half-century of sacrifice on freedom's frontier," the President said. "America salutes you. Mission accomplished." Also, as noted by the *Washington Post's* deputy editorial page editor, Stephen S. Rosenfeld, Clinton recognizes a possible electoral advantage in cultivating a country of 58 million American cousins, since German-Americans are the largest ethnic group in America. Later in this book, I will focus on the withdrawal of the Allied Powers, including the Russians, and how the Germans reacted.

Now that the Allied withdrawal is complete, a new, unified mission is just beginning for the reunited Germany. But the citizenry is skeptical and passive. A 1994 public opinion poll conducted by a leading polling organization, the Emnid Institute, showed that less than half of West Germans, and fewer than one fifth of East Germans favor their troops' participation in international operations, including United Nations missions. Germans recognize that the days of abstaining from military involvement in world affairs while at the same time economically dominating the continent are over. However, they are unsure of their new role, as are some anxious neighbors.

German Chancellor Helmut Kohl knows his people and their fears. Being the skillful politician that he is, he had to show President Clinton who's boss. In response to President Clinton's call for "the full range of Germany's capacities to lead," he immediately followed up Clinton's remarks by telling his leery people: "It is not as if a new mood has broken out that says, 'Germans to the front!' " Is Kohl—at four terms the longest-serving head of state in the world—the new leader of Europe? Will the champion of German reunification also go down in history as the wise statesman who, like Frederick the Great, buffered the interests of East and West, as Russians and Americans openly courted his country's partnership? Just ask Yeltsin who his man in Europe is; we already know who Clinton's is.

But why are Germans themselves reluctant to take the lead? In decades past, the Germans would have loved to fill such a role. They fought two world wars in this century in the name of achieving continental dominance. Partly, German uncertainty and lack of self-confidence are a product of their national identity crisis. They are in shock from the overnight reunification and the responsibilities their position in the center of Europe imposes upon them. One paradox is that most Germans, so involved in the transformations of their everyday life, don't even recognize their own influence and power. This book will attempt to offer insight into how difficult and unprecedented those transformations are.

One of the factors that prevents the Germans from taking a leadership role is the very history of the 20th century. Chiefly because of the devastating defeats suffered in 1918 and 1945, German leaders are slow in picking up the mantle of leadership. In this writer's view, it is less a function of their leaders' unwillingness than of the public's uncertainty and identity crisis (as illustrated by Chancellor Kohl's introduction of German troops into Somalia and Bosnia AWACS missions without approval of the parliament and the German Constitutional Court's subsequent ruling that future operations must be made with a parliamentary majority on a case-by-case basis, as well as Germany's active behind-the-scenes lobbying for U.N. Security Council membership). Kohl is bringing his country along, slowly but surely. This book will first analyze the decision to move the government back to Berlin, then will look at the forces dividing Germans. In conclusion, I will have created a sort of projection, or fantasy if you will: It is the year 2000 in Berlin, and I am walking in the German capital. From inside the committee rooms, from conversations with representatives will emerge a portrait of a German agenda for the future—a supranational European Union in which Germany's reunification problems have abated and the country's dominant role in Europe has been secured.

Acknowledgments

With special thanks to Klaus Rettel, who made the experience I share possible. Also, in recognition of the significant contributions by Frank Zitka, my family, and all my other friends along the way.

Gedacht
wir
werden
wir
gemacht

Savignyplatz train station Berlin

Idee und Erfahrung werden in der Mitte nie
zusammentreffen. Zu vereinigen sind sie nur
durch Kunst und Tat.

— Wolfgang Goethe

Der Gedanke, den wir gedacht, ist eine solche
Seele, und er laesst uns keine Ruhe, bis wir ihm
seinen Leib gegegeben, bis wir ihn zur sinnlichen
Erscheinung gefoerdert. Der Gedanke will Tat,
das Wort will Fleisch werden.

— Heinrich Heine

Introduction

My first visit to Berlin in 1987 stirred fascination and guilt, the kind of guilt you feel on discovering your ignorance about something you believe fundamentally important. Back then, my biggest concerns in life were winning my next high school tennis match and finding the right date for the senior prom. Coming to Berlin, with only a foggy idea of what the place was even about, I was amazed by the city's siege.

I didn't go to Berlin because I was a sociologist or political scientist or journalist. I went to Berlin because I was in love with a Berliner. I first arrived in Duesseldorf, where my girlfriend Helga's grandparents moved from what today is Poland after World War II. Like millions of others, they were uprooted from their homeland.[1] We visited Helga's relatives for a few days before venturing to Berlin, literally a trip into enemy territory.

All of her relatives expressed reluctance, including her aunt, uncle and cousins, about letting us attempt the journey alone. I couldn't understand this. We were both adults and Helga had traveled there with her parents many times before. But her relatives kept emphasizing the risks, repeatedly warning us that with one wrong move we could end up in communist hands.

Driving through the last West German post, I was immediately aware that there were no exits on this highway, only on ramps. On both sides of the freeway were seemingly endless fields. They appeared lifeless. There were no houses, no tractors working the fields, nothing but barren land.

Like many West Germans, Helga thrives on the speed and challenge of autobahn driving. But she was driving cautiously—carefully obeying the 100 km/h speed limit—not by choice but out of necessity occasioned by plentiful potholes, some crater-like enough to break a car's suspension. Helga sat up straight and paid close attention to the road. I became especially alarmed as we drove past a car accident. Two cars were overturned in the ditch, but there was no emergency aid. Other cars had pulled over to help, but from my car window it looked like nothing was being done. Could anyone call for help? Where? Was there even a hospital in the area where the injured could be taken? All of these questions heightened my attention. As we moved through the accident scene, at my urging we slowed down and drove even more cautiously.

As Helga and I approached Berlin, we encountered more and more guard towers. The towers were always centrally located and recognizable by their mushroom appearance on the horizon. Crossing the river checkpoint, I was fascinated by the security setup. It was like visiting a medieval castle.

The East German checkpoint was drab and foreboding. I was aware that Helga was ill-at-ease. She was clearly nervous and obedient to everything said to her by the guards, automatically answering questions in a cold voice.

The next stop was the Allied checkpoint, where Helga seemed to loosen up a little. Meanwhile, I was like a little boy, fascinated by everything. The most incredible part of my first visit was a short trip to the Eastern sector of the city. I was fascinated by West Berlin's status, surrounded by communism and Soviet military divisions. Upon our departure I committed myself to studying more about Berlin's precarious situation. Little did I know that within three years, I would return to Berlin, work for the Germans, and rediscover Berlin as the emerging center of liberated Europe.

During my final year of college, on the triumphant day of November 9th, 1989, I was distracted from memorizing chemical formulas by the fall of the Berlin Wall. It wasn't just a temporary distraction. Seeing those crowds dance and chisel away the Wall at Berlin's Brandenburg Gate changed me. With my B.A. in hand, I abandoned my medical school plans, eager to return to see the New Europe first hand.

When I arrived in Germany in the summer of 1990, I didn't speak the language. After I got to Berlin, I worked as a waiter for the U.S. Army's Non-Commissioned Officers Club in order to survive and pay for intensive language courses.

Working for Americans was odd because I worked inside a familiar bubble. After traveling halfway around the world, curious to experience German culture, I found myself getting paid in U.S. dollars and working for my own countrymen.

If it weren't for my German friends, my girlfriend in particular, I could have closed myself off from Germany altogether and lived a sheltered life, eating all my meals at Burger King, Baskin Robbins, and the local pizza joint on the base. These were surreal days, and because I wanted to immerse myself in another place, and another culture, I proceeded to do just that.

After I learned some German and gained a little more confidence, I put all my efforts toward getting a job working for the Germans. But I kept running into walls. After repeated brush-offs and few returned phone calls, I decided it was time to go home. As much as I wanted to stay in

Berlin, I did not want to continue working for the U.S. Army. After three months of trying to find a job, I felt my time was up and that I should go home.

But then came the historic day, June 20, 1991, when the German parliament voted to return the government to Berlin. In the midst of my uncertainty and insecurity, I found myself in this unfamiliar and vibrant city, where although the Wall had fallen, the city was still precariously divided and occupied. My friends and I hardly ever traveled to the East. Now Berlin was to be the hub around which Germany would unite itself. It was again going to be the full working German capital and possibly the future center for the New Europe.

The news encouraged me to stay. My chances for finding a job must be improving I told myself. The Bundestag vote for Berlin would change this place and its people. And so, together with my growing curiosity about the culture and society in transition, I redoubled my efforts. I went back to every German-American institution and think tank.

I allotted myself another sixty days to find a position. The fifty-eighth day arrived and I was still out of work and low on both promise and money. I booked a one-way flight home. But on the fifty-ninth day, after placing one last desperate call, I received word of my interview for an eight-week internship in the Berlin parliament. I was excited about what this position could mean for me, and what I would be able to learn about the city. Within two weeks, I was working in the central nerve cell of the new German capital's political scene, in the Berlin state parliament.

---

1   According to the German Information Center in New York, a total of 16,558,000 Germans were displaced, including 9,303,000 from East Prussia, East Pommerania, East Brandenburg, and Silesia, 3,000,000 from Sudetenland, 120,000 from Memel, 380,000 from the free city of Danzig, 1,290,000 of Volksdeutsche in Poland without wartime colonizers, 120,000 colonists transferred from the Baltic States, 200,000 from Bessarabia, Dobruja, Bukovina, 450,000 Volksdeutsche in Slovakia and Bohemia-Moravia, 600,000 from Hungary, 595,000 from Romania, and 510,000 from Yugoslavia, with estimated deaths owing to flight, expulsion or deportation to forced labor of 2,120,000. Also, it is estimated that more than two million Germans were able to remain in the home territories, but from 1950 to 1976 approximately one million Germans were allowed to emigrate to Austria, East and West Germany.

Political map of Europe, 1994

xviii

Part One

Moving the Government
Back to Berlin

Chapter 1

Vote for Berlin

On June 20, 1991, Germany's lower house, the Bundestag, voted to move the German government back to Berlin. In a historically close 337 to 320 vote for *"die Vollendung der Einheit Deutschlands"* (the completion of German unification), it was agreed that the functional working conditions for the German parliament should be ready in Berlin within four years, and that within 10 to 12 years, the complete working conditions for both the parliament and executive chancellery in Berlin will be achieved.[1]

With the fall of the Berlin Wall and the end of the Cold War, Europe is free of the shackles of superpower conflict. Traditions that were smothered by the Cold War in Europe are resurfacing. The vote for Berlin moves Germany's emphasis back to its unifying power center in the heart of Central Europe.

Before the founding of Germany in 1871, Berlin had been the capital of the Prussian kingdom since the seventeenth century, through which German unification was forged in 1871.[2] Berlin was the capital of the German Kaiser Reich from 1871 to 1918 and the capital of the German Weimar Republic from 1919 to 1932. Berlin was also the capital of the Third Reich from 1933 to 1945.

After the Soviet Union invaded and defeated Berlin and the Third Reich capitulated in 1945, Berlin was later divided into four sectors, each controlled by one of the Allies. Half of Berlin went to the Soviets, including the heart of downtown, while the other half was divided in three parts among the American, French and British Allies.[3]

Later, in 1949, East Berlin was named the capital of the German Democratic Republic (East Germany). Meanwhile, the West German government took up provincial housing in Bonn. Despite Berlin's isolation and division during the Cold War, Berlin was always the symbolic German capital. During the height of Germany's division, politicians promised that as soon as the Cold War ended, and Germany was reunited, the capital would be moved back to Berlin.

Upon reunification Berliners actively campaigned to move the capital back to Germany's traditional center. Because of Berlin's isolation in the middle of the former East Germany, many Germans will admit that they never thought it would happen. But indeed, less than two years after the triumphant collapse of the Wall and communism, a unified German people represented in a democratically elected parliament voted by a narrow margin for their capital to be returned to its traditional place. As an interesting side note, on June 19, 1991, the Bundestag voted against putting the capital vote for Berlin or Bonn to a public referendum.

Proponents hail the decision to move to the heart of the former East Germany as a major step for healing the scars of Germany's decade-long division, an essential investment in the collapsed Eastern economy and a confident re-assertion of Germany's place in the center of Europe.

The German government's days of provincial exile in Bonn are over. In some ways, the decision to move the German government back to the former Prussian capital symbolizes the completion of the end of World War II because the last time Berlin was Germany's capital, the German government was chased out of Berlin, bitterly defeated and occupied by four foreign nations. The Bundestag voted for Bonn to be West Germany's capital in 1949.[4] It should be pointed out that Germany could not move the government back to Berlin because of the Allied occupation of the city under the Allied Powers' command. Now, the German capital has moved back home again. But back home to what?

The days of Konrad Adenauer's West Germany are generally over. Adenauer was the first West German Chancellor and Christian Democratic Union Chairman from 1946 to 1966. Adenauer's conviction that the only hope for a free Germany was Germany's close association with Western Europe was carried forward, but Adenauer's choice of the North-Rhine Westphalia capital of Bonn was not. The European Union is expanding eastward too, as we will see.

Adenauer favored Bonn not only because his home town, Rhoendorf, was on the opposite bank of the Rhine but also because he believed the quaint character of Bonn was the appropriate image for Germany's post-war government. Adenauer, born in 1876, was a Rhinelander who felt that the customs of his birthplace were superior to Prussian traditions and ideals of the Prussian state. After World War 1, for example, Adenauer proposed the separation of the Rhineland and other western German provinces from Prussia, by far the biggest state of the German Reich.

Later, after World War II, Adenauer's skepticism toward Prussia and its traditional Berlin capital continued. Said Adenauer: "As we started in 1949 with the rebuilding of Germany, then I purposely selected a small German capital, namely Bonn, and not only because Berlin wasn't reachable, rather because political decisions mature better in the quiet atmosphere of a small city than in the hectic atmosphere of the big city."[5]

Berlin certainly is not a quiet city, and no longer will the Soviet threat force Germany to focus solely on Western Europe, which prompts the question: What other influences will Germany's move back to the heart of Europe have? One result will be Germany's renewed emphasis on and interest in Central Europe.

Perhaps we can also gain some insight into what the vote for Berlin means by reviewing the speeches by Germany's most notable leaders in the passionate 11-hour televised Bundestag debate about whether to move the capital to Berlin. Some representatives argued for resisting the temptations of moving their capital away from its secure Western footing, fearing the uncertainty of breaking with their stronghold in the West. Others recalled the promise of the government to return to Berlin as soon as possible—apparently irrespective of what the consequences might be.

On that historic day, I was glued to the television. Every German parliamentarian had the opportunity to take an unlimited amount of speaking time to discuss his or her views on the issue. Following are excerpts from that debate:[6]

Willy Brandt (Social Democratic Party):

> My esteemed colleagues, who would want to dispute that it is pleasant to live and work on the Rhine? But it is not a question of our well-being and the amenities of everyday life. It is a question of setting a course for the nation. . . . Germany will not remain on the Eastern edge of the West, but rather it will be the new center of Europe. Berlin is, indeed, well-placed in both directions, North-South and East-West. Germany does not need a capital solely for cocktail parties.

Hans-Dietrich Genscher (Free Democratic Party):

It is true: it is not a decision between two cities. It is certainly more.
1989 is talked about again and again. Nothing will again be as it was,
neither in the East nor in the West . . . . No one argues that a decision for
Berlin would call into question our ties to our democratic community.
Indeed, we are now experiencing a constant eastward expansion of this
democratic community. It cannot be said too often: Europe is more
than the European Community. Our neighbors in the East mean no less
to us than our neighbors in the West.

Helmut Kohl (Christian Democratic Union):

If Europe were to remain what the E.C. is today—even if we assume a
politically united European Community—it would not be our Europe.
Our Europe has northern Germany in it. When Prime Minister Carlsson
called me last week to tell me Sweden will be applying for [E.C.]
membership, I told him: We Germans will support you. If Norway or
Finland make the same decision in the near future, as I hope they will,
we will support them . . . . But, as I said Monday at the signing of the
German-Polish treaty, it is our wish—an absolutely essential wish—that
the nearby reform states to the East—the Czech Republic and Slovak
Federal Republic, Poland, and Hungary—also find a way into this Europe
. . . . So you see . . . Berlin is not off at the margins, but rather has an
important, central geo-political role. That is the reason I believe that
Berlin will also be a good location in the year 2000 or 2005, when the
idea of a New Europe will have been established, and for that reason I
am voting for Berlin.

The debate about whether to move the capital touched on all aspects
of the German question: what is in the best interests of Germany today,
where should Germany be heading in the future, and what is the best way
to get there?

In response to the historic vote for Berlin, SPD Honorable Chairman
and former Chancellor Willy Brandt called it a "national guiding spirit."[7]
Chancellor Helmut Kohl said: "The decision for Berlin is a decision for
Europe." He also said: "The reunited German capital will now be the
middle point of the federal and democratic Germany."[8] But how could it
be the middle point, when the Polish border is only 80 kilometers away
from Berlin?

In Bonn, a weekly *Montagsdemo* (Monday's demonstration) protest began against the decision. Bonners bitterly fought against the decision to move the capital. Economic investment relating to the capital was one reason why Bonners were upset. Moreover, speculators immediately devalued the property values in Bonn. Thousands of Rhinelanders' jobs and security were likewise threatened by the decision.

But it was more than just a question of money and jobs. Protesters also feared the focus of Germans would shift away from their little town on the Rhine. Demonstrators' protest signs, in the spirit of Adenauer, warned that Germany's attention would shift back to the big and bustling Prussian metropolis in Berlin. The uncertainty of what this would mean for Germany as a nation, considering the results of the last time that Berlin was the capital, scares many. Protestors argued that it was best to keep Germany anchored in the West, and keeping the capital there was one way to counterbalance German focus to the East.

Like a snowball rolling down a hill, the *Montagsdemo* grew every week. Months later, small groups of dedicated protesters still gathered at Bonn's market square to protest the vote. A cult-like following manifested itself and was a premonition of the enormity of the decision and its implications for a new era in Germany and Europe.

Notes

1 Deutschen Bundestag, "Vollendung der Einheit Deutschlands" (Drucksache 12/815): "Die Herrichtung der notwendigen Kapazitäten für Tagungen des Deutschen Bundestages, seiner Fraktionen, Gruppen, und Ausschüsse in Berlin schnell begonnen werden soll. Die Arbeitsfähigkeit soll in vier Jahren hergestellt sein. Die volle Funktionsfähigkeit Berlins als Parlaments- und Regierungssitz soll in spätestens 10 bis 12 Jahren erreict sein. Das heißt, der Bundestagsbeschluß selbst unterscheidet bereits zwischen der Herrstellung der Arbeitsfähigkeit und der Herstellung der vollen Funktionsfähigkeit."

2 Friedrich Wilhelm was the first Prussian King whose Berlin capital, largely due to him, gained the reputation as "the Athens on the Spree River." Sebasitian Haffner, *The Rise and Fall of Prussia*, Weidenfeld and Nicolson, London 1980

3 In accordance with the Yalta agreements, the Americans took over their sector in West Berlin on July 3, 1945.

4 The decision also came after a contentious public debate in which many politicians favored moving the capital to the city where German Kings had been crowned for a thousand years and in which the first German democratic parliament met in 1848-1849, Frankfurt.

5 Deutscher Bundestag, 12. Wahlperiode - 34. Sitzung. Bonn, June 20, 1991, pg 2765 (unofficial translation provided by the German Information Center).

6 Ibid.

7 Berliner Zeitung, June 21, 1991

8 Berliner Morgenpost, August 26, 1992

Chapter 2

Berlin's Reaction

As the favorable news of the capital vote for Berlin reached anxious members of Berlin's state parliament, the place was filled with celebration. Liberals and conservatives stood arm in arm celebrating their united campaign victory and drinking champagne. Even the "stiff and formal security officials" let their guard down for a few minutes and rang the American-donated Liberty Bell at the Schoeneberg City Hall for several triumphant minutes, despite the late hour.[1]

In contrast to the mournful demonstrations in Bonn about the decision, Berliners, including everyone from garbagemen to businesswomen, were encouraged. For weeks after the decision, Berlin reeled in pensive shock. Although details of the move remained vague, it didn't seem to matter, Berliners were just happy to be united Germany's capital again. The national news and newspapers were filled with stories from Berlin about the future of their city. The atmosphere was skeptically positive, which is about as encouraged as Germans allow themselves to get.

Nevertheless, the Berlin markets immediately reacted enthusiastically. Investments and property sales increased overnight. Speculators were quick to jump on the bandwagon and make quick profits on property in the German capital. For example, within a span of two weeks, two large property sales were made on the barren territory where pieces of the Wall were still visible.

First, the government announced the sale of seven acres of Potsdamer Platz to Sony Europe for some DM 100 million. Potsdamer Platz's 17 acres was Berlin's bustling historic center in the 1920s. It is a barren wasteland haunted by Berlin's forced division in the early 1990s. Under the terms of the deal, Sony agreed to rebuild the famous Esplanade movie theater. Nevertheless, Berlin representatives grumbled and moaned that the price was too little, estimating the value to be more in the range of DM 400 million.[2]

In the same week, another spectacular investment in the center of the city was made. Galeries Lafayette confirmed the purchase of one of three blocks of the DM 1.4 billion Friedrichstadt development project. The target date is late 1995 for this redevelopment, which will include 130,000 square meters of office space.[3]

Many architectural plans were announced in the wake of the Bundestag's vote for Berlin that symbolize the promise for Berlin's disconnected landscape. Following the sale of part of the Potsdamer Platz property to Sony, within two months the architectural contract was awarded to Herr Sattler from Munich. His block construction model features Berlin's traditional architecture. After an intensive competition the final contestants placed their proposals on display in the former Hotel Esplanade, one of only two buildings left standing in Potsdamer Platz at the end of World War II.

Prior to the architectural contract being awarded, Berlin's representatives wanted to see for themselves what the architects' proposals were for this historic place. An excursion to Potsdamer Platz included the whole CDU party group and staff members, approximately 130, piling into buses and traveling to the area that had been stripped barren to build the Wall.

My initial eight-week internship extended to two years. At the outset, I participated in all committee, party group, and parliamentary sessions at my discretion, like this trip to Potsdamer Platz. Later, it was agreed that I would work on the Committee on Berlin-Brandenburg, Committee for Federal and European Affairs, and the Committee on Alien Affairs.

In 1991, Potsdamer Platz was a sandy moon-like landscape. One year before it was still split by the Wall and filled with land mines. Before World War II it was Europe's busiest public square. Most famous in the roaring twenties, Potsdamer Platz was known to be an intellectual meeting place and artistic center. Berlin's history seems to orbit around this square. The Third Reich had its headquarters located in close proximity; everything was destroyed, except parts of the strongly re-enforced bomb shelters where Hitler spent his last days before committing suicide.

"We are going to the center of Berlin, this is the traditional square where the town used to bustle, vibrant with life," said my Berlin representative neighbor on the bus. With this in mind, I pictured some grand old place that was somewhat dilapidated.

I was disappointed. After being heavily damaged during the war, very little of the original structure still stands, and because it was directly on the former Wall strip, it was completely abandoned and in ruins. Nevertheless, the representatives were all interested in taking a glimpse into the famous old hotel. To me it seemed as if they didn't see the true nature of this desolate place, but rather their vision was befogged by their memories or pictures they had seen. Or were they envisioning the future? Without any emotional ties or connection to Potsdamer Platz, I was harder in my judgement, although sensitive to their appreciation. Indeed, the only recognizable feature of the place was the old lettering on the hotel's facade.

Walking through the double doors was like entering a ghost house: the hardwood floor creaked and the lighting was terrible. Straight ahead was the well-displayed exhibition of architectural plans for development of this property, all cleaned off: like an oasis in a desert. Some representatives were eager to look around the historic building before moving directly to the exhibition. Eager for the chance to break away from the crowd, I followed them through the hallway and up the stairs, all along the way pulling the cobwebs out of our way. "Look up there," said one representative. "Do you see the old picture on the ceiling and the fine woodwork?" Indeed he was correct, but the condition was deplorable. I wanted to move back into the main group, back to the safer areas of this haunted-looking house, but he continued and I felt somehow responsible for him too. Suddenly we stepped on a weak plank and the whole floor felt like it was caving in beneath us. That deterred even him enough so that he made his way back to the group. Coming through our secret exit path, we were suddenly back in the "real" world, or to be exact, that of the media. I found myself following the senators and the mayor and the television lights to the next room, where the three favored architectural contestant's models were on display.

The room was full of energy and excitement — maybe because of the glitter of the TV lights. Everyone was maneuvering for position — wanting to be on tonight's TV news. Trying to break out of the bustle of people, I accidentally found myself alone next to one of the architectural models and the mayor. We gave each other half a glance. I must admit, I couldn't have imagined that the empty, dusty field from which we had just entered could be of such value and importance. Extravagant models were everywhere, some even resembling space ships. Suddenly the bright camera lights were on me. I tried to get out of the way, but it was too late, the other representatives had already encircled us and were pushing closer to get next to the mayor and the camera.

Although every possible architectural design was on display, Sattler's traditional model clearly won the day. The CDU and SPD entertained the architects in their respective party group meetings and posed a range of questions. I respected the representatives' consideration of history and the consequences on city planning, as evidenced by the representatives' exhaustive and thorough questioning of the leading architects. This concern echoed the many public debates since the architectural competition began and the effects of their decisions on the other parts of town; from transportation to playground sites for the kids, a full range of impact studies and town meetings took place.

As Berlin's building director, Hans Stimman stated: "Berlin is the only city in the world where the inner city is empty. We must bring this city back so that when we look in the mirror, we will know it is our face. If we look like Hong Kong or Tokyo, nobody will come. Berlin must look like Berlin."[4]   Indeed, Berlin has an opportunity other cities can only dream of: the chance to build a capital center literally from scratch, with 1990s technology and 21st century goals.

Beginning in 1994, construction crews started rebuilding Potsdamer Platz. Daimler Benz and Sony Europe are building their new headquarters there; apartments, parks, and shopping centers will also highlight the former no-man's land. The reconstruction of the historic Potsdamer Platz, the biggest private-sector construction project in German history, is scheduled to be completed in 1998 with three high-rise structures among 19 buildings and more than 1.1 million square feet of space.[5]

The Berlin Wall at Potsdamer Platz looking East, courtesy of the German Information Center

Construction begins at Potsdamer Platz, 1994, courtesy of Daimler-Benz

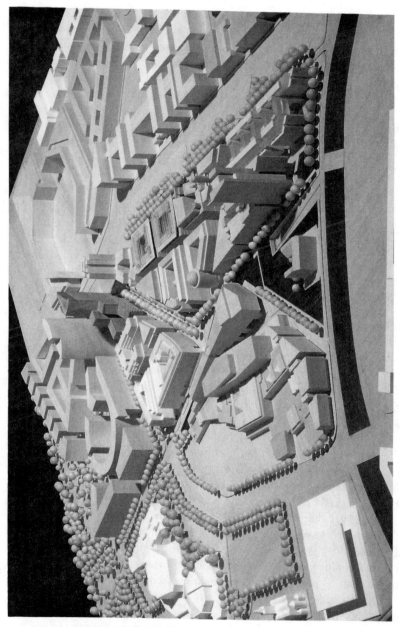

Potsdamer Platz in 2000, courtesy of Daimler-Benz

Walking in 1991 from the Reichstag toward Leipziger Platz I imagined how this desolate sandy field would look in 2000. To me this place is still a no-man's land dividing East and West Berlin. The Wall still exists. Although physically gone, it is socially present. The separation between East and West is very real, as real as the Wall was. One sees it everywhere, in the faces of people, in their contrasting views and conversations. All of the complicated events surrounding this area, from the ominous barren Reichstag to the empty Potsdamer Platz, are landmarks in the spectrum of Berlin's history. On the one side, these symbols represent German tradition and pride, symbolizing their early democratic tendency under Kaiser Friedrich II, whereas on the other hand, these symbols are also reminders of days of terror and fascist military parades.

The forty years of communist division and terror are being added to the dark days of the Third Reich. Already, in some ways, the reunified Germany is overshadowing the horrific symbol of German defeat and division represented by the Wall. Like the stubborn and unforgiving German nature, Berliners, indeed all Germans, are deeply interested in the fate of this area, with all the paradoxes it entails. Despite the political will to overcome this spiritual metaphor, years of modern architecture may never eliminate the feeling of confrontation one faces here.

Just down the street from Potsdamer Platz, the domineering Reichstag sits lonely on the fringe of where the Wall used to extend its horror through the middle of the Spree River. This historic place also received a big vote for the future following the historic vote for Berlin. On October 31, 1991, the Bundestag agreed to move back into the Reichstag. This deeply symbolic decision is an important step for the united German parliament.

Some feel that it is fitting that the German parliament moves back into the Reichstag. The Reichstag's tradition in Berlin and German history is deep; if Germany's elected officials were to ignore this ominous structure it would shame their identity and reject their history. Germany has always been a powerful country, and the old building is a symbol of its strength.

In 1991, the precarious yet domineering Reichstag was the only standing structure in the immediate area. It stood empty on the fringe of East and West Berlin. Formerly the Wall ran right down its back side. Like a sleeping giant the Berliner Bear is awakening from the darker days of the past. What is the Berliner Bear awakening to? In 1993, in direct contrast to three years ago, the activity around the Reichstag enlivens the use of this metaphor. Initial renovations were completed and international conferences are held in this deeply symbolic building since the fall of the

Wall. Large spacious entry halls lead to the grandiose main conference room. On the one side of this large rectangular room, a floor to ceiling glass window looks out onto the spacious fields in front of the building, where enormous Doric pillars are set immediately in front of the 100 foot-square window.

Anti-communist rally at the Reichstag, 1948, courtesy of the German Information Center

Reichstag, 1980s, courtesy of the German Information Center

The New German Parliament in 2000, courtesy of the Bundesbaudirection Berlin, photographer Richard Davies

Situated next to the Brandenburg Gate, the Reichstag's location is crucial to Berlin's inner city dynamic. On one side it is surrounded by Potsdamer Platz and on the other by desolate fields on the Spree River. The decision to move the German parliament back here is a major achievement for the unity of the future German working capital. Being centrally located, this main legislative building will be the hub around which all the working German government buildings will rotate.

Within weeks of this decision, another development plan for the future is announced. From inside the government offices and from listening to the party group spokesman talk, one might think that there is no problem with reunification other than just repairing the disconnected roads and unifying the cities' systems. On the surface, the walls seem to be falling quickly.

City officials agreed on an architectural concept for Alexanderplatz. Named after the Russian Czar Alexander I in 1805, this plaza was a respected city center in the late 19th century and in pre-war Berlin. After being destroyed during the War, a mammoth concrete project was undertaken by the communist regime, including the construction of the 1200-foot-high television and observation tower beginning in 1965. City officials agree that in the future all existing structures will remain but that extensive renovations will occur, including many new buildings. An emphasis will also be placed on adding more greenery to this concrete monstrosity.

In 1991, the coldness of Alexanderplatz was chilling, the atmosphere cosmetic and artificial—as every visit painfully reminded me. Walking across the square one sunny day, I was overwhelmed and disoriented by its size and circular nature. The buildings were all distant and uninviting and I couldn't decide which direction to turn. It was difficult to recognize anything.

Upon hearing a train horn, I re-oriented myself with the whistle bellowing across Alexanderplatz in my ears. There were hardly any objects on this concrete desert, there were no monuments or other appealing cultural amenities. Looking more intently, I realized that there was no natural color whatsoever, no benches, trees, not even a waste basket. I suddenly felt lonely. Thankfully I recognized a clock off in the distance. Like the mirage the lost traveler sees, the clock inspired my progress. I made my way over to this isolated object. The clock is contained in an artist's rendition of the world. The world is portrayed as being black and the atmosphere steel gray. Upon careful calculation, one can tell the time of the world's major cities. But my brief refuge was as real as the desert traveler's mirage; the revolving clock didn't work. And like the clock which wasn't ticking to the right beat, I felt out of rhythm and lost in time. I wanted to leave the abandoned, brutalized place. Then I wondered how the Germans will ever be able to change the socialist architecture and bareness of this place, highlighted by the monumental concrete television tower.

As the three architectural plans illustrated, the German parliament's decision to move the capital back to Berlin is a vote for the future. Berlin's traditional city center will be remodeled with state-of-the-art architecture and construction. However, it also shows that Berlin, like Europe, has a long road ahead of it before it will be rebuilt, let alone reunified. In some ways, Berlin has been frozen in history since the capitulation of the Third Reich.

Germans have a long way to go before they will be united again too. After Berliners' initial shock at the vote to move the capital back to Berlin, their happiness changed to a more pragmatic cynicism. The daily problems replaced the promise of the future and all the self-delusion this can bring. Why? Because the decades of forced division and Soviet occupation have made Berlin a city of two cultures. East Berliners went straight from a brown dictatorship to a red one. The chains of decades of totalitarianism need to be fully discarded in the Eastern part of the country—which will take longer and cost more than any monetary figure can account for. Meanwhile, Western prejudice and impatience are dampening the mood in the West. It will take a lot longer and prove more difficult than many realize to re-emerge from the rubble of the Cold War into a reunified German capital by the year 2000.

Nevertheless, momentum is on Berlin's side. Experts predict that by the year 2000, Berlin will have more residents than Hamburg, Munich, and Cologne together and that Berlin will add two million jobs before the year 2010.[6] Greater Berlin, six times the size of Paris in area with 4.2 million inhabitants is estimated to top six million.[7] People are already talking about Berlin as the largest urban center between the Atlantic and the Urals.

Perhaps more significantly, as Chancellor Kohl, Willy Brandt, and Hans-Dietrich Genscher's remarks illustrated, Berlin is the geographic center and spiritual symbol of Germany's place in the heart of Europe. It is that historically double and divided city—the center of chaos, division and war in the 20th Century—that will be the seat of the most powerful European Union country in the year 2000, and forms the theme of this book: Berlin will be the center of Europe at the turn of the millennium.

Notes

1 Klaus Bruske, Die Neue Zeit, June 22, 1991
2 Ulrich Paul, "Sony-Kauf: Filetgrundstuck zum Hamburger-Preis," Berliner Morgenpost, June 27, 1991
3 Real Estate Perspectives, "Berlin's Property Markets", pg. 8 May 15, 1993
4 Paul Goldberger, "Reimagining Berlin", The New York Times Magazine, February 5, 1995.
5 Ferdinand Protzman, "Companies Join Huge Berlin Project", The New York Times, November 28, 1994
6 Dr. Norbert Bluem, Deutscher Bundestag, 12. Wahlperiode, 34. Sitzung, June 20, 1991, pg. 2737-2738
7 Ibid.

Part Two

Berlin Walls Still in Place

Chapter 3

East-West Divisions

Fall 1991 had arrived. The days were getting shorter, and Berliners' initial euphoria about the German government's decision to move the capital had given way to a more serious atmosphere. People did not cross over to the "other side" as much as those pictures of joy and celebration on November 9, 1989, led us to believe. Instead, after the initial excitement of traveling over to see what the other side was like, the two societies wandered back to what they were used to, to the places where they grew up. Just knowing that one could cross seemed to be enough. For now.

One of the first trips I took during my internship in the parliament illustrates the paradox of the divided but unified Berlin. Imagine getting into two luxury German cars with a group of well-dressed associates. We are all from the West and we're off to visit a sports facility in the East. As the curious American, I asked if I could tag along. Little did I know the discovery this trip would be. "Where are we going again?" I asked one of the representatives I was traveling with. "We are going to East Berlin, to the former Olympic training center of the German Democratic Republic. We're going to the East!" he said with strong emphasis on the last two words and a look of anxiety on his face.

East, I thought to myself, I don't want to go the East either, as pictures of marching soldiers with red flags filled my mind. "Come on, snap out of it," I said to myself, "there is nothing to worry about, those days are over, this is the New Europe!" In a more relaxed state, I experienced a little tingling of excitement in my stomach for what we were about to discover. "It can't be that different," I said to calm myself.

Passing through the guarded gate, the four representatives from West Berlin and I all felt a little apprehensive. "Is it the air, the buildings, the dirt road, or just us?" we all seemed to be asking each other with looks of bewilderment and displacement.

As we were greeted by the training center director and his associates in his office, we looked at our East Berlin hosts like people from another planet. No one knew what to say to each other. After the handshakes were made, the two groups retreated back to their respective sides of the room. We stood at a great distance apart from our hosts, as if we were two opposing football teams on opposite sides of the playing field. Except on this field, it seemed as if there was an invisible barrier between us. It was a very awkward beginning.

In an effort to ease the stilted welcoming reception, the director suggested that we begin our tour. We quickly agreed and made our way to the door. Once we were under way on this cold, cloudy fall day, the director gave us a very detailed explanation of the facility. There was a large velodrome stadium, a complete swimming and diving complex, as well as a gym with weight training and track and field, neighboring the ice arena. Curiously, in the middle of the grounds was a house where the former head of East German State Security, Eric Mielke, used to lounge in his combination bar, TV room, and massage parlor. At this stop, the camp director seemed especially proud to show us around. The West Berlin group and I followed the director in the stuffy, maze-like cabin. I was struck most by the cheapness of everything—the thin walls and spartan furnishings. The only sign of the former police chief's presence was the red, fluffy sofa, from which Mielke used to watch the athletes from his TV monitor, said the director. The director dwelled longer on this part of the tour, as if he were nostalgic for the past.

Next stop was the athletic facilities. Finally, I thought to myself, let's get to the purpose of our visit. As we approached the track and field hall, chills ran up my neck. The cold and damp weather brought out the foreboding nature of the gray structure. The colors were all the same, the same gray walls and roofs. Looking across the fields I saw no one.

Walking through a big double door, suddenly an entire community emerged before us. It seemed to me as if we had arrived in another country, a total contrast to the lifeless landscape we had just surveyed. Athletes were running around the track, springing up on the long jump and throwing the shot put to the side. I had the feeling I had just been sent back in time about 40 years and was deep in the heart of the Soviet Union. The lighting was terrible. It was stuffy and warm in this bubble complex and the air was mixed with the sweat of working bodies. The athlete's equipment was so outdated that the very idea of using it hurt.

The trainers were middle-aged men and women, and they all were large and very strong. The men had mustaches, long hair, and beer bellies. The women had large breasts and buttocks. It was as if the fashions of the 1970s had come back. The athletes were young, no older than 16 years old, but very developed and skilled. As we stood there in our coats, ties, and leather shoes, I was embarrassed. I felt as if we were walking through an exhibition in the Soviet Athletic Association in Moscow, like President Richard Nixon's famous kitchen exhibition visit with Soviet Premier Nikita Khrushchev, or watching a Cold War film about life in the Soviet Union. As I walked into the weight room my mouth dropped open. My high school weight room had double the equipment.

I glanced over to a board on the wall. There were the names of East German Olympic Medalists in weight lifting that had trained here, in this very room. At that moment my mind raced back to my middle school years and the pictures of Soviet and East German weight lifters we used to envy and emulate. The differences in equipment were one thing, but the athletes? People were training everywhere. They were kids, some no older than ten years old, but working the weights with skill and control. They were like a family here, the friendship and happiness was clear to see, like my middle school P.E. classes used to be. But here it was serious, not just an hour of laughing and playing. They were professional-caliber young adults.

Our guide told us that athletes are selected to come to this training camp from all over East Germany. "It is, excuse me, it was, a very high compliment from the State to be selected. They attend school in the morning for around four hours and then train, take a break, and then train some more. This was the central training grounds for all East German Olympic candidates," he said.

We proceeded to the skating rink, where Katerina Witt once trained. The conditions were completely outdated. The supporting technology, from the buildings and bleachers to the overall care was deplorable. Next, we went to the swimming pool, where the European swimming championships took place in 1987. The plaques of Olympic swimmers who trained here showed what a first-class operation this must have been. As I gazed at the swimmer turning his lap, a feeling of surprise that we were still in Berlin came over me. It seemed as if we were years and thousands of miles distant. Just three miles away was a totally different world, and I felt as far away from home as I'd felt since my arrival in West Berlin.

I could have spent the entire day here, but the tour continued. And it was sometimes cruel. Our guide showed us the shower rooms for the swimmers, where they all gathered after training to talk of their days and latest girlfriends. There is something special about locker rooms or team rooms for athletes. Then I heard the showers running and we appeared in a small locker room, surprising the five or so swimmers there. I heard our host and the representatives critically analyze the layout as the boys stood there half naked, cringing and completely horrified. We stood there like tourists at an orphanage. A feeling of total embarrassment and shame came over me. I backtracked as fast as possible while the others looked over the facilities.

Before we made our way out of the sports complex, we stopped by the boxing room and saw some female gymnasts stretching in the sweaty old training rooms. Although some of the athletes were also interested in us, they never came closer than ten feet away, making the tour even more awkward. Two gymnasts standing within a shouting distance, giggled uncontrollably as they pointed at my suit and shoes.

Meanwhile, the director kept giving us his monotone presentation as if he was oblivious to the social collision going on around him. As we moved beyond the boxing room, he pointed out that the complex would remain open and functioning, for now. He and other organized East German sport directors were currently lobbying the government to maintain the complex as a German national training center.

In the coming weeks I thought a lot about this trip. In my dreams I had strange feelings of anxiety, insecurity and embarrassment that I had as I recalled those young East Berlin athletes looking at me across some invisible divide that had separated us. Did they see those red marching flags in their dreams too, I asked myself. Or did they have nightmares from television scenes of violence in American cities? The distance was far greater than the mere ten feet that separated us.

In the days that followed, I couldn't help asking myself questions about what the social collision I witnessed said about the new German capital. What did it say about the New Europe? Why didn't the two groups of re-discovered countrymen warmly greet each other and celebrate the government's decision to move the capital back to Berlin? What prevented us from being able to even carry out simple dialogue with the young athletes we visited? Searching for answers, I found what was certainly a factor contributing to this social divide.

During a CDU party group meeting, the Berlin Senate distributed a recently released brochure entitled "Foreigners in East Germany: a Review."

The startling fact contained in this brochure was that only 1% of the East German population were foreigners and they were mostly isolated from the general population. "Well, no wonder the gymnasts at the Olympic training camp were looking at me like that," I thought to myself, answering one of the many questions I kept inside me. Foreigners were just that to them: foreigners, something that many had never seen or been exposed to before.

The fact that there were few foreigners in East Germany may have been one reason I was not able to communicate better with the people we visited at the training center. But I was the only foreigner with the group. Or was I? All the representatives I traveled with, as well as our hosts, were Berliners. What was preventing the Berliners from being more brotherly?

The cold truth is that the Soviet Union's occupation of East Germany and later the Wall made Berliners foreigners. On August 13, 1961, after more than three million East Germans had fled to the Western Allies' sectors, Soviet Premier Nikita Khruschev decided to stop the drain of the East Germans moving West and strung barbed wire around West Berlin. The barbed wire turned into the permanent concrete Wall that divided the continent.

Thus, after a decade-long forced division, East Berliners became foreigners to West Berliners and vice versa. The Wall symbolized two world views that dominated each side of the Cold War. Westerners had free elections, freedom to travel, and most of all the freedom to live as they chose. In direct contrast, in the East the communist regime restricted every decision and activity.

The Wall survived November 9, 1989. It survived that triumphant celebration in which dancing crowds chiseled away its outer core and bore holes through its concrete. As much as we may regret it, the Wall still triumphs over us today, in our thinking, in our movements, in our prejudices. That is the main reason these former East and West Berliners stood on opposite sides of the field, and were subconsciously inhibited from mingling. It is also the main reason that I, the American, couldn't interact with the athletes.

It was not only the physical separation that prevented us from understanding each other. The influence of East German communist ideology and social systems were far greater than I imagined. The people responsible for erecting that 12-foot concrete snake around Berlin succeeded in isolating East and West, and they carried out their totalitarian plans and social control. They divided East and West Berlin, East and West Germany, Eastern and Western Europe, indeed the world. Although we can say we won the Cold War, the price will continue to be paid for generations.

Therefore, before discussing what post-reunification life is like in Berlin, let's take a step back and try to imagine what life was like in Berlin when the Wall stood. The following stories help illustrate the different worlds in which East and West Berliners lived just five years ago. Whereas the East lived under the control of a communist regime, West Berlin was walled off and isolated in a sea of communism in the middle of East Germany.

One small example of how entrenched the communist indoctrination in East Germany had been, was illustrated by a decree from the Berlin government to all East Berlin elementary schools. All East Berlin elementary school principals and teachers were informed that they should discontinue instruction in *Ordnungsform* (rules of conduct). All throughout the former East Germany, the military, the National Peoples' Army (NVA), required elementary school teachers to lead their classes in military drills, including such things as marching in file, saluting, standing at attention, and marching on the double.

Upon reading this report, I wondered how many teachers still practiced these drills out of pure habit. Is it possible that some teachers are doing that today?

As much as we like to focus on the big names and figures associated with revolutions, governments and regimes, in my view we too often overlook the citizens their countries represent. In the case of East Germany, a long legacy of the social plague and mores associated with a free and constitutional society have been wiped out by the perverse abuse of dictators. Society will suffer for a long time. Integration will be a long process, and understandably so. The definition of right and wrong and responsibility for one's actions will not blossom in the East for a while. The costs Germans will pay for the suppression they have lived under is greater than any monetary figure or one person.

And on the other side of the Wall that divided the European continent, the island of West Berlin became a beacon of hope and freedom for all. Being supported and defended by American, British, and French armed forces, West Berlin was isolated in the middle of East Germany, ironically known as the German Democratic Republic.

What was life in West Berlin like before the Wall fell? What was it like to live encircled by a 170 kilometer long Wall in the middle of communist East Germany? Probably the best place to begin imagining what life in West Berlin was like in those decades of siege is first to envision your town being surrounded by enemy forces. And on top of that imagine the city being literally split in two, randomly divided through the middle, with no concern for existing roads, buildings, or such, with one half being held siege inside a Wall. It is like taking a red marker and randomly drawing a thick line right through the middle of Berlin's city map, everything landing on the line would be divided, split in half, placed in the no-man's zone, in order to encircle the democratic West Berlin.

Such a bizarre idea became reality in Berlin in 1961, roads were barricaded, parks were divided and turned into battle zones, schools were shut down and boarded up, metro stations and even complete lines were shut down. As if an evil spirit cast a dark spell on the city, the torment did not stop there—West Berliners were bombarded with communist propaganda to underline the psychological terror.

Certainly West Berliners could move around in their guarded democratic outpost freely, with the Western Allies always present. Nevertheless it had a surreal nature. It was artificial. This condition of isolation and separation from the rest of Germany, from the West in general, outside of the minimal contact the Germans had with the occupying Allies, produced peculiar results. The people closed themselves off too, they manifested their own culture. The city's stranglehold naturally manifested itself in their character and behavior. Their horizons were closed off, the average things we all take for granted—like freedom of movement, taking trips and long drives—were made impossible with the nature of the city being so brutally violated.

If you can imagine growing up three blocks from where shoot-to-kill orders ruled, then you can imagine what it was like living in West Berlin's Kreuzberg, Wedding, Prenzlauer Berg, or Neukoelln Districts. Imagine living less than ten miles from divisions of Soviet military forces training and exercising everyday for your takeover. Imagine this being the case for 30 years.

One effect of this very artificial and precarious existence for Berliners is that they hardly even know where they live anymore. When they did want to leave West Berlin during the Cold War there were only three freeway corridors possible, as well as three air corridors to each one of the Western Allies' sectors in West Germany.

Now that the Cold War is over and the Allies are gone, Berliners are rediscovering their homeland. They are on a journey back home again, to the places where they were forbidden to go, to the places they lived in as children. They have perhaps grown up listening to their parents' stories about these areas or have seen old family pictures, but haven't been there

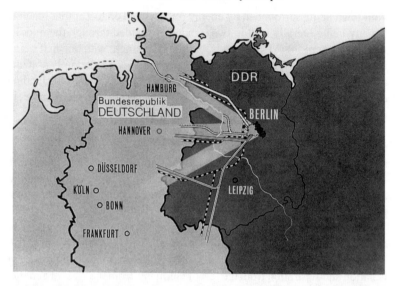

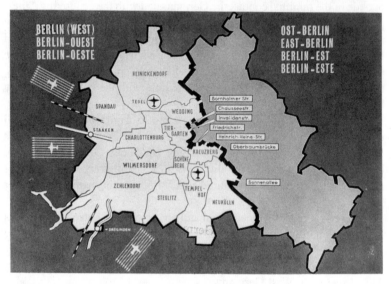

Cold War Berlin, courtesy of the German Information Center

in decades, if at all. Many West Berliners never imagined that the day would arrive when they could possibly decide for themselves to take a trip out to the famous countryside, only 10 miles from their door.

Now Berliners are taking small steps into the former East Berlin, like the Berlin representatives' visit to the former East German Olympic training center. But in addition to the obvious cultural clash existing in Berlin and ghosts of prejudice prevalent on both sides, practical problems are also present. The road conditions in the East are still deplorable compared with West Berlin: hotels and restaurants are few and far between, although new gas stations were some of the first Western enterprises to set up shop on the country roads.

Old historical books and travel brochures offer nice pictures, but when one is actually there, many buildings are run-down and not in good shape at all. Towns are falling apart, but slowly maps and travel books are being rewritten, slowly Western-style infrastructures are being established. With every passing day improvements are being made. Little communities that once looked dilapidated and run-down without hope of recovery are today sporting colorful American cigarette billboards and private enterprises have sprung up in the otherwise fallen buildings.

The degree of separation from the divided worlds that Berliners lived under really only sank in when I accompanied a West Berlin family on an excursion from West Berlin into Brandenburg. The father was so proud of the history of the castle we were visiting. He told us the whole story at least three times before we arrived. "In the later middle ages," he began, "a famous prince had many castles throughout Brandenburg, and this was one of his favorites." He continued with details describing the Prince's influence on the region and his architectural prowess. And it wasn't just the father's enthusiasm: the expectation, the thrill, the adventure was exciting the whole family.

The mother planned for days, food of all types, and we had enough to last us a week. The father scrupulously studied the map. He had to buy a new, more updated one, because his old map included only West Berlin. Although our destination was only 20 kilometers from their home, it took over an hour for us to escape through the traffic jams and find it.

Nevertheless an atmosphere of joy and expectation permeated the car. It was really a family outing, we were three cars altogether, everybody inviting a friend. As we approached the old hunting castle in Brandenburg, the bridge was broken; the only way across the small dike was to jump a little stream.

As the father explained the prince's beloved castle to us one last time, I was inspired, despite the uncomfortable feeling of wet shoes and socks as we stood on the grassy hill. But then I saw the castle's boarded doors. We left in no more than 15 minutes and were safely drinking our tea and eating cake back in West Berlin. And although the journey only lasted over three hours, everyone seemed tremendously fatigued, some were making their way to bed for their afternoon naps. The mother looked as if she had just sailed through a hurricane.

As the above stories indicate, West and East Berliners are dealing with entirely different categories of problems in adjusting to their reunified world. While East Germans are struggling to figure out the value of their new currency and the concepts of banking and insurance, not to mention their new constitution, West Berliners are slowly awakening to their new world without walls and their kids are listening to American, French, and British radio stations. Their problems are of different degrees and magnitude. Due to the fact that their problems are so dichotomous, neither side can understand the other.

The first time I witnessed Berliners' disparate problems was at a public gathering as I was standing alone on Pariser Platz, on the East side of the Brandenburg Gate. On that late summer afternoon, Mayor Diepgen spoke to a sparse crowd in tribute to the 200th anniversary of the Brandenburg Gate. Looking around at the people present, all quiet in solemn reflection, the mayor vainly tried to stir enthusiasm. In his rhetorical attempt to pull Berliners out of their daily problems, he implored them to focus on the symbol the gate provides Germans, symbolizing former East and West division and later the reunification of Germany. No one smiled and no one interrupted him with applause. As the Mayor implored them to reflect on the accomplishment of their reunification and all that it would mean for their future, they all stood dazed gazing at him.

How much longer will that horrific divider continue to haunt Berliners, the *Mauer in den Kopfen* (walls in the mind)? How long will it take before I can look at the Brandenburg Gate without envisioning the Wall? How much longer will the Cold War prejudice me? My head begins to pound as I reflect on these questions. If it is this way for me, how must it be for Germans? The hard reality of the bitter, decade-long division of Germany, is what drowned out the celebrations of November 9, 1989, so decisively.

Chapter 4

Deeper Causes for the Divide

A dark wintry day in 1992 was a big day for Berlin's representatives and for me, the American that got to come along. I knew the representatives had been regretting this forthcoming visit to a Berlin Eastern city district since the announcement was first made. Regular party group meetings occurred bi-weekly in preparation for the Berlin state parliamentary sessions. All legislative business is discussed and an attempt is made to increase party cohesion and understanding.

Normally we met in Schoeneberg City Hall (Rathaus Schoeneberg) in the heart of West Berlin, in comfortable leather chairs in room 110. There, the friendly waitress served wonderful German pastries, *boulettes*, coffee, and other sweets. But not today. Boarding the buses in front of the building, the last-minute scurrying reminded me of the final boarding call at an airline gate. The boarding passengers' nervousness gave the impression we were embarking on a journey into the great unknown. Unknown it proved to be. Some of the Berlin representatives even had their cameras all loaded and ready along with their snack bags.

The representatives had all been to the core of the former East German power: the *Palast der Republik*, Unter den Linden, and Checkpoint Charlie. But to drive further, to explore the city districts beyond the obvious center was unheard of for most West Berliners.

"I don't know why we are going here," said the representative next to me as our bus waited at an ominously long light (East Berlin was well known to have 'dumb lights,' where you wait for over three or four minutes regardless of whether traffic is coming from the other side or not). "We should just stay where we belong, back at Rathaus Schoeneberg in West Berlin." He was squirming and looking out his window as if we were in a dangerous zone.

Interesting, I thought to myself, that he would take such a position. Then to my surprise he changed his tone. "Look at it this way," he said, "you'll get the chance to learn our own city with us, through our eyes," as he chuckled. At the time this remark seemed insignificant, but later as I reflected back, this is exactly what happened.

East Berlin had always seemed too far out of the way for me. What was there to do here, in this run-down and unappealing city? From what I had seen of East Berlin's main attractions, the general atmosphere was uninteresting, the streets monotone gray, the few stores that even existed closed early in the afternoon. There was generally little life on the streets, and the lonely passersby one did see were far from friendly.

Previous to this visit to East Berlin's Weissensee District, I'd hardly ever traveled there. None of my West Berlin friends wanted to introduce me to the Eastern part of town outside of the main attractions. It was only later that I realized why: my West Berlin friends had never been there themselves.

Once we were on our way, we drove by the biggest German-Jewish cemetery in Berlin, in Weissensee. It was not open, but no one seemed very disappointed. "Why would I come here freely?" said another West Berlin representative, as he pointed out his window at the run-down apartment buildings.

We were two buses full of Berlin parliamentary representatives, acting like tourists. The microphone loudspeaker came in handy, as our guide pointed out the sights. Amazing, I thought to myself, that the governing representatives of the German capital have to be taken on a tour through their own city.

As our bus pulled to a halt and we all disembarked, I noticed that the East Berlin representatives were in good form. They were robust and their color was good. In contrast, the West Berlin representatives looked a bit pale and disoriented. They lost their previous arrogance and clamorous behavior, as the Easterners pointed out the sights in their home territory.

These people were arch enemies just five years ago. Berlin's parliament, a mix of East and West representatives since the first common elections held back in 1990, is truly a melting pot of the former competing ideologies. Whether in the committee rooms, the party group conferences, or in the parliament, it is a very interesting process to follow, the process of getting used to each other and blending together. This cooperative work is a sign for the united state government that they are working for. Skepticism and disagreement abound, as they look at each other with crooked eyes and doubtful faces, but each time some progress is being made. It is a hard and arduous process, but they are pushing forward.

After disembarking from the bus, I stood there observing everyone. I imagined that some of the representatives lost themselves in the fantasy of regularly being able to meet in the East, being able to control the decisions, being able to baby "little brother" along, like the Westerners so casually and normally do to their East Berlin colleagues in Berliners' united, but divided, party group and committee meetings. As we all gathered around the front stairs of the building on this overcast fall day, the party group chairman, Klaus Landowsky, was greeted by the district mayor. Landowsky looked at his Eastern subordinate with much skepticism upon the overly friendly welcome. He appeared to be thinking: let's get to work, so we can get home.

But no. First, the district mayor planned a little tour for us as his associates were running to and fro beaming at their Western colleagues. Long stares were exchanged between the West Berlin CDU party group representatives and their Eastern hosts. From my sideline, I observed skeptical glances exchanged between them across another part of the invisible wall characterizing life in Berlin 1992. Walking up the many flights of stairs to the tower of the district city hall was ultimately unrewarding. We looked over the daunting sights of East Berlin's skyline: smoke stacks were everywhere. Many were still working and because we were downwind from one of those smelly objects, we only stayed for a quick overview. Then back down the stairs again and finally to work? Not yet. First came a long-winded introduction from our host. Even when we finally were able to make our own plans, the rigid routine was altered. The normal party group briefing from the Senate and the mayor on the latest issues, followed by representatives' questions and then a run-through the list of issues we would be dealing with in the next parliamentary session, was reduced to the latter—in other words, the bare necessities.

Even the staunch opponents of the mayor and the Senate held back. They all seemed afraid that someone was listening or watching over their shoulders. Could it be that the frame just recently taken down from the wall behind the chairman's back used to house a picture of former East German communist dictator Erich Honecker? Looking around me, I could tell by the looks on people's faces that I was not the only one suspecting this. It was as if they imagined him to still be there.

To everyone's relief, the session, which normally lasted around three hours, was cut in half. Everyone was anxious to go, but the hospitality was not to end. Our hosts prepared a big buffet for us, with all sorts of meats and other items that seemed foreign and unappetizing to me. But it wasn't just me—about half the people went through the line—but no one seemed to put anything on their plates. Next thing I knew we were all back in the buses and on our way home.

Pulling into the parking lot at Rathaus Schoeneberg, I felt the bus take a deep breath in unison, people patted each other on the shoulders, especially the Western representatives. Maybe in its own right this Berlin CDU party group meeting in East Berlin was another East-West bridge opening for the city, when the government joins in and makes a deeply symbolic and not soon forgotten trip to the 'other side.' Regardless, all the representatives seemed to be rewarding themselves for the extra hard day's work.

Going home that night, I thought about this experience with the representatives of the city. How must it be for regular citizens? I fell asleep thinking of the German capital in a different light, I saw a bigger picture, my curiosity and interest for the city and its reunification was only enhanced. If this is the case for Berlin today, for its democratically elected representatives, how must it be for the rest of Germany?

Despite the obvious social divide in post-reunification Germany, little steps are being taken to improve the inevitable social collision course Germany is on. The first place to begin dismantling the social divide is by removing the physical barriers that divided East and West for decades. In a highly symbolic sign of the new Germany, the Berlin government announced the re-opening of the commuter train line between Berlin and Potsdam. This will be a big contributor to improving the distance everyone imagines exists between them, the distance forcefully blocked by the Wall. Since 1961 the train connection between the metropolis of Berlin and Brandenburg's state capital, Potsdam, has been separated by the Wall; today the traveling trains are full again. It is no more than a 12-mile distance from the heart of Berlin to the heart of Potsdam.

That same day after work I boarded the new train connection for Potsdam. I was so curious to see what for so long was prevented by American tanks on one side and Russian tanks on the other. I wanted to experience the feelings associated with crossing a distance as wide as the infamous Glieneke Bruecke that once separated West Berlin from Potsdam. This famous bridge is where captured spies were exchanged in high Cold War drama.

And what a drama it was to cross this short distance, in the post-Cold War era too. I had no idea that a matter of feet could make that much of a difference. As the train squeaked out of the last former West Berlin station at Wannsee lake, from the looks on the faces of my fellow travelers it looked like we were on a journey into another world. People were standing glued to the windows as the train rolled into the first station in the former East Germany, Babelsberg (a suburb of Potsdam). Encouraged to do the same, I gazed out of my window and understood better why everyone was gasping at the sights.

The differences were stark. The old building facades were run down, laundry hung off every balcony and the streets were deserted. In the background I recognized the remains of the famous Babelsburg film studios by the dilapidated welcome sign and the run-down studio houses. From my window seat it looked like a ghost town. I could barely make out the shapes of the old buildings through the smoggy air. The faces of the people waiting to board the train looked different and foreign to me too. They were staring at us and we were staring at them. Looking into their faces, I couldn't see past superficial details, such as their clothes. I never got a good look into their eyes. We were separated by some deeper force.

I had a flashback to the young athletes at the East German Olympic training center. I had the same feelings of collision and distance that I felt then. We were foreigners to each other—mystified by the chance to look at each other like we had been prevented from doing for decades! The stares, the looks of amazement were the same on both sides. It was as if we were looking at each other from opposite sides of a gate at a zoo. "Where does that fashion come from?" I overheard my neighbor say to her mother as all three of us stood gazing out the window at the people on the platform.

The obvious tension decreased somewhat as the train rolled further towards Potsdam. We were all sitting together on the same train, West and East Berliners, Brandenburgers, and an American. The glares turned into prolonged stares. The walls were everywhere to be seen and felt. Before my eyes, in the reflection of my neighbor's eyes, between us, I suddenly saw a vision of the Brandenburg Gate walled off. I tried to remind myself those days were over!

Another highlight of our approach to Potsdam's main station was when I saw rows of old East German trains lined up on the tracks out of my window. They were apparently abandoned. The Western trains would be coming to replace them soon. Gazing over the landscape, smokestacks poked out all along the horizon against a backdrop of dense brown air draped over the valley.

On the first days following the opening, Berlin's papers reported that the commuter trains from Berlin to Potsdam and back were filled with guests, some just riding the historic route because they could.

Despite the obvious social collision occurring, Berlin belongs to Brandenburg and Brandenburg to Berlin like Los Angeles belongs to California. One sees the travelers' astonishment as the train rolls past Berlin's Wannsee District into Babelsburg. Their surprised faces mirror their realization of how close and similar they are, like we always imagined but could never prove. In the end, Berlin and Brandenburg's 750-year history will prevail over the last artificially divided 28 years. However, it will take longer than everyone wants. But the question remains, what will Berlin and Brandenburg be like once it is re-established?

People are flowing in and out of Berlin. The surrounding districts live off the dynamics of the bustling capital. Many have been run down and look irreparable since the artificial division, but now life is springing up like flowers in springtime. This is just one of the many train openings between Berlin and Brandenburg. Like a magnet Berlin is attracting people and ideas back to its center. The flow of ideas, goods, and people has been suffocated during communist occupation. When one sees the old train system map from West Berlin, it is easier to see how artificial it was. New openings and system maps are continually being made to catch up with the pace of freedom. Now Germans can take a direct train ride from the state capital of Brandenburg to Berlin in 20 minutes. The walls continue to fall.

Days later, I discovered another symbolic headline of the rebirth of the German capital. The physical barriers dividing Berliners were falling. The German Army (*Bundeswehr*) announced that the rest of the Wall still suffocating West Berlin would be totally demolished by the end of 1992.[1] Five hundred former East German National Volks Army border guards are responsible for completing the job, which is taking over a year longer than originally planned.[2] Approximately half of the Wall that snaked directly through the middle of Berlin and around the perimeter of the West Berlin has already been removed.

Despite the fact that the physical separation of West and East Berlin is falling day by day, Berliners' souls are still divided. It is due in large part to the legacy of decades of communist social construction in East Berlin, in contrast to the democratic free market capitalism in West Berlin. Juergen

Kocka, a history professor at Berlin's Free University (FU) summed up the reunification results well:

> The transfer of the West German order to the former East German states has worked relatively well on the constitutional, legal, and institutional level. However, it has met with stiff resistance and has not progressed far on the level of social relations, political culture and everyday life. On another level (i.e. the economy), the transfer of the West German order has led to destruction and crisis.[3]

The remainder of this chapter addresses some of the main factors inhibiting Berliners and Germans from embracing their reunification.

Economics

"As far as inner unity goes," said Chancellor Kohl, "the economic and social challenges will admittedly take longer and cost more than most, including myself, had originally estimated." He went on to add, "What I hoped to achieve in three to five years will perhaps need twice that time."[4]

Not surprisingly, the mood in Germany in the 1990s is far from upbeat. Germans are pessimistic. Behind the scenes, each individual has a story to tell of the hardships associated with reunification.

Economics is one of the chief causes for the pessimism. Now, in retrospect, West and East Germans alike agree that in those difficult years of 1989 to 1990—as Chancellor Kohl was hard at work forging both domestic and international consensus for a reunified Germany—his promise of no new taxes and of a "blossoming landscape" in the East was only political rhetoric.

The collapse of the East German economy, and the gigantic subsidies required to keep Easterners working in outdated plants and factories at high wages, produced a propped up economy that was destined to fall—and hard. The conversion of East German deutsche mark to the West German deutsche mark contributed to the huge debt funding that took place upon reunification.[5] Thus, the days before the natural forces of a market economy could take their effect were numbered. Easterners learned the dark side of their new capitalism, as factories shut down and unemployment rose (industrial output fell by 65% in 1990-1991).[6] Said *The Economist*: "The result has been open unemployment of 17.6%; and hidden unemployment of 30-35%."[7]

East Germans have been washed ashore by the free market tidal wave that struck on November 9, 1989. Not only has their rent market been completely demolished and rebuilt, most of what capitalism entails is completely foreign to them. In Germany the government subsidizes much that is not subsidized in the United States, such as health care and generous allowances for the unemployed. Everything is new—their money, its value and all prices are suddenly up to the Western levels.

Job training offers another practical example of the economic walls present after overnight reunification and the resulting forced cooperation. Often, East German certification doesn't meet Western standards. For example, in Berlin former East Berlin school teachers are not allowed to teach in the Western part of the city, because their training is not considered on a par with Western standards. Even then, they are paid less. One Union leader called this "discrimination."[8]

Discrepancies in wages and salaries between East and West Germany comprise one of the many economic barriers in the reunified Germany. In comparison to West Berlin standards, East Berlin salaries are often only one-fifth the Western equivalent. After the fall of the Wall, it didn't take long for free market forces to take effect. Some West Berliners immediately took advantage of this obvious market advantage. For example, West Berliners began to buy groceries and gasoline in East Berlin and go out to East Berlin restaurants to wine and dine on pennies.

And it didn't stop there. Some Westerners also took advantage of the lower income markets in the East in real estate. Mainly students and other members of the lower income echelon have been moving East by the thousands. For example, while Eastern bureaucrats were trying to catch up with the whole philosophy of Western free market principles, people were signing five-year rent contracts still frozen on old East German prices. At approximately U.S. $1.50 per square foot, it was possible to rent prime real estate in the heart of Berlin. This phenomenon lasted for about a year in 1990-1991, before the Berlin Senate stepped in and prohibited such contracts.

And on top of that insult, the political rhetoric continued. "Our brothers in East [Berlin] must receive equal pay for equal work," said Chairman Landowsky in one of the party group meetings in 1991. Sitting in the back row of the conference room, I wondered to myself if this is just rhetoric. This phrase has been repeatedly used in West Berlin to appease East Berliners' demands. Indeed, equality of wages is not the reality. East Germans, doing the same job with the same skills, are paid 80% at most their Western colleagues wages.

But does an East Berlin secretary have fewer of the necessary skills to be a cleaning person, bus driver, or secretary? Maybe he or she cannot operate all the modern equipment at first, will need to be re-trained; maybe the company will initially lose money. But wouldn't this prevent an inferiority complex, an identity crisis, that otherwise might result from such policies? Who should pay for this? In the background of the social chaos the Easterner may be living in, wouldn't such a policy build more bridges and not more dams? Is this discrimination? Nevertheless, another brick in the economic barrier in the reunified Germany fell when the German High Court ruled on July 30, 1992, that East Germans that permanently work in the West, and live in the West, have to receive the same salaries as their Western colleagues.[9]

In some ways East Germans lived in an economic utopia. While Westerners were battling for jobs and working extra hours, most East Germans comfortably worked 35 (theoretically it was 42) hour work weeks and were hardly pressured even to show up. Unemployment was not in their dictionary. Health care was state-financed, as was child care.

Sabina, a 20 year-old student colleague from Berlin's Humboldt University told me that now she will wait and seriously think about it before having a child because there is no security, whereas in East Germany you were always guaranteed help and social advantages when you had children (the East German birth rate fell by 60% between 1989 and 1992, the marriage rate by 65%).[10] According to a demographer from the American Enterprise Institute: "Eastern Germany's adults appear to have come as close to a temporary suspension of childbearing as any large population in the human experience."[11] Brandenburg, in an effort to curb the drop in their citizens' birth rate, announced in 1994 that they will pay parents $650 for every child they have.[12]

For many, such social services were a given, something that society must provide, with no other possibility apparently thinkable. Now East Germans feel paralyzed in a system of cruel competition, deadlines, quotas, big insurance bills, and other hard realities.

Property Rights

The real estate market and property rights in Berlin exemplify a microcosm of what is happening in all of the former Eastern Europe. Since reunification Berlin property values have taken off, appearing to be a five-stage rocket just passing through the second phase. Some East Berliners are getting taken up in the storm of speculation and activity in the free market. And people are alarmed. Nervous renters are filled with fear of the future as the market continues to raise costs and swallow supply. The Berlin government is essentially handcuffed in trying to smooth out the pleas from its nervous citizens. The bureaucratic administration offices are overloaded with demands from all sides: more apartments, renter protection, lower costs. Berlin is known for having some of the most favorable rent laws in Germany.

Property rights are an explosive problem in the reunified Germany, one that will stay with it through the turn of the millennium. It is tearing Germans apart and exacerbating domestic tensions. Like many difficult issues that were frozen in the divided Europe, property rights dating back to World War II are pitting Westerners against Easterners. For East Germans, there is no safe haven from the transitions sweeping all aspects of their lives.

The German reunification treaty of 1990 provided that property owners, whose property had been confiscated or taken from them between 1949 and 1989, could legally reclaim their property. The result has been an onslaught of property claims from the West, most notably from the United States and Israel. Powerful Western lawyers, many of whom were representatives in the parliament, have made a windfall from the legal fees associated with such complex and drawn-out cases. The lawyers end up either winning back compensation for their clients or the property itself.

What about the occupants of the property in question? Current owners of disputed property have few rights other than the right of compensation. It does not matter if the current occupants or tenants may have been born and raised on the property: if the property records of ownership can be found in Berlin's city records, the legal owner under those records has the sole right to repossess the property. And to make matters more divisive, records show that 80% of those who got their property back sold it again.[13] The Brandenburg's justice minister called it "the biggest failure of unification."[14]

This explosive issue is also pitting states against states, and states against the federal government. Huge amounts of money are involved. For instance, the state of Berlin is suing the federal government over former Prussian state properties in Berlin that have been taken over by the federal government since reunification.

The Berlin justice department has processed literally thousands of cases since the fall of the Wall. One example is the IG Farben pharmaceutical company. IG Farben is suing for over 53 pieces of property in Berlin. IG Farben is a well-known company that was part of the Nazi war industry effort; it produced tons of Zyklon-B, the gas with which millions of Jews were killed.[15]

But property rights are also at stake on former Wall properties. This hot and heavy debate is dividing the country among the states more than the people themselves, but the effect is the same, East versus West. Ironically this divisive issue is about property that used to divide Europe.

The lack of the German government's interest in addressing the difficult questions raised by the German Unification Treaty of 1990 became especially clear during a Berlin parliamentary committee hearing in 1992. The Committee on Federal and European Affairs was visited by a citizen's group fighting for the return of properties confiscated during World War II and under the Soviet occupation. The spokesman pleaded with the Berlin Senator for Federal and European Affairs, Peter Radunski, to help the victims of this injustice. The senator told the group that he continues to try to resolve their dispute with the German government over property on the former Wall zone that belonged to them. He went on to outline various legal efforts that the state of Berlin was pursuing in Bonn to obtain compensation for them.

The following account was written after I heard various stories at that committee meeting, all of them deeply affecting.

As the Cold War was climaxing in the summer of 1961, Berliners living in the Russian sector alongside the Western Allies' sectors were evicted from their homes. Some witnessed the demolition of their houses by the Soviet Army. Days passed and soon there was a fence separating East and West, then came the Wall. But in the fall of 1989 the fireworks went flaring and the crowds cheered as the Wall came tumbling down. And although the 2+4 German Peace Treaty paved the way for reunification, it omitted the people on the Wall. All properties on the 1,560- kilometer-long, 50-meter-wide inner-German border and the 170 kilometers surrounding West Berlin became property of the German Defense Department.

As the Wall was being erected, people were thrown out of their houses to make way for the infamous *Todesstreife* (a 180-foot-wide barren strip where shoot-to-kill orders ruled). Now, 32 years and over 400 victims later, these people are demanding justice and restitution of their property. Berlin Senator for Federal and European Affairs Peter Radunski has been hard at work trying to find support for these discriminated-against families. In March 1992, he presented a bill in Bonn calling for the return of the *Mauergrundstuecke* (Wall properties) or at least financial compensation. But the Berlin representatives have still today been unable to find enough political support.

Other new German states aren't as interested in appeasing the unlucky few. One reason is that they don't have as much at stake. The property at issue in new German states outside of Berlin has very little value, consisting mainly of agricultural land. So they were generally uninterested in using their political poker chips for making another exceptional case for Berlin. In contrast, Berlin is a bustling metropolis: in 1992 it was the biggest construction site in all of Europe. And property prices are soaring. Since reunification Berlin office space has doubled or tripled in price. The $1,000-per-square meter ceiling has already been cleared in choice East Berlin locations.

The German government is remaining quiet about this sticky issue. It fears that at this time of rising domestic tension this will be interpreted as a failure in the reunification treaty. Why let another issue compound the already fragile political climate? Another reason the German government doesn't want to open this Pandora's box is that all state properties belonging to the former East German government are now in their hands. Once concessions are made to one interest group, everything will become unraveled and the German federal and state governments will be forced to either return all properties in question or to pay big compensation bills.

The German government isn't the only one with dirty hands. The Berlin Senate itself is not prepared to return private properties which they took over from the East German real estate monopoly. When they ask the federal government to return the Wall properties they are apparently generously foregoing their own possible rights. Or is the Berlin government just passing the buck? If Berlin were to pay compensation for all the private property in question it would be a sum greater than Berlin's annual state budget. The area of Potsdamer Platz, once one of the liveliest streets of pre-World-War Europe, is estimated to be worth $10 billion.

How can the German government just stand by and let this discrimination continue after the Wall is gone? Do they expect anyone to believe their rationalization that the former inner German border is required for military use? Aren't they in effect legitimizing the former military state which built it for this very purpose? Until this issue can be resolved it will continue to hinder investment in the German capital and the other new German states. Investors are wary of putting forth their money where they fear nasty law suits. And who wants to invest their money where property rights can change overnight?

Probably the best way to describe the effect of the property scandal and its role in the divided German capital is to look at it from the perspective of the normal East German citizen, one of Europe's new Germans. I had this opportunity, also through my work, when one of the East Berlin secretaries working in the CDU party group enthusiastically invited me to her birthday celebration. Although it was another trip to the East and I saw the red flags flash before my eyes, I tried to look beyond my stereotypes so that I could celebrate with her.

"Hey, Klaus. Come join us in the kitchen, this guy is an Amerikaner," said Stefan to Klaus, as they looked at each other in disbelief and shock, as if I were a precious foreign object, unstable and reactive. "Wow," he said, and stared at me in wonder as if I was from another planet.

I had the impression that America was as unimaginable to them as Mars and that I'd just arrived by spaceship in their apartment. All the guests welcomed me with the same look of disbelief and looked at me with either reserve or open interest. But clearly Stefan and Klaus were the most interested; they had the courage to speak to me.

"Imagine that, Stefan," said Klaus, "if someone told us three years ago that we'd be partying with an Amerikaner, we'd have laughed him out of here, if not beat him up." To me he said, "You know, then it was different. Don't be hurt, it was a different time." Both seemed to gaze off in contemplation, as I apprehensively stood there, still not sure where the conversation was going. Then they suddenly seemed to snap out of it and looked at each other in disbelief and laughed, slapping each other like good buddies in a beer hall.

In this party of friends, I felt outcast, and marked as the honored guest. I was an outsider looking into an insular community where gestures and words seemed to carry hidden meanings.

As Klaus continued to shake his head, I was overcome with the sincere impression that they were truly moved by my presence, just because of where I came from. As I was thinking this over, Stefan seemed to sense my attention wandering and quickly brought me back. "How unbelievable," he said, with an alarmed expression on his face, "but welcome." He smacked me on the shoulder. It was meant as a welcome, but it hurt and was meant to hurt. "That we would have an Amerikaner at one of our parties, it's just amazing." Smack one more time.

"No, man, he's an Amerikaner, he can't understand," said Klaus to Stefan. "But you've been here since the beginning and you're working in the state government," said Klaus as I nodded my head. "What should I do?" asked Klaus—and with a look of sadness and confusion he started to tell me a story. He told me of a piece of property to which he was given the rights to a building permit. He told me how for ten years he had been saving his money to get started on the project. "I knew people," he said, and continued on to relate how his friends were going to help him lay the foundation, get supplies, and build his dream.

"Today it is all gone. Everything is frozen," Klaus said, "the Senate has prevented me from doing anything. But look, I have the property rights still, I carry it around just in case I have a chance to meet someone who can help, who will listen," he said, as he pulled out his wallet and unfolded a contract, pointing to the official GDR seal. "Look, it is official," he said, as Stefan reminds him that it isn't anymore. "It was mine," he said with a hopeful look on his face, "it was going to be our dream garden, our summer getaway, where the family could go, where we could take a break from hectic city life."

As we stood in the kitchen, with the half-eaten roasted pig still scenting the air, and the American eighties dance music in the distance, I kept trying to remind myself that this was a party. The guests were diverse: the hostess; a secretary; her grandmother; her friends; friends of the friends. There was a teenager at the record player, changing the records at random; he, like the others, couldn't understand the lyrics of the English pop music.

But when he came to the latest pop German single, "Die Da," he played it at least three times, and someone finally had to take the controls from him. The party generally was stiff and uncomfortable. As the guests gathered in the living room, sitting in a circle and talking quietly with their neighbors, a couple got up and danced in the corner. Two boys and a mother with her two-year-old all danced together. The bar was wide open and we were all drinking heavily. It seemed to be the only thing to do outside of smoking.

After taking my break from the two 20-year-olds in the kitchen, I had the feeling I'd just been attacked and stripped. I glanced back into the kitchen and saw them waving me back. I felt obliged—they wanted to be understood, they needed an ear. "Guess what," said Klaus, as I re-entered the playing field, "I'm learning now to fix Chrysler cars. What a car, fast as you can imagine, it is incredible, it is exhilarating."

I asked him what he did before. He brushed the answer off and kept telling me how fast these new cars were, how incredibly quick and thrilling. The atmosphere was becoming increasingly stuffy. The smoke-filled rooms irritated my eyes and the smell of the leftover roast pig lingered. "The Chrysler stuff is fun, but times are tough," continued Klaus, "my wife— here she comes with a dejected look on her face—has been unemployed since reunification. Next week she should start her part-time job as a secretarial assistant."

"But I am lucky, I was trained in electrical work and couldn't do anything else. It has all changed, it is different today, everything is new. I am the minority, at 27 I am too old to be trained any more. What else can I do, so I have been learning the Chrysler repair procedures from the manuals." Stefan suddenly interrupted, after having patiently listened to Klaus spill his personal history. He also wanted a chance to talk to someone new, someone who would listen and sympathize. But Klaus insisted on making one more point.

"Man, you've been here so long, since the beginning, you really should write a book . . . and don't forget to write about how I had to save my money and was going to build a garden house, and how I have still have the deed but . . ." They continued to fill my cup with punch and my ear with stories. I excused myself to go to the bathroom and sat in a corner. I was overwhelmed by their openness. They were telling me personal stories, which I had yet to hear from West Germans I'd known for months. East Germans seemed more open to me, more naive.

Although the music became a little louder, the party activity was winding down, the faces were not half as welcoming, and I could see people slipping out the door. I went to get my jacket, waving good-bye to my newly made friends. I finally stepped out of the door; it felt as if I was just stepping out of a steam bath.

Descending the first flight of steps, I heard Klaus' voice yelling, "Wait a minute." Suddenly my new friends came rushing to the door as I looked up at them from the landing. They had welcomed me, they had accepted me in their normally private party, an American, their first American, and now it seemed as if they couldn't let their new friend go. I felt compassion and sympathy for them. They were genuinely honest. Pulling myself down the stairs was hard, but harder for them it seemed. Walking back to the train station for the long metro ride home, I thought about Berlin. As I went to sleep that night, recalling my visit, it seemed so far away, as if I'd been on a journey in a dream, and not just an hour away on the metro.

West German Prejudice

It should be no surprise that many prejudices exist in Berlin. While Easterners are dazed and in shock from all of the transition in their society since the fall of the Wall, Westerners are busy hurrying on to their next projects. After investing billions of Westerners' beloved deutsche marks into the Eastern economy, the German government, as well as private enterprise, is eager and ambitious to take advantage of their new domestic market opportunities in the new states. Nevertheless, on their unrelenting journey, Westerners are being delayed by their Cold War prejudices. From the Western elected officials down to the garbagemen, the understanding and appreciation for Easterners' past and the sensitivities associated with the division of Germany is negligible.

In this regard, I recall the first time I participated in a Berlin state CDU party group meeting. The main subjects discussed were the future of the 59-foot Lenin Monument in East Berlin and the selection of a new director for the Olympics organization. Berlin CDU Chairman Klaus Landowsky raised his voice and pounded his fist on the table, stating, "The monument must be removed—and quickly. I mean, what are our Eastern brothers to think of us if we tolerate such an abuse of our culture to continue?" As was often the case, his opinion was the locomotive for the whole party group.

And indeed, within weeks the demolition cranes went to work. As 1991 in Berlin came to a close, the Lenin Monument in East Berlin was surgically demolished. Landowsky and other conservatives harshly criticized the liberal parties, who protested against the high demolition costs and lack of sensitivity to history. In their view, the opposition parties' stand to preserve such monuments of the people ultimately responsible for East Germany's totalitarian regime is deplorable.

The Lenin Monument in the 1980s, courtesy of the German Information Center

Demolition of the Lenin Monument in 1991, courtesy of the German Information Center. Translation of sign: Berlin's Senate disposes here of German – German history in connection with a clean up operation against dissidents

The Alliance 90/The Greens' party group proposal to cover the monument with shrubbery, saving money and promoting greenery, would have been a better option. Building on top of existing foundations and what is present instead of trying to level everything the GDR physically left behind would have been more symbolic and representative of today's social and political environment. One should build bridges over the divisions of the past, not cause more destruction. However, the final decision was made and over the course of the next two months the monument dismembered.

It was disturbing to see that the resolve to remove the monument came almost entirely from the West. To many people in East Berlin it was representative of how the West is dealing with the East. As one restaurant waitress in East Berlin ironically put it: "Will they destroy everything we helped build? It seems that way to us." The sensitive subject of West Germans taking over the East erupted as the demolition began. Many protested against destroying East German culture with Western arrogance and resolve.

Despite the fact that many want to dismantle every remnant of the Marxist-Leninist ideological influence in the former East Germany, it is not as easy as sending a demolition team to one of the many monuments or buildings erected during communist reign. The conviction that they should be hastily dismembered illustrates the lack of understanding of its symbolic value to East Germans and a superficial way of dealing with social barriers, epitomizing the social conflict prevalent between West and East Germans.

Although Landowsky and others from the West are burning to tear down the psychological barriers that exist between them, they seem obsessed with such material objects because the psychological ones are so indiscreet and pervasive. Their sometimes fanatical passion appears to be out of revenge and frustration for not being able to break through their own prejudice. In a society where bridges need to be built and compromises found, such acts are destructive.

West Germans seem unaware that it is not possible to wipe away the real differences as easily as it is to destroy a monument. This illusion still exists, but everyday the cold reality becomes increasingly apparent. It digs deeper into what is certain to contribute to Germany's social divisiveness for years to come.

Notes

1   Brigette Baecker, "Minister lenkt ein: Fruehere NVA-Grenzer rauemen Maurreste bis September 1992 ab", Berliner Morgenpost, July 13, 1992

2   Ibid.

3   The Economist, "Germany's mezzogiorno", May 21, 1994, pg. 10

4   Marc Fisher, "In Reunited Germany, Even Taller Walls", International Herald Tribune, June 29, 1993

5   Upon reunification, experts estimated that one West German DM was worth some ten East German DM. The one to one East German DM to West German DM currency conversion up to DM 2000 for natural persons born after July 1, 1976, DM 4,000 for natural persons born between July 2, 1931 and July 1, 1976, and DM 6,000 for natural persons born before July 2, 1931, in addition to the two East German Mark to one West German Mark conversion for all deposits above those amounts have. Source: "Treaty Between the Federal Republic of Germany and the German Democratic Republic establishing a monetary, economic and social union", German Information Center, Official translation, autumn 1989.

6   The Economist, "Germany's mezzogiorno", May 21, 1994, pg. 10

7   Ibid.

8   Peter Mueller, "Ostlehrer duerfen keine Westschueler unterrichten", Die Neue Zeit, March 27, 1993

9   C. Glueksmann/C. Lang, "Volles Gehalt fuer 'Ost-Postler', die im West-Teil arbeiten", Berliner Morgenpost, July 31, 1992

10 The Economist, "Germany's mezzogiorno", May 21, 1994, pg. 10

11 Stephen Kinzer, "$650 a Baby: Germany to Pay to Stem Decline in Births", The New York Times, November 25, 1994

12 Ibid.

13 The Economist, "Germany's mezzogiorno", May 21, 1994, pg. 10

14 Ibid.

15 Otto Joerg Weis, "Heimkehr der Hohenzollern?", Frankfurter Rundschau, February 10, 1993

Chapter 5

The Stasi Legacy

When discussing the barriers present in the reunited German capital, the former East German communist regime and its secret police, the *Staatssicherheitsdienst* (Stasi), deserve their own chapter.

Probably one of the tallest walls separating East and West Berliners is their view of right and wrong and their sense of law and order. East Germans had no basis for respecting the law; East Germany was a police state. The infectious plague of the dictator state reached everywhere — in the justice department, in the police, in the property system. A story from an East Berlin student at Humboldt University illustrates the degree of this social plague.

Sabina was always present and on time to a seminar I attended at Humboldt University on international relations. In fact, often she came early to the small seminar and we frequently exchanged notes. Then in the span of two weeks she suddenly disappeared. I wondered to myself what happened and if everything was okay. When I inquired, none of my colleagues knew of her whereabouts. Upon her return, she did look more pale than usual. I asked her what had happened, what was wrong and where she had been.

With a nonchalant face and in a monotone voice she told me that her father had been killed last year—and that she had had to meet with the district authorities regarding his estate. I was so taken aback by her answer, by the word "kill," that I wasn't sure what to say, where to begin. Killed?

She just sat there, her figure motionless and her face pale, while my sympathy for her, for her suffering and loss washed over me. Then, with my defenses down and my heart open to her, imagining what it must be like to lose one's father, she shocked me: "It was no big loss," she said.

"He didn't love me anyway—I moved out when I was 15 and have had very little contact since then."

After blinking hard a couple of times, I began to question her directly and in detail. Killed? What do you mean, who did it, why, and how? Then in the same tone and the same manner, she said he was killed by the Stasi, because he knew who was who and what they all did. Now my amazement and curiosity were growing. I looked around the room to regain perspective, I was so swept up by her story. I turned to my fellow students. Were they listening? They were all preoccupied with something else.

"Did you go to the police department and report it? How was he killed?" I asked. In a monotone, she said: "I got a phone call one night from the neighbors, they said he was shot in the heart. After they called the police, they had him taken away and until now that is all that has happened. There is no investigation, they are claiming it was suicide, I even had to identify his body." As the tragedy of her story was building in me, I began to become a little uncertain and suspicious. "How can that be? How do you know?" I asked.

"He had been actively involved [with the Stasi] for over ten years, doing all sorts of secret things, they used to watch our house and stuff for years when I was little. He knew too much, knew too many people, maybe they didn't want to take any risks after the Wall fell. I know it is so." I was shocked that she never even thought about asking for justice to be done. It seemed indeed to make no difference to her. The story was incredible to me. As I repeatedly mentioned the police, she laughed with typical Berliner cynicism, and said, "What do mean, should I risk myself too? Don't you see, they are all the same." Fear came over me with these words, the distance between us shining through. After class ended, I quickly shuffled my way out of Humboldt University, through the crowded Friedrichstrasse train station, and with a sigh of relief boarded the first train headed to West Berlin.

For days I was shocked by the story. It seemed so dreamt up, like a film. A week later I was invited to dinner by West Berlin friends, one of whom happened to be a lawyer. I told them the story—I felt it was the least I could do. These West Berliners literally would not believe me. Sitting in my friend's nice garden, it seemed as if we were years away from each other. They refused to believe me, to the point of insult. Although Humboldt University was only two miles away in physical distance from their house, it was worlds apart in their imagination. It seemed far away from me too. The Wall stood higher than ever in our minds. There was a wall standing between us too.

While I tried convincing them of the truth and urgency of this story, they brushed it off as if it were not a concern to them, with the casual flick of the arm to the problems we don't have, as easy as flicking the remote control channel changer. We skipped dessert and coffee, and separated like strangers. That night, I dreamed of the invisible wall that separated me and giggling female athletes at the Olympic training center in East Berlin.

Following the experience with my former student colleague at the Humboldt University, I became more suspicious of everyone.

Since my arrival in the Berlin parliament, I had been following the developments surrounding the Stasi. From the outset, the discussion about how to deal with this aspect of East German history in the reunited Germany interested me. I always wondered how the decisions that are made today will affect the future of Germany. In other words, how will the reunified Germany come to terms with its past? What are the consequences, if it does not?

Since reunification, Berliners have begun to take small steps to counteract this social cancer. For example, the Berlin parliament decided to investigate its own representatives for associations with the former communist regime. In 1991, a Berlin parliamentary special investigation committee was established to investigate possible parliamentary representatives' association with the Stasi.

All representatives would be investigated for possible association through the so-called Gauck Authority (Hans Joachim Gauck is a Protestant clergyman and activist from Rostock who is the custodian of the Stasi files). The former East German secret police archives, filling more than five miles of shelves, are now under the control of the united German government.[1]

There is much fervor in preparation for the study and it has taken the parliament a long time to agree on the course of the investigation. "I'm sure some of my friends—even the people I am sitting next to in the party group meetings—are former members, maybe still real members," said one representative friend of mine as the announcement was made, "I will feel much better when everything is out in the open. Everybody is suspicious." Sitting at the back of the party group meeting, looking at all those faces, I drifted off thinking how many were involved.

The Berlin parliament's investigation of possible representatives' affiliation with the Stasi ended with a recommendation that two representatives resign. Altogether 13 representatives were called to testify.

Six representatives would be subject to further questioning, according to the Berlin parliamentary president.[2]

Also, the Berlin justice department began attempting to triumph over the crimes committed in the former East German police state when the Berlin justice department announced the first justice case for victims of the Wall. According to a government intelligence agency, over 400 people were killed on the Wall.[3] They will try to correct the injustices rendered. Some Berliners think it is insane to even try to prosecute the perpetrators of the crimes committed at the Wall.

The Berlin justice department's first trial to correct the injustices of East Germany's police state began on September 2, 1991. It did not start with the responsible officials on the high end of the chain of command. It was not Erich Honecker, former Stasi head Eric Mielke, or ex-Defense Minister Heinz Kessler who stood trial for the murder of Chris Gueffroy as he attempted to cross the Wall in Berlin's Treptow District (thus becoming the last victim of the Wall).[4] Instead, the public stood dumbfounded as four little-known draftees who happened to be border guards involved in the shooting went before the judge.

Upon reading this announcement, I was angry: Imagine being prosecuted for obeying a command, while your commander sits free in the same city. Is the Berlin Justice Department prosecuting the wrong people while the "big fish" are swimming free? But overwhelming all of those important questions, especially prevalent in the East, is the cynical question of whether it is possible to judge the acts of the former regime in the reunited Germany?

This first case against the border guards illustrates Berlin's unique position in relation to the question of the divided Germany, but it also offers another insight into the legal, political, and moral complexities that arise from the overnight unification of diametrically opposite systems of government. To begin with, Honecker and his cohorts could only be punished for individual violations of the law, not broad decrees which defined East German life—including the decision to build the Wall and the subsequent orders to shoot and kill attempted escapees. Also, the legal framework of the unified Germany complicates the attempt for justice. According to the German Unification Treaty, criminal offenses committed in the GDR could only be prosecuted if they were also punishable under GDR law. In its conviction of the border guards, Judge Seidel had ruled (and the Constitutional Court later upheld) that the deadly use of firearms by the border guards contravened the universal human right to life and freedom of movement, established at the Nuremberg Trials. Therefore, even under GDR law it was illegal.

During the trial, one of the suspects, Herr Kuehnpast, reminded the court of his company commander's praise for his action after the deadly shooting. "You behaved wonderfully," he had been told. After the shooting incident in 1989, the draftees were considered national heroes: they were given national medals, a vacation and some extra spending money. In his defense, Kuehnpast said that he obeyed the shoot-to-kill command out of anxiety and fear of authority.[5] The bricks of the Wall that are falling today are most certainly falling harder on some.

Then, weeks later, the Berlin Justice Department completed the indictment of over 100 cases against former inner German border guards for deadly firing on the Wall. More importantly, indictments were served against Eric Mielke, Erich Honecker, and other high officials. Nobody knows where these trials will lead, and I myself speculated on their duration and chance for success. Even if 100 people are prosecuted, how many others are roaming the streets of Berlin free despite their crimes against humanity committed behind the Wall?

With reunification, many former informers for the police state and the regime's collaborators have taken refuge in low-profile bureaucratic jobs. Meanwhile, their legacy lives on in a society that grew up with a skewed sense of justice, and a system filled with corrupt lawyers and judges.

Former lawyers and judges in East Germany have abused the idea of justice and they will be inclined to do it again if the circumstances are right. Some action is being taken today to weed out these criminals, but the search is destined to be incomplete and the legacy of injustice is likely to continue.

Weeks after the Berlin Justice Department announced its indictment of 100 former border guards and higher officials like Erich Honecker, another indictment was served by the Berlin Court against the lawyer who sentenced the accomplice of an attempted Wall escapee to three years in prison for breaking the East German justice code. It was also stated that the Justice Department is currently processing over 1,000 indictments against other lawyers and judges in the former East Germany for perversion of justice.

Out of the 370 lawyers and judges from the former East German capital that applied for continued public service and credentials, only 41 have been approved by the Berlin parliamentary independent commission for the election of lawyers.

In this regard, I recall a CDU party group session, in which the case of one former East German Judge was discussed. Her case was approved by the Berlin parliamentary independent commission to continue practicing. In response to the news, a number of CDU representatives pounded their fists on the table and complained to the mayor and party board members about this decision. Many representatives are lawyers themselves. They passionately debated the decision and appealed to the CDU mayor to somehow overturn the ruling. "How can a free, democratic society, let alone our own integrity as defenders of freedom and justice be preserved if we allow former servants of the repressive communist dictatorship to receive legal credentials in a Western constitutional society?" they asked.

The German magazine *Der Spiegel* summed it up best: "The dilemma of the investigative commission in Berlin and the other new German states was easy to see: all judges and lawyers in the German Democratic Republic were the henchmen of the SED-state. Their first objective was to serve the state and its laws."[6]

As the examples illustrate, East Berliners' relationship to the former communist regime is not only a result of the legacy of bygone days. Whether through investigations of association with the Stasi, crimes committed on the Wall, or for the election of former judges and lawyers into the reunified German justice system, Berliners are making hard choices about the way in which those decades of terror are being dealt with in the reunified German capital. Perhaps Germans' ability to forthrightly dismember the former East Germany's feared security apparatus, the Stasi, will indicate what lessons Germans learned from the post-World War II era. What influence did the Nuremberg Trials have on Germans, now that they are presented with a somewhat analogous situation in which a police state persecuted and violated citizens' basic rights?

With these questions in mind, I was delighted to receive an invitation to attend on May 11, 1992, a panel with members of an independent commission set up to investigate the Stasi. "Hopes and Fears from the Stasi Past" was appropriately held in the Reichstag.

Now that we are aware of how Berlin has begun to deal with this complex aspect of their history in reunification, perhaps this discussion group would offer some insight into how the German government is dealing with it.

These are some of the questions that were running through my mind as I made my way to the Reichstag: What views do these federal officials hold of the Stasi problem, and *die sogenannte Aufarbeitung der Geschichte* (the so-called rehabilitation of history) that is taking place to forge consensus of the divided past in the reunited Germany?

Arriving at the lonely Reichstag on a windy fall evening, I walked into the ominous building curious what this evening would bring. I was immediately overcome by the emptiness of this powerful and impressive building. The only people present were the security guards. After climbing the giant staircase and reaching room 2003, I opened the heavy doors. Suddenly, a small crowd appeared before me. After quickly scanning the room, one thing was clear to me: there were people from all walks of life attending. The contrast between the lifeless atmosphere in and around the Reichstag and the bustling atmosphere in the meeting room was immediate and stark. I quietly took my seat and immediately noted that nervous expectation filled the room. Then the panelists appeared and after making their formal introductory remarks, the first speaker, Rainer Eppelmann, took the microphone.

Eppelmann, the chairman of the commission, stated that the only way to successfully work through individual rehabilitation cases of former East Germans terrorized by the Stasi was with the help of former East Germans. The decisive question is not whether the rehabilitants were engaged with the Stasi, but rather why they were, he emphatically remarked. Further he expressed his concern that both a predominant number of rehabilitation cases as well as the entire subject of Stasi terror are being overshadowed by such high profile cases as Erich Honecker and the current governor of Brandenburg, Manfred Stolpe. Eppelmann concluded his statement by pleading with the guests to approach the whole subject of the Stasi terror with heart and understanding. Only this way, he said, is it possible for "us" to properly work through the problem.

The next speaker was Herr Poppe, a Alliance 90/The Greens Bundestag congressman and a former East German church leader. He complained that many East Germans have forgotten their own history. He stated that East Germans have become complacent and uninterested, and warned against letting the river of history continue forward without looking backwards. Poppe concluded by saying that it is now a totally new beginning for Germans. Germans need to properly deal with their respective East and West German history, as well their previous united history in order to make lasting progress.

After each panelist made his respective remarks, the discussion was opened to guests for comments and questions. It offered another insight into the degree of suffering present in the reunified German capital. From the outset, the open floor discussion started off with a bang and continually lit up the room like a fireworks show. Some former East Berliners recounted their days of terror, from being continually followed by Stasi agents and German shepherd dogs to receiving late-night check-up calls. They complained vociferously about the fact that today, in a so-called *Rechtsstaat* (state under the rule of law), so many of the same people who they once feared or were forced to report to because of their Stasi connections, are roaming free in a democratic, reunified Germany. Many former Stasi workers, they complained, today sit in the same bureaucratic offices they held in the East German capital. Others guests were more tolerant of the past. Instead of criticizing the former East Germany, these tolerant guests vented their respective frustrations with the reunified Germany by lashing out at West Germans for conducting a witch-hunt.

As the above example illustrates, the diversity of guests was very striking—from retired politicians, church officials and plumbers to young lawyers—and offered a broad spectrum of ideological conviction and opinion. At the same time, it illustrates how pervasive the state police structure was because such a broad spectrum of society was interested enough to attend.

Raising my hand, I asked Herr Eppelmann what he personally feared to be the worst development of such divisive and complicated investigations like the one surrounding Brandenburg's governor, Manfred Stolpe. Stolpe was a senior official in the East German Lutheran church who, according to records found in the Gauck archives, was a Stasi informant who received an East German medal for his distinguished service. Stolpe has been under investigation for his contacts with the Stasi for over a year and has been in a bitter legal and public struggle with Hans Joachim Gauck about his Stasi association. "My greatest fear is that we will come to the point and just say 'enough is enough' and that this difficult period will be covered up and brushed aside. We should learn from our history [our dealings with former Nazis after World War II] and not make the same mistake twice," he said.

Hearing the pleas and personal stories recounted by these fellow guests at the discussion group in the Reichstag, I was overcome with pity and a feeling of helplessness. So many victims of the dictatorship were suffering. But proof is very hard to come by, if not impossible, and the chance that these people will have their cases brought to justice is very small. Many documents are missing from the famous East German Stasi records and therefore testimony is hard to come by. In the critical days following the dissolution of East Germany, many former leaders had unlimited access to the Stasi records. Gossip has it that during the chaotic and turbulent days after the fall of the Wall, many high ranking officials broke into the Stasi headquarters and destroyed their personal files.

Back in the conference room, the atmosphere is near boiling with people interrupting speakers and making sideline comments. Suddenly I recalled another story of suffering from the hands of the Stasi. During one Berlin parliamentary committee visit with the Committee for Federal and European Affairs, we visited the former Stasi prison in Berlin-Hohenschoenhausen. At that time, the site was under consideration by the Berlin parliament for placement under memorial protection.[7] I was impressed by the torment and suffering embodied in the dark cells we'd visited. The memory of the visit haunted me for many nights. Eager to share my compassion for the people who were imprisoned in that hateful place, I asked one of the representatives on the sidelines of a committee hearing whether he had been there before.

In response to my question, the representative immediately pulled away from me in a nervous fashion as he flinched. My first reaction was that he thought I was just about to hurt him. I stood there, a little insecure that perhaps I'd said something wrong. I asked him if everything was all right. Then, with stern eyes and a cool tone, he said: "I've unfortunately already been there for a long time and don't need a tour to imagine what it is like." Taken aback by his words, I asked him what he meant. Pointing to a couple of chairs on the wall, and pulling out a cigarette, he waved for me to sit down as he continued:

"I was imprisoned there from 1976 until 1978 for anti-government propaganda," he said. "Why, what did you do?" I asked him as I moved closer. With a nervous twitch and lighting his cigarette, he told me that in East Germany many people were apprehended by the Stasi for propaganda against the regime, including himself.

"My friends and I used to gather together, we would talk about our views against the government and everything. The Stasi got a hold of some of the pamphlets we had distributed and as a result, my friends and I were sentenced to indefinite confinement. At first the confinement was very difficult. The prison cell was just big enough so that you could turn around and take a step, but that was all. On some days they would take us to what was known as the "u-boat," where we would descend these awful steps into a dungeon-like pit. It was cold and dark down there. After two of us were lowered into the pit, then they would leave. Then, a little later the water began to run. It kept coming and coming, I thought they were going to drown us, but then just as the water reached my knees it stopped. Then a half and hour later it began to run again and we thought this was it, but as it reached our hips it stopped. The coldness and smelly nature of the place was pitiful," he said.

As his eyes nervously twitched, I saw him reach for another cigarette. I must honestly say that after having observed this committee for over a year, I was always taken back by his curious nervousness. I always held him in contempt for this. Today I still feel ashamed for having looked upon him as if I was psychologically so much stronger. "They always wanted to break you, wanted to get you to conform," he said. "And so after a year of such regular treatment," he continued, "then another year of confinement, I lost some of my rebellious motivation. Sure, the core of my idea never disappeared, but the whole nature of the stuff just changes. I had to be more careful when they let me out, otherwise it would have been over. Some of my friends never made it out, and I don't know what has happened to them nor where they are now." [8]

While his cigarette butt was burning his hand, he sat there motionless, looking in a daze down the hall. I felt like he had just taken me with him on a journey into a dark cavern. Then another representative came storming to the doors, telling us to hurry our way in, they would be voting on a proposition shortly. As he slowly snapped out of his dream, he threw the rest of the butt in the ashtray, as if he were unaffected by the spark burning his fingers for the last minutes and motioned that we'd better get back into the committee room. Taking my place against the wall of the hearing room, I looked at this man entirely differently and wondered to myself, how many others have such histories, in Berlin's united parliament.

Blinking my eyes, I roused myself after my mind had wandered, remembering that story. I was alone in room 2003 gazing out of the bay windows onto the barren Pariser Platz. "Where did everyone go," I casually thought to myself, "I must have spaced out." Regaining my focus, I saw the Brandenburg Gate through the window. It was the only symbol of life on the dark fields outside the Reichstag.

Suddenly, a security guard came by to lock the doors and asked me to leave. Picking up my things, still half in a daze, I exited the room and found myself gazing up at the high ceilings, those big, powerful empty halls of the Reichstag. After finding my way to the exit, I suddenly found myself at the lonely Brandenburg Gate. I was subconsciously pulled there to find it sleeping in the darkness.

Berlin's great symbol of East meets West was still, in 1992, balancing tenuously between West and East. The surroundings were quiet; the Brandenburg Gate is poorly lit in the middle of Berlin. What better place to stand and contemplate the new Germany? After standing in the silent evening air for minutes on end, gazing up at the poorly lit gate, my mind began racing back to the meeting. Looking up at the chariot on the Brandenburg Gate, I was overcome by the stories of suffering I had just heard in the Reichstag. Despite the efforts of federal commissions, support agencies and the like, nothing can atone for or compensate the victims of the East German regime still suffering, like the Berlin representative I had just spoken to.

Well-meaning and hopeful, the state and federal commissions established to prosecute Stasi crimes in the reunified Germany are facing a long up-hill battle with few supporters and many opponents. Their noble intentions seem rendered futile by politicians and society who prefer to focus on rebuilding the country through might, rather than by addressing the legacy of their past. Courageous and prominent figures like Herr Eppelmann and his colleagues are battling many obstacles and opponents, deserving the fullest support and respect. They are the only hope that many of the Stasi criminals will be brought to justice, and the cancer lurking beneath German society will be removed.

And Herr Eppelmann's fear has proved just. In a 1994 public opinion survey, 57 percent of former East Germans favor closing the Stasi secret police files. In response to this development, Hans Joachim Gauck said:

> We are hearing appeals for an approach to the past which reminds us of West Germany in the 1950s. The total silence about Nazi crimes in those years created one generation that refused to face the truth and another that struck out with excessive violence against the rule of law. We don't want this to happen again. Instead of taking the easy path of nostalgia, we must confront difficult truths. There can be no peace without honestly and maturely confronting the past.

Not all feel that way. Said Manfred Stolpe in response to the poll: "We have to put an end to this discrimination against Eastern Germans."[9]

One possible reason that some Germans are inclined to ignore the past is the legacy of WWII. On top of West Germany's failure in the 1950s to come to terms with Nazi crimes, East Germans didn't feel at all responsible for those same crimes. For one, the two German states dealt completely differently with their shared Nazi past. While West Germany paid compensation to Jewish organizations and to two million claimants amounting to upward of $80 billion and, in addition, developed relations with Israel, East Germany denied any historical responsibility for Nazi crimes.[10] The German Democratic Republic claimed that because the communists themselves opposed and were persecuted by the Nazis, that their country was not a successor state to the Third Reich, and therefore East Germans bore no historical responsibility. Also, East Germans maintained that anti-Semitism could not exist in a Socialist society and that East Germany had purged all former Nazis. Thus, the reunified Germany began with a divided perception of their shared Nazi past, as well as what lessons were learned from West Germany's shortcomings in weeding out former Nazis from power. This directly affects East and West Germans' respective willingness to confront the legacy of the police state in the former East Germany, and is a recurrent source of division between East and West.

East German Dictator Set Free

German's collective unwillingness to deal with the difficult questions of the past was poignantly illustrated on January 10, 1993, when Erich Honecker was freed. Honecker was East Germany's ruling dictator from 1971 to 1989. As late as 1989, Honecker said: "The Wall will remain as long as the conditions that led to its construction remain unchanged. It will be there in 50 years and also in 100 years.

After spending over 30 days in Berlin's Moabit high security prison on manslaughter charges, East Germany's former leader was released. Based on what the Berlin Court called humanitarian grounds, the ruler of the former East German terror regime was freed. Within a day he was in the arms of his wife and daughter, who were waiting for him in exile in Chile.[11]

I joined the many in shock. How could they let this convict go? If his physical condition prevented him from standing trial, as the prosecution proclaimed, why couldn't he be treated in Berlin, in a special cell with all the advantages of modern German medicine? Was Honecker to be distinguished from the Nazi war criminals who were either executed or sentenced to life? Perhaps Germany wanted to avoid an embarrassing repeat of the incident involving Rudolf Hess, who waited for his death in

Berlin's Spandau high security prison before taking his own life? Or did the court hope to spare the much divided German society the trials and tribulations of such a divisive East-West issue, preferring to wash its hands clean of the past? The memory of the red carpet treatment Honecker was given in Bonn by Chancellor Kohl as the East German national anthem was played still lingers on, along with other tolerant relations in the détente era.

Much to my disappointment, Germany is not prepared to work through the difficulties of the past and deal with them resolutely and with certainty, especially relating to the former communist East Germany.[12] Or were former President Reagan's words "the evil regime" taken by Germans as token Cold War rhetoric? Tragically, Germans are choosing to put their difficult past behind them and go forward without resolving certain issues. One of the many ironies of this decision is that the subject of bringing Honecker to justice filled the press since his "secret" escape to the former Soviet Union in 1990. Since reunification many Germans have been obsessed with making Honecker stand trial for his crimes, loudly proclaiming that justice must be done. The result sent shock waves around the globe. He was not in the hands of the West German officials for 100 days before he was set free.

All that energy and effort seemed to be in vain. Outcries and protest flooded the media. Like many other sensitive issues of the day, this one tore at the frayed fabric of German unity. Do East Germans feel once again deceived by the West? After all those years of propaganda and heavy campaigning against the corrupt East Germany, the reunified German court lets the leader of this regime go! How can the West expect to be taken seriously by East Germans looking for justice?

Only ill can come from this. Is it not ironic that as Honecker flies in a first-class seat to Chile, people are being detained and court cases are proceeding against guards who worked on the inner-German border, the border he commanded? It just doesn't make sense, but unfortunately it makes good politics.

Honecker represents the pinnacle of injustices committed by the East German police state. During the Cold War, he and his cohorts didn't just sit back in their walled-off communist state and terrorize its citizens. They were busy training their troops for the grand invasion that never happened. They were diligently preparing themselves for the Cold War attack on the West. And the plans were real. Within months after Honecker's release, the Berlin government revealed materials that describe in detail how evil the Cold War dictator and his comrades were. On March 2, 1993, the Berlin government released to the public Stasi plans for the takeover of West Berlin.[13] These one-time highly classified papers are just some of the secret Cold War documents that have recently been released by the Gauck Authority.

Nevertheless, justice for East German criminals is hard to impose. One concession West German politicians made in the German Peace Treaty was that only the GDR canon would be valid in Eastern criminal cases, not Western law or natural justice. The trial of the former East German Stasi Chief, Eric Mielke, offers a case in point. Despite the numerous offenses that have been recorded against him, he is only being tried for killing two Weimar policemen in a 1931 riot.

Because of the problematic nature of the Honecker decision, it is probably a good thing that Honecker died of cancer over a year after the court's reprieve.[14]   Because the longer the dinosaur East German communist dictator sat on the beach in Chile with his millions of stolen German deutsch marks, the greater the damage would have been to the German people, the more divisive the issue would have become, and the more of a burden it would have been to the German democratic institutions that pardoned him.

Conclusions

As outlined above, economics, property rights, Cold War prejudices, justice, and of course the East German communist legacy are dampening Germany's ability to forge a national unity. As a result, the two cultures of East and West Berlin are only living beside each other in the reunified German capital. After the fall of the Wall, the two cities stood up, looked at each other, and then sat back down. With this background in mind, it shouldn't be surprising that a poll taken in 1992 found that one in ten East Germans between 18 and 30 will move to West Germany soon and that more than 66% of Germans think the psychological wall is growing between East and West.[15]

Berlin is a city like no other city in the world, with two separate societies. The German capital's struggle with reunification is exemplary of the entire countries. It is a delicate synthesis, one which needs to be carefully handled in order to grow over time. Deeper bonds of unity may need to be uncovered to help Germans overcome their divisions.

Notes

1   Der Bundesbeauftragte für die Unterlagen des Staatssicherheitsdienstes der ehemaligen Deutschen Demokratischen Republik, otherwise known as the Gauck Authority, has developed into the place of judgment for former East Germans. This mammoth complex employs over 3,400 employees and contains 202 km's of book shelves as well as a card index with over 6 million names. (footnote: Berlin "Der Bundesbeauftragte fuer die Unterlagen des Staatssicherheitsdienstes der ehemaligen Deutschen Demokratischen Republik" pages 266, 267, 268)

It is also a fascinating look into the complete secret service apparatus of one of the well known headquarters of the Warsaw Pact. The official job of the still heavily guarded complex is to collect, to arrange in an archival fashion according to relevance, to close, and to manage the files. The office is also providing documents for the rehabilitation of victims of the communist regime and studies cases for persons in church circles or public service. These well documented files contain information on those citizens who either worked for the former East German regime, or those who are regarded as its enemy. Although every person has the right to look into their file, it is hard to know if one exists on you or not, and only by demanding access can one discover the answer to this life-influencing question. People who have filed their applications have to wait tortuous weeks, sometimes months, before they receive permission or a notice stating that no file exists.

Every employer has the right to demand a report on his/her employees. Where the joy of reunification once prompted many employees to hire their newly discovered countrymen, many are now standing trial. Employees having their so-called files studied have been on the verge of a nervous breakdown, knowing perfectly well that if they have something remotely incriminating in their files, then it's straight to the unemployment lines.

Some critiques ask how the West can place so much value on these files, treating them as if they were authentic and legal, when West Germany didn't even officially recognize East Germany until 1972. However, others ask, why should they be nervous if they did nothing wrong.

There are about six million dossiers, almost a third of the former East Germans had a file. That means there is a 33% chance that one may have been classified as a collaborator, supporter, or opponent to the communist regime. This nightmare for some is another barrier in the already problematic union of East and West Germany. On the other side of the coin, these files also offer the German justice system important information on the East German secret police crimes, and the identity and activities of the STASI's 91, 000 agents and 173,000 informers. (source: Stephen Kinzer, "Pictures From a Spy Camera at an East German Exhibition", The New York Times, December 16, 1994, pg. A18)

Considering the numbers involved, it was no surprise, when after the public was allowed to apply to see their files as of January 1, 1992, that the place was flooded with applications.   In the first quarter year after they were opened to the public, over 300,000 applications were filed to look into their personal files. In March alone, 400 new employees were added to handle the overwhelming numbers of applications.   Knut Pries, "300,000 wollen Stasis-Akten sehen," Sueddeutsche Zeitung, April 3, 1992

2   Frankfurter Allgemeine Zeitung, "Der Berliner Ehrenrat empfiehlt zwei Abgeordneten Mandatsverzicht", July 1, 1992

3   Dieter Rulff, "Uber vierhundert Tote an der DDR-Grenze", TAZ, January 4, 1993

4   Der Tagesspiegel , "Mauerschutzen wollen anebengezielt haben", September 3, 1991

5   Ibid.

6   Der Spiegel, Justiz: "Grosste Schnauze", December 30, 1991

7   Christian Fueller, "Vom Stasi-Knast zum Denkmal", TAZ, May 16, 1992

8   As noted by Marc Fisher in his book, *After the Wall*: "Anytime the East Germans determined that someone had stepped too far out of line, the offending party could be sold to the west, eliminating the problem and earning hard cash in one single step. . . . Before the Wall finally fell, West Germany bought freedom for 250,000 East Germans and opened the gates for thousands of elderly people, freeing the East of expensive pension obligations.   The west's willingness—eagerness even—to take in troublemakers as their own was seen in Bonn as a humane, liberal policy. But it allowed the Honecker government to prevent the development of the angry circles of professors, journalists, writers, scientists, women and students who corroded totalitarianism elsewhere in the East Bloc in the 1970s and 1980s."

9   Stephen Kinzer, "Pictures From a Spy Camera at an East German Exhibition" The New York Times, December 16, 1994, pg. A18

10 Peter Heidenberger, "Germany Offers Fair Holocaust Reparations", The New York Times, October 4, 1994

11 Melvin J. Lasky, "The Trial of Erich Honecker", National Review, March 29, 1993

12 Later, in a separate development, on May 23, 1995, Germany's high court ruled that former East German spies can't be charged for espionage against West Germany — thereby granting amnesty for over 5,000 former East German intelligence officers. According to *The Economist*: "Since the Constitutional Court's decision . . . it is logical to expect that it will lead to leniency for East German judges, prosecutors, Stasi functionaries, letter-openers, phone-tappers and all the other agents of a disgraced and repressive regime. . . ."(sources: Frederick Kempe, "Now a Free Agent, Master Soviet Spy Tells Rich Tales", *The Wall Street Journal*, May 25, 1995, and *The Economist*, "Unspooked", June 3, 1995, pg. 46)

13 In the mid-1980s, under the auspices of the Warsaw Pact's plans for attacking NATO, specific plans were drawn up for the takeover of West Berlin. General lieutenant Schwanitz, the director of East Berlin's state security administrative branch, published a document in 1985 with details of the invasion, including the capture and imprisonment of city leaders as well as members of the economic, media and police circles, and other communist enemy leaders. Also included in his report were the outline to takeover all important enemy centers, and the establishment of a communist city administration.

Recorded conversations from East Germany's NVA (National People's Army) officers and their reports provide an insight into their former top secret strategy. They estimated Allied enemy strength to be around 12,000 soldiers with an additional 6,000 Berlin police officers. The invasion troop strength was 32,000. They planned to divide the city in two sectors, with the border running from Konradshoehe to Lichtenrade with the freeway in the middle. The first goal was the takeover of Berlin's Allied-controlled Tegel, Tempelhof, and Gatow Airports. Sector One was to be invaded by the National Peoples Army, while Sector Two was to be invaded by the Soviet Army stationed in Potsdam. In order to facilitate their invasion practices, a ghost Berlin town was constructed at the Lenin troop training grounds, with a model airport, U-Bahn and S-Bahn exits, banks and canals. Source: Otto Wenzel, "Die Eroberung von West-Berlin", Zitty, March 17, 1993, pg. 36

14 Erich Honeker died on May 29, 1994

15 Der Spiegel, "Erst Vereint, nun entzweit", January 18, 1993, pg. 3

Chapter 6

Berlin's Darker Side

When addressing the walls present in the reunified Germany, this subject would be incomplete without mention of the last time Berlin was the working German capital.[1]   The holocaust of approximately six million Jews was decided and coordinated in Berlin. Now that Berlin is free again, the reunified region is beginning to grapple with the difficult questions posed by the legacy of the Third Reich that had been smothered by the Cold War.

As described in the chapter 5, East and West Germans emerged from the rubble of WWII with polar opposite interpretations of responsibility and the lessons learned from the Nazi past. Although Berliners share uncommon perspectives on the lessons learned from WWII, they do share the devastation the war brought to their capital: At war's end, Berlin was 80 million cubic yards of rubble. Everywhere one goes in Berlin, one is constantly reminded of the devastation and crimes committed in this capital center of the Nazi regime. Whether manifested in bombed fields in the desolate city center, or plaques commemorating houses where noted Jewish writers and artists were arrested for deportation to concentration camps, the legacy is still part of the city.

Once you look behind the facades of the gray buildings, Berlin offers the paradoxical promise of the new and the hope of the future, juxtaposed with reminders of its shameful years as the capital of the Third Reich. One of my first encounters with this Berliner paradox was discovered upon reading a newspaper announcement, in which the Berlin mayor laid a memorial plaque at Gruenewald train station in commemoration of the 50th year anniversary of the deportation of Jewish citizens from Berlin to labor and concentration camps. On October 18, 1941, the deportation of

Berlin's Jewish population in cattle wagons began from Putlitzstrasse and Gruenewald train stations.[2]

Upon reading the article, I was captivated and I re-read it twice. Gruenewald! After having crossed over this train station every time I rode into the main part of the city, it never occurred to me that this old train depot, characterized by large red brick warehouses and run-down switch points, was used for this purpose.

Evil looms over the station after one becomes aware of the fact that thousands of Jewish Berliners were shipped to concentration and forced labor camps from 1942 until the end of the war. Many questions and a perverse curiosity pervade my thinking as I became aware of this. Is that why some of the warehouses are completely let go and why there are so many unused train tracks? Being one of my favorite stations because of its central location on the edge of a lush forest, I begin to regard this stop with mixed feelings, something that one does often in this city of many contradictions.

Berlin's relation to its past and its responsibility as the former capital of the Nazi regime was well illustrated weeks after the capital vote for Berlin, when I stumbled upon a very sobering report in a small newspaper column, tucked away in the back pages, about another development plan. This was not a plan like many others. The difference was that this development project was on the site of a former Ravensbrueck Nazi concentration camp, approximately 35 miles from downtown Berlin.

Although a small memorial existed at the Ravensbrueck camp location in Brandenburg, the development plan called for building a shopping mall, including a full service supermarket and car lot. The article read as if there were already a green light for the project. Despite the haunting nature of the place, in which over 92,000 women and children were killed, investors were not inhibited.

The announcement shocked me. How could Germans build a shopping mall on the site of a Nazi concentration camp? Is this symbolic of their disregard for the crimes once committed at the former concentration camp and their interest in forgetting the last time Berlin was Germany's capital? Was this healthy for the reunited Germany and its new capital, from which Berliners were once shipped in cattle cars and subsequently murdered?

Previously, I had disregarded various commentators' opinions about Berlin's association with German Nazism and warnings about history repeating itself. To me such reports were crazy. Everything has changed, the Germans too. Or has it?

As these questions were churning in my stomach, I was thrust back to the memories of primary school history lessons, and my viewing of the Holocaust television programs, in addition to the less subtle propaganda associated with Germany in the 1930s and 1940s. How could these Germans be so insensitive, and choose to build on such sacred ground, where thousands of people were murdered during the Holocaust?

Perhaps more baffling than the project itself, I was shocked by the lack of attention the announcement of building a shopping center on a former concentration camp received. Why was it on page 10 of the newspaper, for instance, and only reported in three small paragraphs. In response to my alarm, I read the announcement out loud to my Berlin friends; they all shied away from my confrontational remarks. They were obviously at a loss for answers.

My anxieties were soon relieved that this would become just another oversight. Days after I discovered the horrifying announcement, protest reports filled the front pages of the newspaper media. By the end of the week, it was the top story in the German capital. Meanwhile, rumors had been reported from Furstenburg town council meetings that the Brandenburg state officials had given their final approval for the project's completion. At the time of the public protest and media coverage against the development project, a leading supermarket chain, Kaiser's, had almost completed construction of their future grocery store, only 500 yards from a small monument to the Holocaust victims.[3]

Furstenburg city district spokesmen rationalized their actions by noting the need for jobs, stating that although the land is of historic importance, it was also an ideal development location and that this development would help the community.

As days passed and the dark reality of the project set in, a public debate erupted. Also public pressure was mounting in Brandenburg, with arson attacks being threatened and public demonstrations from Jewish and Gypsy groups in many European countries. International pressure ensued in the form of newspaper editorials and television coverage. Nevertheless, it seemed as if no one was going to stop them.

With echoes of the past stirring in the former Nazi capital, the Berlin Senate finally appealed to the Brandenburg government to withdraw the building permit. It worked. Days later, the Brandenburg state government bought out the owners and placed the area under memorial protection. Brandenburg officials later admitted that they had "made a mistake."[4]

The announcement by the Furstenburg officials points to one piece of the German puzzle, something that proves itself over and over in the coming pages: the paradox of Germans reconciling their past crimes against humanity and their openness to deal with the difficult questions that arise from them. Wound up in this complex pattern is Germany's unrelenting drive forward. Germans are free, yet chained by the ghosts of the past. They are ambitious and self confident, but defensive and self-conscious. They are divided. The stark dichotomy of these developments provoked my curiosity and seduced me to look deeper — to try to understand the direction in which they are collectively moving.

My discovery of the train station's darker past and then the development project on the former concentration camp were some of my initial discoveries of the legacy of the Third Reich. They poignantly illustrate the social and political walls present in the reunified German capital. Some are walls that Germans are born with, like their history. Other walls, like prejudice and discrimination that we all have in us to a degree can be overcome through education, leadership, and personal will. Regardless, they continually haunt their consciousness and lifestyle. No wonder Germans are so complicated, some say difficult.

Wandering and thinking about places, and the roles they served and the evil they witnessed, was an awakening for me.

With my eyes open to Berlin's legacy as the capital of the Third Reich, I discovered more skeletons of Berlin's past. My best friend in Berlin, Ulf, lives in the city district of Tempelhof. Because I always preferred to live in the green southwestern sector with the lakes, it was always cumbersome for me to visit him, and vice versa. Often, I would take the underground train to the Tempelhof airport, and then ride the bus from there. But I don't like to wait for buses, so I would always walk to the next bus stop. This is how I discovered the next skeleton in Berlin's war chest.

Walking along the street parallel to the airport, I was overcome by the size of the buildings, and their emptiness. They were gigantic, bigger than any other airport terminal, or hangars I had ever seen. There were no signs or markers indicating a historic site. At first impression, I thought they were just empty warehouses. Only after the third or fourth time passing by, impatiently looking for the next bus, did I realize that they were all empty. How many people have walked this path before, how many soldiers? One night I asked my friend what they were.

He told me that Tempelhof had been Berlin's central airport since 1923. The hall complex was constructed in 1936-1939 under the Nazi regime. Upon its opening, it was celebrated as being one of the biggest buildings in the world, one of the new architectural wonders of the Nazis' future capital city, Germania. Just being in the proximity of these buildings, of this entire airport, is a frightening experience: the sheer mass and volume these buildings occupy is unimaginable. I was always unsure why I had such strange feelings when I rode my bike or even walked by this airport. The buildings seem so disproportionately big for an airport, one doesn't even think an airport could be there. Even the landing turboprops are out of place, not big or loud enough to be using this powerful and impressive facility. I had always wondered why the buildings were always empty, why there seemed to be no activity. There are few windows and their concrete construction is cold and unwelcoming.

Upon realizing that the American Air Force has control of the complex, I began to reflect and understand better. Since World War II, these gigantic buildings have only been partially used by the Americans. Walking into the base for the first time, I couldn't help noting the large halls and big sinks in the marble bathrooms.

The Americans have influenced Tempelhof, they have taken all of the life out of the one-time bustling and busy *Luftwaffe* airfield. Even the American flag waving in the air at the main gate is out of place, appearing artificial and inappropriate in the shadow of the mammoth square entry hall. Now that the Americans are departing, a controversial discussion has erupted as to what should be done with these fortified buildings that look like they would laugh at an earthquake. Working through the history is a big problem in regard to buildings such as Tempelhof.

Not only did the Americans cover up the Nazi ghosts to be found at the Tempelhof Airport, but most of the bases that the Americans took over, as well as the French, British, and Soviets are tarnished. For instance, the American Army's Andrews Barracks was the former site of the Royal Prussian Cadet Corps and later the headquarters of the Nazi SS.

With my eyes now wide open, I found Berlin to be littered with many different tributes to this period in history. Relics of World War II exist throughout the city. Like Tempelhof Airport, it is hard to know what something is from the street, you need either a historical guide book or to ask someone. The Olympic Stadium, the current site of the Treuhand (the state trustee company established in 1990 to privatize former East German government holdings), as well as countless other buildings are relics of the Nazi regime. In more recent history, buildings like the *Palast der Republik*, and more are relics of the former police state of the East German communist regime.

Therefore, it is a good German history lesson to take an architectural tour through Berlin. The contrast and confrontation of styles in architecture, and the variety of uses these places serve is both haunting and educational. There are mammoth fortress-like concrete structures built under the Nazi regime, as well as the paper-thin apartment buildings of the former East Germany. Nevertheless, these 1930s and 1960s architectural relics hardly compare to the power and impressiveness of the Reichstag or the rest of the Kaiser Wilhelm Gedaechtniskirche.

Only now with the departure of the Allies, are the World War II ghosts coming out and the people confronted with these one-time important locations.

Other than pointing out some of the ghosts from the Third Reich who are still breathing in the German capital, this also provokes further questions. For instance: What other places of terror have I so casually glimpsed over, not knowing what once lay behind their bordered-up doors? How have Berliners collectively come to terms with this part of their city's history, especially in light of their divided views on their roles in WWII? These questions will be addressed in coming chapters.

Notes

1   Nevertheless, it is interesting to note that in the last somewhat free Reichstag elections on March 5, 1933, Berlin's 31.3% vote for the National Socialists was the second lowest percentage of 35 voting districts. source: *Das Dritte Reich* Dokumenten-Verlag Dr. Herbert Wendler and Co., Berlin, Neunter Band, pg. 76

2   Ekkehard Schwerk, "Es geschah unter den Augen der Berliner Bevolkerung", Der Tagespiegel, October 18, 1991

3   Marc Fisher, "Germans Allow Market At Site of Death Camp", International Herald Tribune, July 19, 1991

4   Weeks after the Brandenburg government's buy-out of the principal investors for the development project at the former Ravenbrueck concentration camp, Kaiser's supermarket started a major publicity campaign in the newspapers to improve their image following an embarrassing week in the press.

Chapter 7

Berlin's Nazi Museum

Some of the ghost-filled fixtures of Berlin's landscape played surprising roles in the German capital in the early 1990s. On January 20, 1992, the Berlin government announced the opening of the famous Wannsee Conference House in Berlin's Wannsee District as a memorial and a permanent exhibition to mark the 50th anniversary of the Wannsee Conference.

In 1942 the 'Final Solution' was decided upon concerning the organization and implementation of the decision to deport the Jews of Europe, Gypsies and homosexuals to the East and to murder them.

My first reaction on reading this announcement was horror. Little had I known, but after more closely reading about the location of the memorial just opened, I discovered that it was near the same place where I used to relax in a sailboat. I had seen it, walked by it, sailed by it, and not even known.

Why did it take over 45 years for Germans to open this house as the rightful monument of terror that it is? From 1952 to 1989 the house was used as a school vacation home for Berlin's NeuKoelln District. But days after the opening, record crowds visited the memorial and documentation center. Perhaps enough time had passed.

Where is the German national museum, let alone a national museum covering the period of the National Socialists rule in the German capital? Indeed there are places to be found in and around Berlin that pay tribute to this time, including exhibits and documentation, but there is still no central museum or monument to the Holocaust. Most of the memorials are in places where synagogues used to stand.

Nevertheless, the more questions I began asking, the more critical I was becoming. I was astonished to discover that there exists no national museum dealing with Nazi Germany. One needs to look very hard to discover that there is no standing museum. The answer one receives is that there will be one. In the Eastern part of the city there exists nothing other than Soviet memorials of soldiers killed in the liberation of Berlin or statues of Lenin, Stalin, or other communist heroes.

Berlin needs to fully deal with its history as one city now, with all of the difficult questions and steps that implies. But how simple that is to say and how hard it will be to actually enact. First of all, consensus must be reached on all the practical aspects of being a single city again, like re-connecting the streets, unifying the public transportation system, promoting contact and fusion. The biggest and most pressing issue for German history is to try to find some reasonable solution to the justice problems associated with the long-term division of the country and the dictatorship that ruled its Eastern portion for so long. Once again Germany must heal itself, in a situation analogous to the post-World War II era.

Shamefully, German society excused itself from eradicating Nazis from society. As mentioned, East Germany all but put the entire blame on West Germans for the Holocaust, and it still haunts them. In East Germany the Nazis were tolerated, and the lower ranks disappeared under the cover of occupation. But that happened in West Germany too. The main difference is that West Germans were led to feel responsible for their crimes, whereas in the East, communism was the answer and the fascists were considered to be in West Germany. On top of that, Germans were divided after WWII. East and West Germans under 50 have been raised differently. But until the more contemporary questions are answered, it will take a long time before Germans incongruous views of World War II can be addressed.

In fact, the discussions and debates surrounding a possible centrally located monument in tribute to the Holocaust is a good indicator of how divided the people are. The debate started back in 1983, when a consensus could not be reached about erecting a monument on the bombed-out site of the former Gestapo headquarters. At that time, proponents of a central monument called for a monument that paid tribute to all victims of National Socialism. None of the over 200 proposals were approved. Instead it was decided to build a temporary documentation center, the Topography of Terror, which opened in 1987 for Berlin's 750-year anniversary celebration. This temporary exhibit was received with such enthusiasm and continued public interest, that the Berlin government extended the exhibit indefinitely.[1]   At the exhibit, one can walk into former prison cells and read documentation and literature about the deportation of prisoners to concentration camps. On March 25, 1993, the Berlin government announced its plans to expand the Topography of Terror exhibit into a permanent documentation and conference center.

The 1987 provisional exhibition hall was to be replaced by a number of fixed buildings, including a permanent exhibition documenting the National Socialists' institutions and crimes including a visitors' center, library, and documentation center. Planners were intent on creating an exhibition for people of all religions and countries, a place where people could meet, discuss, and study the National Socialist movement in Germany.

But the debate about a central monument continued. A citizen's initiative called "Perspective Berlin" continued to carry the banner for a central monument to be built in recognition of the Jewish Holocaust. In response, Gypsy, Russian, homosexual, and other minority groups threw up their arms, in protesting their exclusion. In this debate, the conflict was clear: on the one side was the problem of how to remember all victims of National Socialism, and on the other, the unique character of the Jewish persecution.

Berliners are far from having come completely to grips with their past. In a broader perspective, the debate also shows how far Germans are from arriving at a national consensus on their shared history.   In 1994 there were over 60 memorials and museums dealing with the time of National Socialist power, 1933-1945.[2]

The German government is slowly beginning to address this issue more vigorously, to ensure that their capital's reawakening also reflects the tragic results of the last time Berlin was the working German capital. For instance, I recall when the funding for Daniel Libeskind's new Jewish Museum in Berlin was discussed in a party group meeting. Annexed to the Berlin Museum, this bold piece of architecture prods Germans to recall their painful past. Libeskind refers to the most important space of the museum as the "void," an atrium at the center of building that one cannot enter, only peer into, which symbolizes the absence of much of Berlin's Jewish community.[3]

But misunderstandings and stereotypes persist. In "Reimagining Berlin" (February 5, 1995, *The New York Times Magazine*) Paul Goldberger stated: "It is too soon to tell how much of Berlin's architecture will be of world importance. For now only Libeskind's Jewish Museum seems certain to be, although the renovation of the Reichstag, by the British architect

Norman Foster, may turn out to be brilliant." This, of course, completely overlooks the Topography of Terror and the Wannsee House.

Perhaps the most important piece of Berlin's landscape in the year 2000 was decided upon in the spring of 1994, when an architectural competition to erect a monument for the European Jews murdered during the reign of the National Socialists began. Funding of over 15 million deutsche marks has been set aside for the project, more than for any other monument in Berlin, and it will stand on five acres between the Brandenburg Gate and Potsdamer Platz. An architectural contract to build the monument was awarded to Simon Ungers and an art collective led by Malerin Christine and Jackob-Marks on March 17, 1995. Building is scheduled to begin in 1996 and be complete by the time the government moves to Berlin.[4]

But why has this important piece of the German landscape only been decided on in 1994? Is it in response to the success of the National Holocaust Museum in Washington? Why have the other competitions taken precedence, including the renovations on the Reichstag, the building design for Alexanderplatz and Potsdamer Platz, and for the location of the federal government's office spaces?

And if that is the state of affairs at the pinnacle of political, social, and cultural life in Germany, imagine how long will it take before such questions will reach down to the average citizen.

In my view, this debate illustrates the government's failure to lead a discussion about the past. In the last decade before the beginning of the new millennium, after a century in which Germany fought two world wars in the name of continental dominance, and in which the Holocaust took place, the country has the chance to deal properly with this aspect of its history. Especially in 1995, the 50th anniversary of the end of WWII, Germany's leaders should use the painful reminders of their nation's collective history—including the liberation of concentration camps such as Auschwitz and Buchenwald and the Nuremburg Trials—to galvanize a collective national confrontation with the past. This historic year offers the leaders a chance to overcome one of the causes of their country's deep social and political division. Nineteen-ninety-five offers Germany a unique opportunity in it's difficult reunification to establish national consensus, based on their shared history. However, the window of opportunity in this transition-filled Germany to shape a national consensus is quickly closing. As stated by Chancellor Kohl: "There is no collective guilt. But any young German who stands at Yad Vashem [Israel's Holocaust memorial] or the cemetery in St. Petersburg — unfortunately, I could name many such places — cannot say this does not concern him."[5]

In this regard, perhaps by erecting a national museum in their capital, the government would satisfy the public need for a national position on the past, expel the heretics who want to use the ambivalence to their advantage, and thereby set Germany on a path forward.

With these questions and ghosts looming, Germany is moving full steam ahead, paving roads that were blocked off, selling off the former state-owned properties like hot cakes, privatizing, unifying the tangible, disposable, bombable. Disturbing winds blow in, like the Wannsee Conference memorial opening and the whole debate surrounding a national museum and memorials commemorating the crimes of the Nazi regime, yet they seem to push Berliners to increase their drive forward.

Nevertheless, one step forward was taken on May 14, 1993, when the Bundestag approved Berlin's *Neue Wache* (New Guard) to be the national

"Neue Wache", 1993, courtesy of the German Information Center.

memorial for the victims of war and tyranny. A line was drawn in post-war Germany with this decision. Another chapter was closed.

For decades, Germans have also been bickering amongst themselves about whether or not to have one memorial for the victims of Germany's tumultuous twentieth century. Now, with the reunification of their country, continent, and capital, with the drive homeward, Chancellor Kohl was able to push through a consensus to put this issue to rest in their reunified capital.[6]   Now all they need is a museum to explain the memorial. This seems a bit like putting the horse before the carriage.

The inside of the building built in 1816, designed by the famous Berlin architect Friedrich Schinkel, features a life-size sculpture of "*Mutter mit totem Sohn*" (mother with a dead son) by Kaethe Kollwitz. The president of the largest art school in Europe, Dr. Olaf Schwenke of Berlin's Hochschule der Kunste, criticized the selection of Kaethe Kollwitz's sculpture: "This memorial is a bad beginning for the new government center. That one thinks of monuments in the conventional form after Auschwitz is very problematic for me."[7]

The *Neue Wache's* inside right wall is inscribed with a remembrance to the victims of war and tyranny, from the soldiers killed in action to the murdered Jews, homosexuals and disabled persons.[8]   However, this also was the subject of much controversy. Jerry Kanal, the chairman of Berlin's Jewish Community pronounced the memorial very troubling, stating: "One cannot recognize the perpetrators and victims in the same memorial and mix everything together."[9]

Chancellor Kohl was quoted as stating that the decision was very important because "a third of the German population lived the chaos of the wars."[10]   He concluded his remarks in the Bundestag by stating that the decision must be made now.[11]   The opening ceremony for this first national memorial took place on November 14, 1993, a national day of mourning.

Despite criticisms, the *Neue Wache* is a good place for reflection because it truly embodies Germany's incongruous and difficult history. In 1818 the *Neue Wache* was erected for the Prussian King, Friedrich Wilhelm III, as a guard house and served this function until 1918. In 1931 the government remodeled the house to be a monument to the fallen soldiers from World War I. Then, shortly before the end of World War II, the Neue Wache was heavily damaged during the bomb raids.[12]

Since 1960, the German Democratic Republic constructed a monument in the name of "the victims of fascism and militarism." Since 1965, a burning flame stood in the middle of the room. In 1969, the remains of an unknown soldier and an unknown concentration camp prisoner were laid to rest in the *Neue Wache*, in soil taken from a battlefield and a concentration camp.

But I am skeptical about whether the *Neue Wache* memorial is necessarily a good thing. Today in Germany, there are little memorials all over the country; one is repeatedly reminded of the victims of this century's wars. From small plaques in parks to numerous former concentration camps to monuments in children's playgrounds, one is accidentally, yet consistently, reminded. Will this new, all-embracing national memorial be regarded as sufficient and thus make it easier for the smaller ones to be removed?

There is a danger that the reunified Germany will be content with one monument. And what does the memorial stand for if there is no neighboring museum to clarify the time period? One may have a national memorial, but what does it represent when there is no national consensus on the roles played in the war.

Perhaps Germans have too much pride and ambition to want to look back. Rather, they choose to march forward, which may be the bond that links them. They seem obligated to make the sacrifices necessary to reach their goals. For instance, I've yet to hear that they are being asked too much. On the contrary, Berliners always want more and are willing to make the sacrifices and pay the costs necessary in order to achieve it. On some days I find myself completely forgetting that this city was once divided by military might. It is easy to get swept up by all the planning and projects going on. Berliners are very focused on the future, obsessed with their goals and the fulfillment of their history.

By accident I experienced another small, albeit significant step taken by the Berlin government to come to terms with the past. It offered me an inside view of the problem at hand, and the work that still needs to be done.

Climbing the steps of Rathaus Schoeneberg on a gray and drizzly morning, I was on my way to a meeting with the CDU representatives in preparation for a Committee on Federal and European Affairs hearing. After drinking my morning coffee and trying to shed the sleep of the previous night, I trailed behind the representatives as they filed into the small conference room.

Taking my seat, I realized that I'd forgotten to pick up a copy of the bills that were to be marked up in the committee hearing. Instead of getting upset about it, I just sat back. I sipped my coffee and listened to the rain tapping at the window pane.

Then out of the corner of my ear, like one hears one's name called out from a distance or in a crowd, something caught my attention. Funny, I thought to myself, no one ever bothers me, as I set my coffee cup on the table and looked up. I saw my boss' normally warm blue eyes coldly looking down upon me as he told me to make copies of some protocol sheets, with a look of contempt, as if he were asking me, "What the hell are you doing here anyway?"

I felt his eyes drive through me as I turned to exit the room. Returning from making the copies, I slumped in my chair, feeling especially insecure upon recognizing that I had inadvertently sat at the head of the table. Oh well, I said to myself, it's too late now, don't be so sensitive, as I tried to accelerate my pickup by slugging another dose of coffee. With my head somewhat shrunk down, I overheard them discussing an opposition party group's proposal to make a permanent exhibit out of the former East German Stasi Berlin-Hohenschoenhausen security prison. From what I could make out they were all addressing the subject with much emotion and passion; I could feel it in their intonations and their body movements, if not their words.

Although moved by the intention of the FDP to make a memorial out of the former central prison for East German criminals and political enemies of the communist state in East Berlin, the representatives were reluctant. "It just can't be that we finance all of such a memorial," said the CDU committee spokesman. The other representatives nodded their heads in agreement. My boss also stated that it would not be a good idea because it would set a precedent for the Berlin parliament, and the next thing we knew, the Berlin parliament would be asked to finance every similar initiative, including from the Nazi period. He went on to express the need for a general policy to deal with such memorials of Germany's past, including Nazi and East German socialist memorials.

Overhearing this exchange in my outsider's position and smiling occasionally to lighten my foreign presence, suddenly my half sleep, half conscious attention sprung to life. I thought I saw an opportunity and an omission in their arguments.

This feeling intensified as representatives began discussing their strategy for rejecting the proposed bill. Just before the last consensus was reached and the next committee bill proposal was up for discussion, I sat up straight in my chair, and interjected that a similar proposal for a complete concept to fund memorials and monuments of the former Nazi regime and the East German communist dictatorship was made last year. It was an unresolved case, I continued, in which the Alliance 90/The Greens party group proposed an immediate DM 100,000 grant to assist refurbishment of the Auschwitz concentration camp in Poland, where over four million people were murdered. Their faces went from irritation and contempt for my interruption to interest. As I opened my mouth, I saw my boss' face cringe as my American-accented German filled the room. But after he comprehended what I was saying, his face loosened and became relaxed.

This transformation, all occurring in a matter of seconds, supported me as I continued. Is it not true that last year our committee agreed that the Berlin Senate should report to the parliament on a policy program for dealing with both Nazi and East German socialist memorials [which was agreed upon when the Alliance 90/The Greens party group initially proposed the additional grant for Auschwitz last year]? In response they looked at each other first, with general perplexity, but a hint of recollection, a hint of the possibility, and finally they looked at my boss who, in response looked at me and said, "Are you sure, can you find the corresponding protocol in the next fifteen minutes?" I hurriedly retrieved the protocol.

Upon presenting the material, I suggested that we make a new proposal out of the opposition's original, reminding the Berlin Senate that they still hadn't informed the committee of the state government's policy report, that they were three months over the deadline, and to also include in their report the Berlin-Hohenschoenhausen prison. My boss looked at me and smiled, as his sharp blue eyes flashed, I could feel him apologizing for his stern glares at the outset of the meeting.

Now I was fully awake. As we entered the official committee room I was curious to see if anyone from the other party groups had discovered this oversight. I had just discovered the treasure map and was totally insecure to find out if anyone else had discovered it too. The CDU committee spokesman presented the amended proposal with a careful lucidity and an air of confidence. I also sensed an air of reproach in the tone of his voice that none of the other party groups had remembered to consider last year's proposal. The SPD committee spokesman, Alexander Longolius, leaned back in his chair, dropped his head, and consented that some of us had good memories. The committee voted unanimously for our proposal and that the Berlin Senate was required to report to the committee their policy for dealing with both Nazi and East German monuments. Later, the initiative to make the Stasi prison in Hohenschoenhausen a permanent memorial exhibit of the former communist East Germany was approved. The DM 100,000 for Auschwitz was approved too.

Notes

1   Said the Director of the Topography of Terror exhibition, Mr. Lutz, in 1993, 1,000,000 people visited the exhibit, of whom 500,000 were foreigners

2   In a September, 1994 document released from the United States Holocaust Research Institute, "AN OVERVIEW OF THE WORK OF GERMAN HOLOCAUST MEMORIALS", Mathias Hass described the memorials: "In Germany currently, there are approximately 60 memorials and museums which address the period of National Socialism from 1933-1945. They range from memorials at former concentration camps such as Dachau, Buchenwald, Ravensbrueck, Neuengamme, to institutes in various former centers of the Nazi State such as Hadamar (the euthanasia killing center), Wewelsburg (the SS cult and reception center), Topography of Terror (located on the Gestapo grounds in Berlin) to the memorials and museums which were established in almost forgotten realms of the Nazi terror, such as the Emsland Camp Documentation and Information Center (documentation of 15 concentration camps in Emsland) or the Sanbostel memorial (Stalag X B Sandbostel)." Source: Matthias Hass, "An overview of the work of German Holocaust Memorials", United States Holocaust Research Institute, September 28, 1994

3   Paul Goldberger, "Reimagining Berlin", The New York Times Magazine, February 5, 1995

4   The architectural competition's jury for the monument, under the chairmanship of the Berlin-Brandenburg Academy of Arts President, Walter Jens, awarded two first prizes from the 528 applicants on March, 17, 1995. source: "Wettbewerb fuer Holocaust-Mahnmal in Berlin entschieden", Deutschland Nachrichten, March 24, 1995

5   Rick Atkinson, "Anniversary of V-E Day Stirs Conflicting Feelings in Germans", The Washington Post, May 7, 1995, pg A31

6   There was much debate in the German Bundestag about who the memorial represented. Over ninety minutes of floor time was spent debating the issue. Although all representatives were of the opinion that it should be a place of remembrance and reflection, few knew how to furnish the memorial to represent all of the victims. Kohl warned the representatives against listing all of the ethnic groups who were victimized in the catastrophic twentieth century, because it would ultimately only lead into the labyrinth of modern German history. source: Karl Feldmeyer, "Zur Errinerung, Trauer und Ermahnung", Frankfurter Allegemeine Zeitung, May 14, 1993

7   "Plaene sind problematisch", Der Tagesspiegel, May 14, 1993

8   The inside wall of the memorial is inscribed with the following:

Die Neue Wache ist der Ort der Errinerung und des Gedenkens an die Opfer von Krieg und Gewaltherrschaft.

Wir gedenken der Voelker, die durch Krieg gelitten haben. Wir gedenken ihrer Buerger, die verfolgt wurden und ihr Leben verloren. Wir gedenken der Gefallenen der Weltkriege. Wir gedenken der Unschuldigen, die durch Krieg und Folgen des Krieges in der Heimat, die in Gefangenschaft und bei der Vertreibung ums Leben gekommen sind.

Wir gedenken der Millionen ermorderter Juden. Wir gedenken der ermordeten Sinti und Roma. Wir gedenken aller, die umgebracht wurden wegen ihrer Abstammung, ihrer Homosexualitaet oder wegen Krankheit und Schwaeche. Wir gedenken aller Ermoderten, deren Recht auf Leben geleugnet wurde.

Wir gedenken der Menschen, die sterben mussten um ihrer religioesen oder politischen Ueberzeugung willen. Wir gedenken aller, die Opfer der Gewaltherrschaft wurden und unschuldig den Tod fanden.

Wir gedenken der Frauen und Maenner, die im Widerstand gegen die Gewaltherrschaft ihr Leben opferten. Wir ehren alle, die eher den Tod hinnahmen, als ihr Gewissen zu beugen.

Wir gedenken der Frauen und Maenner, die verfolgt und ermordet wurden, weil sie sich totalitaerer Diktatur nach 1945 widersetzt haben.

Source: Presse- und Informationsamt der Bundesregierung, "Neue Wache Berlin" 1993

9   "Plaene sind problematisch", Der Tagesspiegel, May 14, 1993. Translation provided by author: "Man kann nicht die Taeter und Opfer mit dem gleichem Mahnmal ehren und damit alles zusammenwerfen."

10   "Zustimmung im Bundestag fuer Gedenkstaette Unter den Linden", Berliner Morgenpost, May 15, 1993

11   "Gedenkstaette Neue Wache: Der Kanzler sprach ein Machwort", Bild Zeitung, May 15, 1993

12   Presse- und Informationsamt der Bundesregierung, "Neue Wache Berlin" 1993

Chapter 8

Capital of Multi-Ethnicity
or Xenophobia?

Another obstacle to German reunification is foreigners. Right-wing violent crimes are on the rise in Germany. In 1991, there were some 1,500 reported violent crimes from right-wing radicals, up from 300 in 1990 and 71 in 1986. In 1992, up to October 23, there were some 1,500 reported cases of violent crimes. A violent crime is defined by the German constitutional protection agency as bodily injury, arson, or heavy material damage.[1]

Although I didn't feel threatened as a foreigner in Berlin, when I read the statistics, I began to question when I should be going home. For example, a poll conducted by the Infas sociology group found that more than one in four Germans consider the saying *"Auslander Raus"* (foreigners out) justified. Also, the same study found that 37% of East and West Germans fully agree that "the foreigner problem in Germany had developed to such a degree that Germans have to arm themselves against foreigners in their own country."[2]

Tragic reminders of Germany's past association with racism and discrimination were everywhere in Berlin in 1992. For instance, on August 25, 1992, part of a former Nazi concentration camp near Berlin's Oranienburg District, Sachsenhausen, burnt to the ground. Later, officials determined the cause to be arson. The timing of this felony couldn't have been more symbolic. Ten days previously, Israeli President Yitzak Rabin paid an official visit to one of the only original buildings in the former camp where an estimated 10,000 Jews were murdered.[3]

German Jews, in response to rising xenophobia and violence against foreigners, are fearful. In Duesseldorf, Eugenie Brecher a board member of the fourth-largest Jewish community in Germany, said: "The 2,200 Jews

in Duesseldorf now have downright angst."[4] Ignatz Bubis, chairman of
the Jewish Central Committee in Germany, shifted some of the blame to
the German courts, stating that the justice system had "played down the
crimes committed up till now."[5] He went on to say, "Neo-Nazis are
celebrating their cowardly crimes with *Heil Hitler* cries. Those are signs
that are very thought-provoking."[6]

In addition to the arson fire at the former concentration camp at
Sachsenhausen, the Berlin city district Jewish cemetery in Weissensee (the
same one I drove by with the CDU party group on the way to East Berlin)
was vandalized. According to police reports, numerous gravestones were
overturned.[7] In response to these events, Berlin's newspapers were filled
with horrific news stories of both these tragic acts of terror. And the effect
is the same on Germans. Like a lead weight, the past bears down on
Germans, embittering the sweet taste of their plans for their new capital
metropolis and deepening the divide in the society searching for common
ties.

Then, within months of these events, I found another disturbing
announcement indicative of Germany's stormy social atmosphere. For
the fourth time a memorial for Jews deported to concentration camps from
a Berlin train station near the Putlitz bridge was vandalized. At the scene,
police reported finding a black plastic bag containing a pig's head, a
swastika, and a note with profanity against the chairman of Berlin's Jewish
Community, Heinz Galinski, as well as against asylum applicants.[8]

How can these events be explained? Sitting in my office in Rathaus
Schoeneberg, gazing out my window onto the busy streets of Berlin, I was
overcome with a feeling of bewilderment and confusion.

This whole development disturbed me because there were no easy
answers. While the major newspapers, including the more prominent
papers, carried sensational stories of the neo-Nazis' ascent, I was more
skeptical. I had never felt threatened because I was a foreigner. Germans
had embraced me very warmly in their Berlin state parliament, as well as
the other new German state parliaments I had visited, like Thuringia and
Mecklenburg-Western Pomerania. German politicians have also included
me in activities, including some of their closed party group meetings. Or
is that just because I am an American?

Regardless, on the streets of Berlin, I never felt threatened, anywhere,
anytime, in direct contrast to the caution I wear on my sleeve in American
cities. So what is it then? "Maybe it is because you look German," said a
friend in a local cafe that night after I had vented my frustration. "If you

were black I think you would know better through personal experience," he concluded.

Riding the local train home that night, I was more disturbed than before meeting my friend. Ironically, that meeting—which I expected would bring me support and understanding—made me more upset than before. Could it be as easy as my friend said? Am I too biased because of my skin color to fully appreciate the problem? From reading the *International Herald Tribune* and the *Wall Street Journal Europe*, one would have thought that Germany was on the verge of a time warp, a rebirth of the 1930s. From the inside, I knew this wasn't the case. But then what was the cause of these horrific acts of vandalism?

From that point forward, I followed the related developments more closely, including the politician's speeches, the government's reaction to the increasing violence, the international reaction, as well as the grass roots scene in Germany's capital. It became another intriguing aspect of the reunited Germany.

The Asylum Scandal

As a group of people gathered at a Berlin bus stop on my way home, a young boy, who looked as if he was non-German due to his skin color and his accent, began harassing the waiting passengers for a little money. His German was sketchy, his style relatively arrogant and flamboyant compared with the well-behaved German children waiting for the bus. Nevertheless, his innocence and age made up for the clamorous disturbance he was creating.

The presence of the boy and his sister was an aberration in the otherwise homogenous mixture of Caucasian passengers waiting at the bus stop. The question came to mind: where did the young boy and girl come from? Immediately, I thought to myself that the they probably lived in the crowded house for asylum seekers close to my apartment just three bus stops away. For about six months, an entire apartment complex had been used to house asylum applicants, noticeable due to the crowds of foreigners standing before the house, where the children used the sidewalk as their playground and the adults played cards.

The Germans waiting for the bus were clearly disturbed by the boy's begging. They brushed off his advances with cold stares and the silent treatment. Looking to my left, the bus was approaching. I liked to sit in the back of the elongated bus and as usual I took my place. But when I began to hear loud talking and protest from the front of the bus, my curiosity compelled me to stand up, move forward, and see what was happening. Here is what I witnessed.

A heavyset German man was yelling at the begging boy's sister while the boy was making faces at the man, which was clearly increasing his anger. "You are all here on our cost, we don't want you here, why don't you just go home?" said the man. The young girl of perhaps 13 or so looked openly insecure at his aggressive remarks and tried to shrug them off, looking at the faces of her fellow passengers for refuge. She found nothing but empty glares in return.

Meanwhile the outspoken German kept laying into her: "You are all just using us, taking our money and doing nothing but causing problems in our society." I had the impression that he was letting out his pent-up anger for the first time in public, and that he was somehow feeling justified in his behavior. Could his accusations of the boy and girl be due to the German government's debate about the misuse of Germany's asylum laws?

The German man began looking at his fellow passengers and preaching like someone who had something important to say. Meanwhile the other passengers just sat there listening, some nodding in agreement. The older grandmothers were agreeing with the man, the young man next to me was looking at the soapbox preacher with a look of intense reproach and contempt. "You know where they all live. Look, there is the children's parents and friends standing on the road raising havoc," the angered German said. "Go on to your clan of foreigners, get out of the bus and go back to your homeland," he continued as the girl stuck out her tongue at the man as she exited the bus.

But even after the boy and girl departed the bus, the anti-foreigner rhetoric continued. In fact, as soon as the boy and girl were gone, all of the passengers seemed to join in. "We all know that they are breaking into the corner supermarket, and have been placed under house arrest after dark," said another bus rider. The older ladies nodded their heads in agreement, now standing by the outspoken German man's side. At that moment, I didn't pay attention to these people. However, it was clear that they began exchanging their own personal stories among themselves. Then, as if out of the blue, the same German who started this onslaught of intolerance and protest, spoke again, but this time louder, as if he were addressing the whole bus; "The problem is that no one trusts themselves to say anything." Many shook their heads in agreement.

As the above story indicates, in the background of Berliners' domestic struggle to overcome the walls in the reunited Germany, there exists an outside influence that is complicating matters. It is an additional challenge contributing to the post-reunification difficulties. The major difference is that this is a foreign challenge: namely refugees. To most Germans, refugee is synonymous with asylum seeker, due in large part to Germany's extremely liberal asylum law. The evolution of this issue is critical to an analysis of what Berlin is and will become, because Germany's refugee crisis is likely the biggest challenge to face in Germany since reunification in 1990.

Since reunification, the number of persons seeking asylum in Germany has increased dramatically. One disadvantage of Germany's long and open border to its Central European neighbors is the overwhelming number of refugees crossing into Western Europe through Germany. And because Germany offers the best deal for refugees of all European countries, many never go further West. The timing of this foreign pressure couldn't be worse for a stressed German society consumed by its reunification problems.

To learn more about Germany's asylum law, I visited the Berlin state office for alien affairs. When the office director told me that as an American I could also apply for political asylum in Germany (in other words receive free housing and a monthly stipend, although at the same time I was earning a monthly stipend for my CDU party group internship), I studied the subject more closely to try to understand the reasons for such an open law.

Also, my motivation to learn more about Germany's immigration laws were rooted in an effort to counteract the international media's portrait of Germany's rising xenophobic violence.

With this background in mind, I wrote the following article for *The Seattle Times* in 1992.

"Foreigners Welcome"

Would you like to travel with your family to Germany? Surprisingly the best deals are not to be found at the local discount travel agency. Rather the German government's offer includes free housing, free monthly pocket money, free health insurance, and free traditional German schooling for the kids. Upon receiving your application receipt, you can get those amenities and more, including free integration language classes. It's the law. But like all good deals there is one restriction. From which country are you being politically persecuted? Come on, don't be shaking your head and tearing the application form to pieces. Today you'll claim to be a Marxist and that you're being persecuted in the capital of capitalism.

How long will this vacation last? How long do you want it to? The official German statistics office says the average asylum case requires 8-12 months before the first decision is made, but you can always prolong the stay if you want to. Take a minimum of 6 months to get adjusted and if you're dissatisfied, you can always decide to go. This is not like the Hotel California, you can check out and leave.

You aren't the only one getting excited about traveling to the center of Europe, to the land where the government subsidizes everything from health insurance to Airbus airplanes. In 1991, 250,000 people came on exactly the same deal you're going on. Already in this year alone, around 400,000 people have applied for political asylum in Germany and officials estimate it will top half a million before year's end.

Germany has the most liberal asylum laws in the world today. Articles 16, 19, and 24 of the German constitution provide every person with the individual right to claim asylum in Germany, regardless of where you come from. These laws were written and adopted by German lawmakers and politicians persecuted under Hitler's Nazism, like the honorable Konrad Adenauer. For over 45 years they have humbly been politically supported and held up for the world to see.

With the fall of communism and a guarded East-West border, the migration of people across the European continent is approaching the shores of Western Europe like a tidal wave. Germany's border with third world economies of former East Bloc countries is attracting people from Eastern and Central Europe looking for a better life. Today Germany has the highest quota of asylum applicants in the European Community, absorbing over 50% of the E.C.'s total asylum applicants. And the system is completely backlogged. "There are over 300,000 applications still sitting in Nuremberg waiting to be processed," said Herr Kramer, assistant director of Berlin's Alien Office (Nuremberg is Germany's central office for immigration and asylum cases).

Most asylum applicants are coming from the rubble of what was Yugoslavia, with Romania and Bulgaria claiming second and third place. Until each individual case can be examined from the court, you are guaranteed support by the German taxpayers. When the final decision is made from the German court, the "recognition quota (for true asylum) lies between 3% and 5%," said Herr Kramer as he smiles and shakes his head.

That's not all. If your case is rejected, you also have the right to appeal, prolonging your all-expenses-paid residency for two or more years. While you have the express right to an individual court case, stories from the McCarthy days will surely pass for at least a couple of years. When the court does finally decide that you have *kein Recht auf Asyl* (no asylum rights), then what? The government naturally tries to get you to leave the country, but that opens a whole new set of problems. Travelers have caught on that it is advantageous to lose your passport, if not destroy it. When the day comes for Germany to send you home, the country of origin refuses to accept you without an official passport. Once you are in the system, it is almost impossible to get you out.

The overwhelming misuse of Germany's asylum laws is complicated by the lack of specificity they entail. There is no system in place to funnel out applicants from the war torn Yugoslavia, economic refugees, or world travelers. While the laws are so unspecific, many are taking advantage of them.

Social tension in Germany is already high due to the stresses and burdens associated with reunification. And the corruption and misuse *"auf Asyl"* (for asylum) is like dried cedar branches rekindling nationalism in Germany. In the upheaval of the social and political stability some social groups feel disenfranchised and betrayed. They are searching for something to identify themselves with and tack onto. Some of these groups are using the obvious misuse for asylum to vent their anger and frustration.

Average Germans still support the right to asylum, but due to the extreme corruption taking place, it is forcing them to re-consider their extremely liberal ways. Until this anachronism is changed, it will continue to provoke frustrated social groups to extreme ideological views and terrorist action. Politicians are under tremendous social pressure to create new asylum laws. It is without question the hottest political issue in Bonn at this moment and the debate is raging. The major parties are getting closer to reaching an agreement to change Article 16 and establish a clearer asylum definition; immigration quotas and a list of countries without political persecution are being discussed along with other proposals.

Also the German Foreign Minister, Klaus Kinkel, announced a bilateral treaty last week with Romania that allows asylum applicants who have been rejected for asylum to be sent home without passports. This is another step to defusing this social time bomb. But can the problem be solved with a change in the law? "That's one step, as are the treaties with individual countries," says Kramer, "but we also need to begin to tear down the social benefits we continue to give. As long as people know that their life will be better here than at home, they will keep coming."

Germany has politically supported the right to asylum admirably for over 45 years. Today, due to the enormous corruption and misuse taking place from over 95% of the applicants, a false impression is developing regarding Germany's social landscape. With the facts in mind, perhaps Germany's difficult transition phase will not be judged so much from old stereotypes but as the 1990s problem it really is.

Looking for the Solution in Bonn

One of the highlights of my experience working for the Berlin CDU party group was being invited by the Berlin government to visit their state delegation in Bonn. Especially now, when there is so much pessimism and uncertainty flowing through the German capital about everything from the traffic connections between East and West Berlin, to the ever increasing numbers of foreigners in the capital. Change is in the air. It is a heavy air. No wonder no one is smiling.

As the train from Berlin to Bonn rolled into the provincial capital on the Rhine, I immediately sensed I was somewhere new. It was small, I could have mistaken the clean train station to be one of the metro stops in Berlin. But the air was heavy here too. In other words, I knew I was still in Germany.

The main talk of the town upon my arrival was the number of asylum applicants coming to Germany and what could be done to stop it. Rumor had it that the conservative parties would be trying to push through a joint resolution to change the abused law in the next parliamentary session. Maastricht was hardly mentioned.

On my way to the German parliament on a cool fall morning with my host from the Berlin state delegation's house, I was impressed by how small everything was: the buildings, the houses, the streets and the amount of traffic. In comparison to Berlin the proportions and dimensions were much smaller, like comparing Washington to New York. From the delegation house on the residential Joachimstrasse, my host and I crossed and walked down an avenue in less than 10 minutes to arrive at Germany's national parliament. Along the way, my host told me that the Berlin delegation's suspicion was correct and that the CDU-CSU coalition would be proposing a procedural vote on a bill calling for a study to change Germany's asylum law. Upon hearing this news, I just couldn't wait to get inside the parliament and hear Germany's representatives debate the refugee issue.

Approaching the Bundestag, I was immediately taken back by its quaint character. It was small in scale compared to what I had imagined. Walking through the entrance was a very memorable experience: the security personnel were friendly, after passing through one metal detector, I was brushed away under the stairs, through a maze-like hall, and then suddenly I found myself standing next to the speaker's podium of the German parliament. The representatives were milling about as Bundestag President Dr. Rita Suessmuth appeared and took her podium seat and officially opened the parliamentary session. I was so taken back by where I was, I was expecting to be seated way at the back row, maybe just to observe for a moment or two—as I had been permitted to as a guest at the United States House of Representatives.

But when my host showed me where to sit, I settled down somewhat, that is until I realized that I was the only person sitting in the front row on the left side of the podium. Later I found out that normally the state representatives from the Bundesrat (Germany's upper house) sit there, but that didn't help me get over my shock at the time. Then Dr. Suessmuth called for the speeches of the parties on the CDU-CSU resolution for amending the liberal asylum law. Slowly I observed the CDU parliamentary chairman Dr. Wolfgang Schaeuble, receive help pushing his wheelchair up the inclined podium. There, he eloquently spoke of the misuse of the asylum law. The logic of his arguments was clear and supported with fact. He didn't talk about what he wanted, rather about what needed to be done to alleviate the obvious abuse of Germany's asylum laws. The facts spoke for themselves.

Nevertheless, I was really looking forward to hearing the main opposition speaker. As the SPD parliamentary chairman Klose sat up right in front of me and approached the speaker podium, my curiosity was intense. My anticipation ended up being the most stimulating part of his speech. He spoke of not wanting to upset the liberal tradition and warned against taking rash constitutional action. "The constitution has worked very well all these years. Therefore, we shouldn't jump the gun and look to change the constitution when that is not where the problem is," he said.

His arguments only solidified my position and convinced me that the problem was going to escalate, as was the violence against foreigners. The opposition parties were debating the issue away from the facts with heavy partisanship. They were out of touch with reality and unaware of the tensions their positions were creating in the streets of Germany.

Standing on the train station's shiny-clean boarding platform, after walking with my suitcase from the Berlin state delegation's house, I felt somewhat suffocated by the town and its provincial nature. Bonn was an excellent German capital when Berlin, Germany, and Europe were divided during the Cold War, but Bonn isn't a reflection of German life in the 1990s. It was all so clean, so quaint and fine. Even Bonn's train station, with its eight tracks, was clean and proper. Everybody in the station was well-dressed. Is the richness of the city of Bonn representative of the reunified Germany?

In direct contrast to Bonn, Berlin's main train stations, Zoo, Hauptbahnhof, or Lichtenberg, each of which is twice or three times the size of Bonn's main station, are dirtier and noisier. In Berlin, passengers are coming and going, to Warsaw, Moscow, and beyond. In Bonn it is quieter, more orderly, and appealing—like everything in Bonn compared to the German capital of 2000, Berlin.

As the train pulled out of the shining train station on its way toward the bruised-up German capital, I thought about what an eye-opener my stay in Bonn was. From the conference rooms, to the Bundesrat, the Bundestag, and the state house, everything was so perfect, small, and stuffy. I saw the whole debate in a different light upon boarding the train and looking out the window. I was happy to be going back to Berlin and upon my arrival, the stinky smell and the aggressive begging child who didn't even speak German, was welcoming. Now I understood better how some German representatives were so convinced that there is no problem with the current asylum laws. Perhaps they had never walked the streets of Germany's reunited society in the workshop of unification, Berlin.

Are the horrific violent acts against foreigners just a function of the increased numbers of refugees in Germany since reunification? Is the liberal asylum law the cause? No, but this is contributing to it.

Within days of my return from Bonn, on October 26, 1992, Berlin's Interior Affairs Senator, Dieter Heckelmann, announced to the Committee on Alien Affairs that a new asylum office was being opened in the East Berlin. Taking part in that committee hearing, I couldn't help being amazed at the fact that a new asylum office had not been opened sooner. Over the last year the number of asylum applicants in Germany has multiplied drastically. And the papers had been consistently reporting over capacity at the only existing facility.

As the representatives asked the Senator questions about the opening, I drifted back in reflection to my first visit to Berlin's Alien Affairs office to receive my visa a year before. Standing in a waiting line for four hours beginning at six in the morning on a freezing winter day, the diverse crowd made a strong impression on me. We were from all over the world, like no other place I had ever seen in Berlin. My fellow foreigners were of many races, and speaking many unfamiliar languages.

In retrospect, the impression I received there was the beginning of my realization and appreciation for Germany's future domestic crisis and of the magnitude of the issue. In the course of the next six months over 200,000 additional asylum applicants arrived in Germany. Slowly, I became more and more aware of the increasing numbers of foreigners in Berlin, from the city streets to my doorstep. Shopping on West Berlin's famous boulevard, Kuerfurstendamm, one increasingly saw peddlers from all over the world, with all sorts of goods. Meanwhile, I could hear Berliners sometimes grumbling and complaining about their presence over my shoulder. The New Europe had arrived.

Although I wasn't grumbling or complaining, this element of Berlin's social landscape was new to me as well. I had only been in Berlin for a year and a half. Nevertheless I had become slowly aware of more foreigners, from the groups of families walking the streets to young boys and girls selling roses in restaurants, and of course the Gypsy music being played on Berlin's streets and in Berlin's commuter train stations.

Then, to my bewilderment, the Berlin SPD announced on October 31, 1992, that they were fully against changing the asylum laws in the German Constitution. What a mistake, because violence is rising, and quickly. Whatever the exact cause, the numbers of refugees must certainly be contributing to it.[9]

Lower Saxony's Minister for the Interior pointed out that 80% of the violent crimes committed in 1991 were against asylum applicants or foreigners. Seventy-percent of the convicted criminals were between 16 and 21 years old. This development runs directly counter to the trend of violent crimes from left-wing groups. In 1991, some 700 cases of violent crimes were registered, up from 600 in 1990, but down from almost 2000 in 1986.[10]

Paradoxically, while Germans are becoming less and less tolerant of foreigners in their country, there is also an increase in the number of foreigners being legally accepted to work in Germany. In 1991, some 900,000 work permits were given to foreigners, which is 300,000 more that in 1990.[11] Also, there were eight times as many work permits issued to asylum applicants in 1991 than in 1990.[12]

Also, the Berlin Senate stated in the parliamentary session that foreigners from 169 different countries live in the German capital, for a total of 386,000 in 1992. Turkish citizens comprise the largest foreign group in Berlin, with 139,000 citizens, secondly citizens from the former Yugoslavia with 120,000, and thirdly, Poland with 29,000. The percentage of foreigners in Berlin is 11%, in West Berlin 15 % and in East Berlin 3%. Also, there are over 10,000 foreign companies in Berlin.[13]

Nevertheless, tension is brewing in German society as the foreigners keep coming to the richer Western Europe and the international urban center of Berlin offered a good place to observe these developments. In order to meet the rising numbers of asylum applicants, on March 22, 1993, Berlin's Spandau District was announced to be the new center for all arriving asylum applicants in Berlin (so-called Phase one in the humanitarian asylum process). The new house will also take over part of the functions of the Berlin-Hohenschoenhausen asylum office. Hohenschoenhausen was temporarily the center for all asylum cases, but now with the newly completed center in Spandau, this office will only process asylum applicants who have been federally distributed to Berlin (Phase two). Every German state has to take on an equal percentage of asylum applicants according to population.

On March 24, 1993, over 50,000 people have applied for asylum in Germany. This is 40% more than applied in February and an absolute monthly record. It is one thing to talk about the refugees in sheer numbers and such, but what are the practical effects? Why would Germans be adverse to foreigners coming here?

One dimension of the asylum problem that is not so well-known is the smuggling market. Caravans come from Eastern Europe to the German border. Refugees are selling off all of their possessions just to pay the traders for their journey, sometimes for entire families. Like the merchant ship traders of the 18th century, there are risks involved. But unlike the courageous and faithful travelers of the oceans, unsure of what was awaiting them during the hard and treacherous journey, these travelers have the inspiration of knowing that a warm bed and food awaits them as soon as they fill out the right forms.

The German Federal Office of the Interior reported for the month of January that more than 36,000 asylum applications were filed, 676 of which were accepted as true asylum applicants. But that is not the whole story, even if your case is rejected, you can find a loophole, a way to stay.

Thus, the system is overloaded and Berlin is struggling to meet the demands necessary to accommodate the numbers of applicants. On February 22, 1993, the tension manifested itself in violence once again when conflict broke out at the newly opened asylum center in East Berlin. During the Berlin Committee on Alien Affairs, many people openly criticized the director for instigating the outbreak by not efficiently processing the applicants, questioning him as to why he employed a two number waiting system. Shaking his head with a serious look, the director replied that tensions are high at the center due to over capacity. Nevertheless, every visitor who receives a number before 1:00 p.m. is guaranteed same day service.

There is definitely a cause and effect relationship that is often selectively overlooked for sake of politics. Why? Because as referred to in "Foreigners Welcome," in 1992 alone, over 400,000 asylum applicants were being fully supported by German taxpayers and misuse was in upwards of 95%. Of the 15,000 asylum applicants in Berlin in 1992, the recognition quota for asylum applicants was less than 5%.[14]

The problem is not just the money required to support them. There are housing problems too. One of the biggest problems communities are facing with increasing numbers of asylum applicants is where to put them, especially in the smaller communities. This was well illustrated when the local community of Koenigs Wusterhausen, approximately 70 kilometers south of Berlin, was forced to house 1,500 asylum applicants at a recently vacated former Russian air force base, for lack of alternative housing.[15]

Leasing out houses or property to the state governments has turned into a profitable undertaking. The state governments are strapped for public housing. Therefore some private owners are leasing their houses to the city districts under a pay per night arrangement.

All Germans are affected, the neighborhoods and streets of Germany have changed in degree because of the increased presence of foreigners, as already mentioned. Before I moved to my own apartment, I rented a room in a garden house in Berlin's Zehlendorf District. One of the main reasons I moved away from the idyllic lakeside house was because of the changed environment the house underwent, due in large part to foreigners, as the following experience illustrates.

Opening the door after someone repeatedly pounded on the door, I was surprised to meet a strange young man about my age. With gold chains around his neck and a half unbuttoned shirt on this warm summer day, he provocatively started off with. "We are the new owners and you have to move out before next week. If not then, then we will throw all of your stuff on the street."

Taken back by his aggressive attitude and seeming disregard of my rights, I tried to explain to him that I had a rent contract to live in the house and that I had no intention of moving out. He brushed off my reference to my contract and rights as if they no longer applied here. Then I proceeded to politely ask him why we couldn't reach some agreement and that I was willing to negotiate with him. In response, he arrogantly told me of his great plans to remodel the main house and the garden house and that it was going to be a exclusive hotel, which he said I'd surely never be able to afford.

Upon recognizing that our conversation wasn't going any further, I retorted with a defensive remark that I was staying under the original contract I had moved in with. He laughed at me with an arrogant manner about him as he ordered two of his larger friends to get to work in some language foreign to me. I felt overwhelmed by the whole turn of events and upon leaving the house for a walk on the lake, I saw my new friend sitting in his sparkling, black Mercedes parked at the front of the house and laughing at me as I walked off.

I stayed away from the house as much as possible in the next days. I wasn't interested in being around his aggressive behavior. From that day forward, somehow the house had taken on a different air, one that made me anxious and uncomfortable.

Upon returning one evening after a hard day at work, I was looking forward to a quiet and peaceful evening in my room. But as I exited the local train, a strange premonition came over me, that there was something forthcoming which made me uneasy.

Approaching the house, I was immediately confronted with music blaring out of the second story window of the main house and lines full of washing on practically every balcony of the three-story house. There was a scene of activity in the front of the house as a child was screaming and the other children were looking on. I was moved from within and suddenly overcome with anxiety.

As these and other questions filled my mind, suddenly I was relieved to see that none of my belongings were in the street as he threatened.

Upon passing through the gate, the normally elegant and peaceful-looking house was filled with screaming children, music and more, all within the span of a day. Where did all of the these people come from? From the looks of their dress, the color, their lifestyle, it was obvious to me that they were not German, they all were speaking a language foreign to me. Seeing my garden house door open, it was normally closed, I was immediately filled with anxiety. Did my room even exist? What had he done with all of my things? Climbing the stairways, I was comforted to find that my door was still locked and my room intact. From this day forward, what used to be a quiet and peaceful place turned into a nightmare for me. Neighborhood complaints to the police became a regular occurrence.

Next door to this house were very expensive apartments; the area is well-known as being one of the most exclusive districts in town. I couldn't help asking myself how the neighbors felt. I had to move out. Although I am also a foreigner, I had the feeling that I had just moved somewhere else, to another country with another language. Everything climaxed one evening. Going to bed early, because of an important meeting early the next day, I just couldn't fall asleep, the house was shaking with music and pounding walls. My new housemates downstairs (a family of four in two small rooms) were intolerably loud, despite the fact that it was well past midnight. I tried to talk to the father, but he could not understand me and his sons only seemed to laugh at my entreaties.

Anger grew inside me. My fellow foreigners living in the downstairs apartment were not allowed to work in Germany, they were just waiting for their cases to be decided upon, they lived by no regular schedule and therefore it was practically round-the-clock activity. In response, I began to hate the house, I began to hate the people in the house, it grew inside of me. I knew it was wrong. Was I being fair? Was I stereotyping all these people against any right of asylum in Germany?

I couldn't help it, reading the daily newspapers and knowing that over 95% of the asylum seekers have no right to asylum in Germany. I began to see all asylum applicants through the prism of abusing the system, although I knew that I wasn't being fair.

And after sharing my personal story with my Berlin friends, they all shrugged their shoulders and bit their lips, telling me their similar experiences. "There is one of those places in my neighborhood too," said another grimacing. Bitterness and helplessness is mounting about how this element of the reunified German society will be solved.

But it is hard to keep an overview of the developments when one is wrapped up in the daily goings-on. It is everywhere, affecting everyone. The bus trip story that I began this chapter with was not an exceptional situation. Tension is brewing from the grassroots up in German society against the increasing numbers of foreigners living with German support. The strain on Germans is manifesting itself in explosive outbursts like the one I witnessed on the bus, against foreigners on the streets, in Berlin's cafes, and in the parliamentary discussion groups. A mixture of helplessness and frustration has taken hold. In short, foreigners have become the scapegoat for a stressed German society.

As already shown, some Germans are reverting to violence to take action into their own hands. Most Germans are turning their shoulders from the conflict. It has become a regular part of post-reunification Berlin, in contrast to 1991, that violence against foreigners fills their daily papers' first three pages. No one can explain why, no one wants to try. It is even in vogue to express your discontent for the *Unruhe* (noise) refugees bring to the otherwise quiet society. Just pick your group, it doesn't make a difference, everyone has a story to tell about how their lives have been affected. On top of that, history bears down on them, muddying their resolve and self-confidence that something can be done.

The consequences of the increased intolerance against foreigners is not only a local problem. It is a nationwide epidemic. The developments in Rostock, a sleepy port town on the East Sea in the state of Mecklenburg-Western Pomerania, from August 29 to September 3, 1992, offer an insight into these grim consequences on a larger scale. In this coastal town with 300,000 citizens, near anarchy rained as neo-Nazi proponents and disgruntled citizens waged a five day assault on the overcrowded refugee hostel where refugees were sleeping on the lawn for lack of space. The attack culminated with hundreds of radicals storming the overfilled refugee center with Molotov cocktails. Only after successive warring standoffs with policemen, were the violent demonstrators turned back.[16]

As a result, Rostock was out of control for days. The city was on the verge of anarchy. As these developments were being broadcast throughout Germany, one prominent German politician stated in a press conference: "This could just as easily happen in any other German city." Days later the wildfire spread across the country and many similar atrocities took place, with arson fires being set to various immigrant homes and violent confrontations occurring between foreigners and right-wing German radicals.[17]

Conclusions

The asylum crisis, and the rise in German intolerance for foreigners is a domestic crisis that will affect Germany into the next millennium. It is tragically ironic that after decades of a very successful refugee policy for asylum seekers, German politicians allowed their law to become so abused, and rising xenophobia to be one of the results. While politicians are wrapped up in their tremendous plans for the future, they have lost contact with the people who elected them.

Unfortunately, this movement in Germany is on the one side understandable, however, under no terms is it justified. Increasing numbers of refugees from Eastern and Central Europe continue pouring into Germany.

Foreigners are tipping the scales in a society in transition. And there is no easy answer to the flow of refugees pushing their way into the richer Western Europe. Although at the end of 1992, the German government began debating an amendment to their asylum laws, it was as if they were working in clay. Politicians are mainly in a helpless role, only reacting to the latest waves of nationalism and right-extremism. They visit refugee centers, take steps to tighten the justice system, go to great lengths nationally and internationally to improve their image, but are nevertheless incapable of bandaging the injury. Thus, the meteoric rise in xenophobic violence in Germany since reunification can be attributed in large part to the increasing number of refugees in Germany.

By 1993, the asylum crisis in Germany was almost old news and no longer interested many. Germans had literally given up trying to influence their obstinate politicians. And even then, few Germans even make the association between politics and refugees anymore. But certainly it is something more, it is not just the presence of foreigners, there is a deeper reason for the intolerance.

Notes

1   Johnny Erling, "Steigende Kurve der Gewalt", Die Welt, November 20, 1992

2   Peter Scherer, "Immer mehr Deutsche fordern: Auslander raus", November 25, 1992

3   Die Welt, "Sachsenhausen: Anschlag auf die 'Juedische Baracke'", September 28, 1992

4   Die Welt, "Deutsche Juden sind besorgt", November 25, 1992

5   Ibid.

6   Ibid.

7   Der Tagesspiegel, "Juedischer Cemetary in Weissensee geschandet", September 7, 1992

8   Weso, "Juedisches Mahnmal an der Putlitzbruecke wieder geschaendet", Der Tagesspiegel, November 7, 1992

9   The German Federal Crime Institute stated in their 1991 yearly report that the asylum debate in the Bundestag was a factor to be considered in the increased violence.

10   German Federal Crime Institute (Bundeskriminalamt) 1991 yearly report

11   Der Tagesspiegel, "In Deutschland arbeiten wieder mehr Auslander", April 4, 1992

12   Ibid.

13   Der Tagesspiegel, "In Berlin leben Menschen aus 169 Nationen", June 22, 1993

14   Berlin Senatsverwaltung fuer Inneres, Senator Hecklemann, May 27, 1993

15   Der Tagesspiegel, "Auf frueheren Flugplatz entsteht grosste Asylbewerberunterkunft", December 18, 1992

16   456 people were ultimately investigated in connection with the incident, 32 of which were sentenced to prison terms, the longest of which was three years. Source: Reuters, "German Port Marks Anniversary of Racist Attacks", August 23, 1993

17   In the state of Baden-Wuerttemberg, the state interior ministry reported that for the month of August, 1992 there were 28 incidents of violence, in September, after Rostock, they documented 118 incidents of violent acts against foreigners. That is more than a 400% increase. In Mecklenburg-Western Pomerania, the statistics showed 166 violent crimes through October 27, 1992, two thirds of which took place after Rostock. Also, in North Rhine-Westphalia the number of violent crimes increased by a factor of 5 between July and September 1992. Source: Silke Lambeck, "Die Signalwirkung von Rostock", Berliner Zeitung, November 6, 1992

Chapter 9

Berlin's National Demonstration

In response to Germany's dramatic increase in violent crimes against foreigners, Germans are again pressured from the outside world to prove they are against these developments.

And Berlin had the remedy. When the Berlin government proposed hosting a national anti-violence demonstration called the "Dignity of Man is Inviolable," most were thrilled by the idea. Berlin Mayor Diepgen invited all of Germany's prominent leaders, including every German governor. Overnight, a move of humanitarian goodwill evolved into one of the biggest public demonstrations in German history, with Chancellor Kohl and Foreign Minister Genscher jumping on the bandwagon practically overnight. Like a brushfire, the idea raged through the country.

I couldn't help getting caught up in the excitement of the upcoming demonstration. Workers in Berlin's state parliament seemed like students in a high school in preparation for Friday night's big football game— everybody was standing together behind the united goal. "Finally," I overheard one colleague to another in the lunch room, "we have a unified effort!" Every state governor warmly accepted Diepgen's invitation.

That is every governor except Governor Max Streibl from Bavaria. He was against the idea from the outset. Governor Streibl was outspoken in expressing his view that this was not the proper way for Germany's elected officials to solve the country's problems. In his view, Germany's elected officials should rather be working in Bonn to change Germany's anachronistic asylum law rather than demonstrating in the streets. Like most black sheep, as a result of his position, he was heavily criticized by many of his colleagues and ostracized.

With the upcoming demonstration capturing all of the political and social attention in Germany, I couldn't help but ask myself why everyone was suddenly so motivated. What is the difference between today and six months ago? The whole demonstration production seemed like a Hollywood production, not so much for domestic consumption, but rather to counter anti-German foreign media propaganda. Exports were at stake! Berlin's parliamentary president, Hanna-Renate Laurien, stated in preparation for the demonstration she helped organize that the time had come for a "peaceful and fun demonstration that will change the image of the ugly Germans."[1]

But it was more than just that. Another reason the demonstration was received so favorably was that Germans are insecure about who they are. It doesn't take much to rock the boat in Germany in these post-reunification days. Many well-established radical minority groups in Germany can upset the balance in Germany easily. In tough times like these, when everything is possible, it is as if the majority doesn't know what to be. Rather the majority of public opinion reacts to every new development as if it were a direct threat.

In response to all of these insecurities, and Germany's pocketbook, Germans staged a huge public demonstration to prove to themselves and to the world that they are against violence against foreigners. In an effort to promote this message worldwide, the Berlin state and German federal government heavily promoted the event to the international media.

The whole country knew of the upcoming demonstration. It grew exponentially in importance since the first announcements were made. The fervor generated by the idea was like a giant wave swelling with increased momentum toward November 8, 1992.

I had already decided that I would not march for something that would have no effect other than perhaps alleviating one's own guilty conscience or bolster an effort to find a common identity. Rather, on that Saturday I visited one of Berlin's beautiful cafes with a Berlin representative who was also not interested in attending the national demonstration. Despite our nice discussion, good coffee, and full stomachs, we couldn't help being curious to see how the demonstration went. Upon our return to his apartment, we immediately turned the television on. And what a surprise. Thousands of visitors came to Berlin for the special occasion. Expectations predicted the crowd would be around 100,000 people, but over 300,000 people were present. They marched through the streets of Berlin toward the place where a podium was erected in the city center for the German

Federal President Richard von Weizaecker, and the mayor of Berlin to give their climactic speeches.

But the plan almost backfired, not only for promoting Berlin as the capital but also for supporting Berlin's international Olympics 2000 campaign slogan of being "a place of freedom, fairness and peace." In the otherwise peaceful demonstration, Chancellor Kohl bailed out and headed back to his hotel when protesters swarmed around him and allegedly threw eggs and other projectiles at him. And his instinct proved to be tragically correct, again.

As the great mass of people made their way to the stage area, the peaceful march found its tragic conclusion. As the distinguished speakers began their addresses, projectiles (including rocks and eggs) in addition to boos, filled the air around the stage. Riot police swarmed in front of the stage and fended off the debris thrown at them with their battle shields. Meanwhile, German Federal President Weizaecker continued addressing the majority of peaceful German demonstrators. However, it was only in vain — as his sabotaged microphone was drowned out by hissing and booing from the minority radicals at the front of the crowd.

At that climactic moment, chaos broke loose. In response, German riot police assumed a more offensive posture. They jumped off the stage into the crowds of people and attacked the rock-throwing protesters. The panic spread. In the pandemonium that resulted, people fled wildly, screams filled the air. Meanwhile, back on stage, the distinguished guests were escorted off stage by rows of riot police officers.

After the dust settled, Bavarian Governor Streibl made no comment to the press regarding the misbegotten demonstration. The atmosphere at work was of one of great loss and depression. In response to these developments, and to summarize the social mood in 1992, I wrote another article for *The Seattle Times*:

"Berlin's National Demonstration"

"It was a nightmare," expressed a frustrated demonstrator. "Our Federal President was bombed with eggs and his speech was completely drowned out by left wing radicals." A small minority of demonstrators succeeded in spoiling the otherwise peaceful gathering of over 300,000 citizens at Saturday's internationally publicized anti-racism demonstration in Berlin. And it isn't the first time — as the attacks on refugees' homes in Rostock, Hoyelswerda, or arson attacks on the Sachsenhausen concentration camp testify.

Anti-establishment is a hot trend in Germany. Whether one looks to the left or right of the political spectrum, small, well-organized groups are disrupting the disciplined German social order and political stability. But the democratic parties also need to be watched, if not more so.

The asylum crisis in Germany is one of the most splintered domestic issues in the history of post-World War II Germany. This year alone, over 400,000 asylum applicants are being fully supported by German tax payers and misuse is upward of 95%. A thousand mayors wrote to Chancellor Kohl that their communities are overburdened with the numbers of refugees.

Germany's democratic parties have been arguing about this issue for years. The goal has been clear: change the law in such a way as to permit asylum for politically persecuted persons and prohibit the misuse from non-politically persecuted refugees. However, ideological party strife is preventing the necessary majority required to amend the constitution.

The Social Democrats and the Federal Democrats continue to oppose amending this liberal pillar of their constitution. Only now, after the system is practically worn down, are they beginning to change their views. It is five minutes before midnight.

Chancellor Kohl has been so pushed up against the wall, that he is prepared to take "state of emergency" measures if Germany's political parties cannot overcome their differences to defuse this social time bomb. He asked the parties to return to the negotiating table and to reach a timely solution "without ideology."

Meanwhile citizens are becoming increasingly frustrated with their leadership and political apathy is on the rise. "I feel like the trust we gave to our politicians is as abused as our liberal asylum laws," expressed another frustrated demonstrator, "We've been waiting for our politicians to stop talking and do something — but we seem to be no closer to solving the problem today than a year ago — with a half a million more refugees to care for."

Even if the parties do reach an agreement, how long will it take for them to regain the people's trust? Is Germany's democratic culture terribly injured or is it only a scratch on the surface? Will Kohl's conservative government hold onto power, or is this crisis a watershed of a new era of leaders?

One possible consequence could be the formation of new political parties. "Many of my friends are ready now," expressed a state representative to me, "but we think it is better to wait just a little longer (to form a new party).

As in the Weimar Republic, it was the democrats' ineptitude that damaged democracy. Maybe we should fear them more than the minority of radicals we often see on the news.

Although I waited for someone in the Berlin government (e.g., the Interior senator, the Police chief) to be held responsible for the failed security at the demonstration and to lose their job, to my bewilderment, this never happened. Perhaps the responsible officials were too busy preparing for the next day. November 9, 1992, was a big day for Berlin, symbolic in many ways.

The show must go on, and commitments fulfilled, rain or shine. And sure enough, the next day, the parliament was bustling with activity. This time the much anticipated Berlin *Ehrenbuergerschaften* (honorary citizenship) award was being given to Chancellor Kohl, former President Ronald Reagan and ex-Soviet President Mikhail Gorbachev in the Reichstag. History is being written every day in Berlin.

Exiting Rathaus Schoeneberg with an assistant friend of mine, we hopped in his car for the drive over to the ceremonies. Pulling out of the parking lot, I asked him what he thought about yesterday. "I was there with my wife and kids—it was terrible. We got caught up in a stampede, I just don't believe it happened," he said.

Pulling up to the impressive parliament to be, I put in a positive word about the day's celebration to change the subject. Oddly, the whole place was full of life, there were people on every corner, security people all around, checking our invitations and passports. Waiting in line, I turned around and glanced over to the Brandenburg Gate. In contrast to six months before, that day cars were dripping through the Roman pillars. There was a bustle of activity surrounding the Brandenburg Gate.

This was an exciting day for Berliners — to reflect back on their reunification. Meeting in the Reichstag were representatives from the political scene in Germany, including Allied military officials. But in the shadow of the previous day's tragic event, the heavily anticipated celebration was in typical German style, serious and contemplative.

Watching the ceremony was like a time warp. Seeing Mr. Reagan's representative, Mr. Gorbachev, and Chancellor Kohl, standing side by side at the podium, it felt to me as if we were paying tribute to their achievements of ten years ago. Today Germany is in a totally different state than the one these politicians helped create.

In the tragic background of the previous day, everyone appeared a little uncertain and shaken up. I saw it in the faces of Bundestag President Dr. Suessmuth, and Mayor Diepgen as they welcomed the guests. Something had to be said about the previous day, all the fine edges of their speeches had to be re-adjusted, to pay homage to the recent tragedy when describing Germany's accomplishments since reunification.

A spoiled feeling lingered not only over the whole city in the wake of the failed demonstration, but especially in the Reichstag, where the leaders responsible for making German reunification possible were congratulated. Before the individual awards were presented, a short historical film was played, showing the highlights of the revolution that led up to German reunification.

Nevertheless, I did my best to see above it. The work of these men was truly remarkable. The Berlin Philharmonic Orchestra played a benefit concert and in conclusion a reception was given. But on the lips of at least half of the people I spoke with at the post-ceremonial reception was the previous day's mishap. One just couldn't get away from it.

I remembered the preparations for this celebration and how the political officials wanted to use this opportunity not only to reward these men but also to promote Berlin and Germany's achievement since reunification. But this was 1992 Berlin, not 1989 Berlin. Walking out of the all but empty Reichstag, I looked up to the German flag waving in the air.

November 9 is a very important day in Germany. On November 9, 1918: Germany abolished the three class voting right and entered the democratic league of Europe by announcing the birth of the Republic. On November 9, 1938: The Jewish pogrom (*Reichskristallnacht*) began. And on November 9, 1989: The Berlin Wall fell.

Note

1 Dietmar Rietz, "Streibl-Absage machte Demo populaerer", Neues Deutschland, November 6, 1992. Translation provided by author: "friedlichen und frohlichen Demo, um das Bild von haesslichen Deutschen im Schaufenster zu veraendern."

Chapter 10

Integration of Foreigners

On May 26, 1993, Germany's liberal asylum law was amended by the German Bundestag. The new law still provides asylum for politically persecuted people, but not applicants from "safe third countries," defined as member states of the European Union (E.U.) and states in which the application of the Status of Refugees and the European Human Rights Convention and the Geneva Convention are guaranteed.[1] Also, the new legislation provides that persons entering Germany from "safe states of origin" may be turned back at the border or returned immediately to the "safe country."[2] "Safe states of origin" are countries in which the German government feels it is safe to assume that neither political persecution nor inhumane or degrading practices take place. To date, these states include Bulgaria, Gambia, Ghana, Poland, Romania, Senegal, the Czech and Slovak Republics, and Hungary.[3] Thus, all of Germany's Eastern border countries are "safe states of origin." Germany's amended asylum law only provides protection for refugee applicants where political persecution by the state is evident. After years of acrimonious debate among Germany's political parties, as covered in previous chapters, this amendment was a major first step to addressing the causes of Germany's increased xenophobic violence.

However, upon reading the asylum law amendment, I felt a mixture of hopelessness and relief. The damage, in large part, was already done. Interior Minister Rudolf Seiters reported in 1992 that over 430,000 people applied for asylum in Germany, an increase of 70% from 1991, when some 250,000 people applied. Germany already takes on over 60% of all refugees from the war-torn former Yugoslavia (over 400,000 since the outbreak of violence) in the European Community. By letting the asylum law exacerbate social tension in the reunification-torn country, as well as define much of the public debate in 1991-1992, the German government has been an accomplice to the rise of violence against foreigners becoming a defining part of the reunified Germany's social culture. By tolerating the rise of extreme groups until the violence and insecurity in society were well rooted, the German government has overseen the seed of xenophobic anti-foreigner violence be planted. Despite the asylum law amendment, the problem is not over.

I am also pessimistic about the time it will take for this law to bandage the wounds of intolerance and racism in German society, wounds that have been re-opened by the mishandling of the abused asylum law. If I have noticed such a strong trend of intolerance in Berlin, Germany's largest and most international urban city, then how must it be in the smaller towns, the places where very few foreigners have lived in the past, and in the new German states in particular? Rostock, Hoyelswerda, Moelln all come to mind.

The results of Germany's rising foreign intolerance was painfully illustrated to the world three days after the asylum law was amended on May 29, 1993, when five Turkish women were killed in Solingen as a result of another arson firebombing against foreigners.[4]

As if in response to the horrific arson attack, the government reported that there are currently 41,900 German right-wing radicals in 82 different organizations and parties, of which the German People's Union, the Republicans, and the National Party of Germany are the strongest. Right-wing extreme groups have capitalized on the economic cost of asylum applicants to German taxpayers in their racist platforms. Which provokes the natural question: why is it that the German government has not prohibited such organizations and parties from the outset? According to the German Constitution, political parties are deemed unconstitutional that seek to abolish the free democratic order or endanger the existence of the Federal Republic of Germany.

On June 2, 1993, an opinion poll found that 79% of Germans are for a total prohibition of the far-right parties.[5]

For weeks after these tragic murders in Solingen, the entire nation was in mourning. Chancellor Kohl refused to attend the victims' funeral service and the liberal parties heaped criticism on him. Nevertheless, few seemed to recognize that the asylum law had been changed. And if they did, few were drawing associations between the law and violence against foreigners anymore. Despite the obvious connection between such violent felonies and right-wing extremism, especially in light of German history, these groups are not the only factor contributing to increased violence against foreigners. Nor is Germany's refugee policy and asylum law the only factor involved.

Despite the asylum law amendment in Germany, one thing is clear: foreigners will keep on coming to Western Europe. The same migratory forces are at work in 1995 as they were in 1992, i.e. the discrepancy between rich Western Europe and poorer Eastern Europe.

And foreigners have kept coming, although in decreased numbers since the asylum law amendment. Fortressed Western Europe, through its strengthened Eastern front in Germany, has shut its gates. Nevertheless, in 1993 Germany was the main goal for refugees in the E.U. In 1993, some 320,000 foreigners applied for asylum in Germany, down from roughly 430,000 asylum applicants in 1992. That corresponds with a reduction of almost 80% of all asylum applicants in the E.U. in 1992 to 70% in 1993.[6] Also for comparison, the second ranked main goal country for asylum seekers in the E.U. was the Netherlands, with roughly 35,000 asylum applicants.

Since the asylum law took effect in July 1993, the number of applicants for asylum has dropped off substantially, from 37,000 a month to about 10,000.[7] The year 1994 saw a further decrease in the number of asylum applicants in Germany, with a 60% reduction from 1993.[8] Said German Interior Minister Manfred Kanther: "The figures from 1994 show that the asylum compromise is taking hold."[9]

Violence is decreasing too. In 1994, through October 20, there was a 35% reduction in the number of violent offenses against property and individuals.[10] Also, in the first nine months of 1994, there was a decrease in the number of anti-Semitic violent crimes from the same period in 1993.[11] Finally, the number of right-wing incidents was down by 45 percent compared to 1993.[12]

Therefore, now that the asylum law is taking hold, and anti-foreigner violence is decreasing, the next level of questions to remedy the refugee flow and the violence against foreigners need to be asked. "There's an attitude elsewhere in Europe that as long as refugees are going to Germany, let the Germans handle it, Germany is the sponge," said Hans Braun, a sociologist at the University of Trier.[13] Chancellor Kohl called the refugee crisis in Germany Europe's "biggest challenge." Said Judith Kumin, head of the U.N. High Commissioner for Refugees' office in Bonn: "Europe needed to have a European debate on asylum long ago, the debate is now taking place very late. It's a bit like locking the barn door after the horse has been stolen."[14]

Although Europeans have not achieved a level of joint action on asylum through multilateral agencies even in the context of the European Union, they have harmonized their policies to a degree. Since the numbers of refugees and asylum applicants has been rising steadily since the early 1980s, European countries began to meet more frequently and discuss the implication of these changes for Europe and for the institution of asylum. By 1991, more than 100 meetings took place in 30 different forums in that year alone.[15] The Dublin Agreement and the Schengen Agreement among the European Community states addressed issues of control of asylum applicants and their removal if denied permission. The Schengen Agreement went further toward implementation of the Single European Act by adopting policies related to the crossing of frontiers and borders, visas, the movement of aliens, police and security matters related to the movement of persons, and operation of the Schengen Information system.[16] As of March 26, 1995, seven E.U. member states abolished immigration controls on travel between their territories in conjunction with the Schengen Treaty.[17] The "Schengen States" are Belgium, France, Germany, Luxembourg, The Netherlands, Portugal, and Spain.

In contrast to North Americans, Europeans do not think of themselves as immigrant countries. One major resulting issue is how to deal with racial and ethnic diversity in Europe. In spite of changes in immigration laws, European countries have and will continue to have racially and ethnically diverse populations.

Not only are more foreigners coming to Germany since the fall of the Wall. Germany is already one of the leading European countries for foreigners, with 8.5% of the 80 million German population being foreign, or roughly 7 million foreigners. Only Switzerland, Belgium, and Luxembourg have a higher percentage of foreigners in Europe.[18] In 1960 less than 1.5% of German society was composed of foreigners.

Therefore, Germans must find a better way of dealing with increased foreigners in their country in the New Europe without walls. Few would argue against the fact that Germany's policy of integrating foreigners is ineffective at best.[19]

Germans know this intellectually, but in practice few have any solutions and most are too conservative to change their traditional ways. At this time, a European solution doesn't seem likely. Therefore, in order to relieve this obvious social burden in the reunified Germany, some Germans have suggested following the example provided by the American immigration program, and shipping off asylum applicants to a distant shore, perhaps some leased property in Eastern Europe, far away from causing any stress on Germany, like the Americans seem to have done at their refugee camp in Guantanamo, Cuba. More liberal Germans suggest a re-evaluation of German immigration policies, as well as the whole process of integration of foreigners living in Germany.

And despite the increasing numbers of foreigners living in Germany, the whole perception of foreigners contributes to the rise in xenophobic violence. Domestically, there is still a barrier between how West and East Germans view foreigners, for the former they are a more accepted part of life; for the latter, they are yet another new adjustment. One reason why violence against foreigners is more acute in the former East German states is because for East Germans it is another new social reality to live with foreigners.

This became especially poignant to me during a visit to the Thuringia state parliament's CDU party group meeting in the spring of 1992. Among other topics, the party leadership discussed strategies of how best to inform and educate their constituents about living with foreigners [in light of the rising numbers of asylum applicants being allocated to Thuringia]. Of the roughly 16 million persons living in East Germany, approximately 170,000 foreigners lived in the German Democratic Republic, of which 90,000 had jobs.[20] They came from all over the world, stemming principally from treaties with other communist bloc countries in the 1970s, of which the majority came from Vietnam, Mozambique, and Angola.[21] These foreigners were hardly integrated into the community, rather they were purposely and consequently isolated from the mainstream of East German life. Thus, East Germans are completely unused to integrating different cultural and ethnic groups into their mono-ethnic society. It is a reality of history, communism, Stalinism.[22]

Great strides have been made and one shouldn't underestimate the achievements of West German politicians and citizens to improve Germans' perception and tolerance of foreigners since WWII. However, East and West Germans are both at different levels of social maturity. East Germans are going through a psychological metamorphosis. One product of this social crisis is that there are many unhappy and discontented people. Jobs and money are only part of the remedy for these rehabilitation cases. Competition characterizes all walks of life in reunified German society, and many feel threatened by the competitiveness of cheap labor that the foreigners bring with them, sometimes with better skills.

While times are tough, some Germans are looking for a scapegoat on which to vent their anger. With this background in mind, perhaps the causes for increased violent attacks on foreigners can be better understood.

Nevertheless, the heart of Germany's problem with foreigners is its ability to integrate foreigners into their society. In light of the growing wave of violence against foreigners, many are blaming Germany's immigration laws for their growing social intolerance and violence against foreigners. Chancellor Kohl has repeatedly made it clear that "Germany is not an immigration country." Why is the integration of foreigners in Germany, one of Europe's most diverse ethnic states, such a big problem? If Germany had a less stringent naturalization process, would the violence stop?

Perhaps one place to begin looking for solutions to Germany's foreign integration problem is by analyzing its current integration system. Of all European Union member countries, only Ireland, Luxembourg, and Germany do not permit double citizenship. Shortly after the Solingen firebombing, Berlin's Justice Senator, Juta Limbach (today Germany's Constitutional Court President), spoke out again for double citizenship rights in Germany. Nevertheless, the issue of double citizenship is splintered among the parties; the conservative parties are against granting double citizenship rights, the liberal parties are for double citizenship.

To be German is only possible if your ancestors come from Germany, not if you were born there or if you have a paying job. This racial thinking is based on the 1913 German Reich's citizenship laws and two decades later led to a catastrophe that still lives on today. A Russian-German boy, whose great grandparents come from Germany, who doesn't speak their language, and whose culture he does not know, is recognized as German, while the girl who is born and raised in Germany, whose parents are Turkish, is only accepted in the community as a *Auslaender* (foreigner).

Nevertheless, more and more Germans are demanding equal rights for all following the surge in racially oriented crimes. Juergen Strohmaier, the foreign speaker for the Alliance 90/The Greens party group, has initiated a nationwide referendum to amend this provocative law. What first and second generation immigrants silently swallowed, has developed into a provocation for younger *Auslaenders*. Of the 150,000 Turkish citizens living in Berlin (the greatest number of any German city) in 1991, only 2% had been given German citizenship. 75% of the 16 - 25 year old Turkish Berliners would like to receive German rights if they did not have to relinquish their Turkish citizenship.[23]   Turkey will accept such a law, Germany will not.

Over two-thirds of Turkish citizens living in Germany have been here over 10 years, with over 900,000 persons in the German school system. Germany's former President of Germany's Federal Constitutional Court and today its federal president, Roman Herzog, is appealing for new rules regarding nationality rights, including permitting double citizenship rights.

This anachronism should be changed soon. It will continue to plague the nation unless the integration system becomes more in tune with present realities. Germany should reconsider its age-old naturalization process because there is no question that this is also contributing to the increased violence against foreigners.

But, on the other hand, why should Germans give foreigners citizenship when they don't want to be German—rather take advantage of the good in German citizenship and their second citizenship—in other words half and half? Like the American naturalization process, they should make the choice as to whether they want to take on the full responsibility of the country. Nevertheless, responsible politicians use such tragedies to reinforce their reactionary argument of "cause and effect."

Walls still stand in the reunified Germany. Germany's immigration laws have prohibited the successful integration of foreigners (e.g. no voting rights, only guest visas, etc.). They must do something to deal with the largely unintegrated foreign population living in Germany and the public's perception of them. Considering the fact, for instance, that almost 50% of Germany's foreign residents have been living in Germany for ten years or longer and do not plan to return home, and that more than two thirds of their children were born in Germany, wouldn't it ease the whole system to just give them full citizenship rights, including the right to vote?[24] Then finally Germany can get one monkey off its back and deal with the other factors contributing to rising xenophobia.

Chancellor Kohl knows that Germans are adverse to such a sensible, but fearfully painful step. While they pay high taxes, have one of the most exclusive and comprehensive social systems in the world, most Germans feel that their own standard of living would suffer by such a shotgun citizenship ritual. And while German tradition still runs strong in this regard, there would probably be a reactionary national movement against any such an initiative. In societies built on a ethnically based national identity, threats to that identity, which is seen as the foundation of social integration and legitimacy of the state as a protector and enhancer of the people and their culture, are serious.[25] They would rather proudly hold up their slippery *Volk* citizenship and pay the high price.[26]

But are Germans aware of the bigger costs involved at this time of transition? History books will be written, and next to German reunification, we will see rising violence against foreigners, not just the increased numbers of asylum seekers. The world has changed and so must their laws. They cannot avoid addressing this issue, because it is a bleeding wound that needs repair.

Incidents such as that in Solingen are a painful and tragic reminder that intolerance for foreigners in Germany is a major problem and one reason is the country's lack of realistic immigration laws—whether asylum or citizenship, not to mention the whole process of integration itself. However hard this criticism may be, it is a far cry from making comparisons to the rise of the National Socialists.

In conclusion, the flood of refugees that have to come to Germany since the fall of the Wall is a precursor for all Western countries. The social backlash that we are witnessing in Germany could also spread, in a manner akin to California's Proposition 187—the broad initiative that would deny health care and education services to illegal aliens as well as facilitate their deportation. However, Germany, due to the way in which they have managed their asylum crisis and the social ill it breeds, in addition to their anachronistic naturalization process, will be plagued by their relations to foreigners into the twenty-first century.

Notes

1   "Foreigners in Germany and the New German Asylum Law", German Information Center, June 1994

2   Ibid.

3   Ibid. Also, Germany signed an agreement with Poland to accommodate the rise in rejected asylum seekers in Germany for DM 120 million.

4   The perpetrators were juveniles.

5   The German Federal Constitutional Court has banned the following political parties to date: the *Nationalistische Front* (NF), *Deutsche Alternative* (DdA), *Nationale Offensive* (NO), *Deutsche Kameradschaftsbund* (DKW), *Nationaler Block*, *Heimattreu Vereinigung Deutschland* (HVD), and *Freundeskreis Freiheit fuer Deutschland* (FFD).

6   "In der Europaesichen Union nimmt Deutschland den groessten Teil der Fluechtlinge auf", Deutschland Nachrichten, November 4, 1994

7   Rick Atkinson, "German Law Discourages Asylum-seeking Migrants", The Washington Post, November 15, 1994

8   "1994 kamen 60 Prozent weniger Asylbewerber - Aussiedlerzahlen bleiben stabil", Deutschland Nachrichten, January 13, 1995

9   Ibid.

10   "Right-Wing Violence and Hate Crimes in Germany", German Embassy, Washington, D.C., September 20, 1994, pg. 1

11   "Antisemitische Gewalttaten", Frankfurter Allgemeine Zeitung, August 10, 1994

12   Bill Powell, "Living With Ghosts", Newsweek, May 8, 1995, pg. 49

13   Rick Atkinson, "German Law Discourages Asylum-seeking Migrants", The Washington Post, November 15, 1994

14   Ibid.

15   Druke, Luise. 1992. *Asylum Policies in a European Community without borders*. Geneva: Churches Committee for Migrants in Europe. (CCME Briefing Paper no. 9)

16   "Multilateral efforts to harmonize asylum policy along regional lines in industrial countries", Sharon Stanton Russell and Charles B. Keely, March 31, 1994, pg. 9.

17   "Austria, Finland and Sweden Join the European Union", The Week in Germany, January 6, 1995

18   Ibid.

19   According to the German Information Center in New York, Germany's policy on foreigners adheres to three principles: the cultural and linguistic integration of foreigners living legally in Germany, restriction of further immigration from non-European Union countries, and encouragement of foreign workers to return to their native countries. Foreigners in Germany can be broken done into asylum seekers, refugees, and foreign workers.

20 Frankfurter Allegeime Zeitung, "Vertragsarbeiter der DDR duerfen bleiben", May 17, 1993

21 Ibid.

22 Nevertheless, East Germany was a top place to live in the communist World. For example, some rumors state that it was a reward for successful and diligent North Korean military officers from the Korean War to receive permission to come live and retire in East Germany. In 1993 there was a German federal debate occurring as to what should be done with the Koreans granted visas by the East German Honecker regime. Nevertheless, even those foreigners who were given permission to live in East Germany were in large part isolated in separate communities, and little or no integration took place between the East Germans and their foreign guests. It was just another part of their communist society that they accepted.

23 Juergen Strohmaier, "Neue BuergerInnen braucht das Land!", Zitty Magazin, March 17, 1993

24 "Foreigners in Germany and the New German Asylum Law", German Information Center, June 1994, page 4

25 "The future shape of developed countries asylum policies: National security concerns and regional issues", Saron Stanton Russell and Charles B. Keely, December 27, 1993

26 See Marc Fisher's *After the Wall*, Simon and Schuster, 1995, pages 264-266 for more information.

Part Three

The Emerging Center
of the New Europe

Chapter 11

Berlin's Universities

Despite the intangible walls present in Berlin after decades of separation, city officials are taking steps to unify the city's public systems, and plan for a common future. One of the government's initial efforts to reunite their city and people in 1991 was to reorganize the Berlin University system.

Founded in 1800 by Alexander Humboldt (a famous ecologist), Humboldt University was traditionally Berlin's only university. Many famous people have studied at Humboldt, including Hegel, Marx and Lenin. After World War II the Soviets used Humboldt to make political statements during the allied confrontation. Humboldt University was only for 'selected' socialists and good communists. Eastern Europeans considered it to be one of the best universities in the world. Professors, assistants and students were mainly chosen because of their correct political character.

In response to the takeover of Humboldt University by the communists, many students and professors left out of protest. These students and professors wandered to West Berlin, where they began a provincial university.[1] The resulting ideological standoff in the occupied capital was illustrated by the name these protesters chose: Free University, founded in 1948. Since its conception, the Free University has remained the counterweight to the Soviet-controlled Humboldt University.

Temporary classes for the Free University in West Berlin were set up in old villas in the sector occupied by the Americans to assist the protesting students and professors establish themselves. It should also be noted that the United States was the chief proponent and supporter of the Free University after World War II.[2]

Since the fall of the Wall, and throughout 1991, the Berlin government has announced that the properties returned to the state from the occupying allies should be immediately integrated into the city's development plans. Citizens at large are unaware and poorly informed about what plans are on the horizon. Only by attending political meetings and listening to the various statements, could I sense the positive undercurrent at work in a city still separated by walls.

One piece of property that the Berlin government has waited to integrate into its plans is the American Army's McNair Barracks in Berlin's Steglitz District. They are proposing to use the former Army base for a future united Berlin university campus setting.

The development plan calls for moving the Free University out of Zehlendorf, one of the richest and most beautiful districts in West Berlin.[3] Over the decades of division since the Free University was first established, modern lecture halls have been constructed to house the more than 50,000 students at the university. However, beautiful villas still house over 50% of the Free University's departments.

The government's plan to unite Berlin's University system is to many a symbol of the arrival of German reunification. There are practical reasons for the move. But walking into turn of the century villas at the Free University to attend my classes gives the campus such a personal character like a private college. Instead of huge lectures with over 500 students in a concrete auditorium, here one sits under the linden trees in front of the literature department and walks into a villa to classes crowded into a one-time living room.

Changing classes at Berlin's Free University today often means having to walk a block or so to the next mansion. Many of the social sciences have their own departments in one villa, with their own libraries tucked away in the basement or attic. These one-time luxury villas are now being used in the public interest and not just for the privileged few. Now the Berlin government wants to give them back to congressmen and cabinet members. With reunification, the intimate charm may disappear.

Like many parts of the once insulated Berlin, such an idealistic situation will vanish. There are many economic reasons favoring the move. Apartments in Berlin are hard to come by and real estate prices are soaring. Also, with Berlin named as the reunified German capital, the demand for good housing has exploded. As an alternative site, McNair Barracks is being proposed as the new home for the Free University. Building an intact university campus in contrast to the current patchwork setup with departments scattered throughout the city district makes this alternative very cost effective.

But seen from a broader perspective, Berlin's University system is a good example of the sweeping changes that characterize life in the German capital in the early 1990s. For instance, entire curriculums have been merged together, enabling any registered student at one university to receive credit for classes taken across town at another university. Just five years ago, these campuses had no interaction whatsoever, in fact, they were ideological battlefronts of the Cold War separated from each other by divisions of Allied soldiers.

For example, Humboldt University illustrates the dramatic transitions occurring in Berlin today with the University's compromised ideological past. "The University was like every other institution, in the hands of the Stasi," said Markus Obstuck, a student at Humboldt University who works in a student group that reads in-depth reports about the university in the Gauck Authority files. According to the information they have discovered, there were over 160 unofficial workers of the Stasi at the Humboldt University, and 17 official workers. The Stasi used its close faculty and student network to build a network of informers for them.[4] Many employees, from student assistants, to the university's president are under investigation for previous Stasi contacts and the university is being completely reorganized. Later, in a dramatic East-West debate, the president of Humboldt, Heiner Fink was fired because of documents found in the Gauck Authority testifying to his connections with the Stasi dating back to 1968.[5]

Due to Humboldt's reputation, I was fascinated to take some courses there when I first arrived in 1990. However, I didn't know the Cold War nature of the University or the degree of its communist infiltration until later. I was very naive. Upon entering Humboldt at the beginning, everything was so new to me, the contrasts were stark from part of the beautiful country club-like Free University campus at which I had often visited seminars. Everything was out of another world. The run-down condition of the building, the large inspiring quote from Karl Marx on the main stairway *"Die Philosophen haben die Welt nur unterscheidlich interpritiert, es kommt aber darauf an Sie zu veraendern."* (Philosophers have only interpreted the world differently, it is up to you to change it) the smell, the chairs and such, the dress and style of the student body and teachers — I let my imagination run wild, taking in the socialist campus lifestyle.

But that was a far as I could go — in my imagination. As expected — although I tried to be objective — everything the quote embodied was hauntingly absent. The professors were cordial, however clearly reserved (were they concerned that they were going to lose their jobs with all of the changes?) The lectures were very staid. The greatest amount of class participation occurred when the students took their seats in the beginning or got up from their seats at the end. As I curiously observed their note taking, it was if the professor was dictating to them, they seemed to take his lecture down word for word, like a secretary. No one asked questions during the lecture, rather we all sat back and listened as the professor read his notes. I wondered to myself when was the last time that he re-wrote his notes.

Finally my impatience got the best of me: I raised my hand during my French history lecture. The professor was so taken aback by the interruption, he seemed completely thrown out of whack, a contemptuous look came over his face. The professor dismissed my remark with a wave of his hand and suggested that we talk later after class. Even the students gave me a look as if I had just broken the cardinal rule. They glared at me in collective disappointment and surprise. After class ended, one colleague came over to my desk and said: "Please don't be such a goody-goody next time. It's forbidden to ask a question during the lecture. Didn't you see how you disrupted everything?"

With time, I began to find my way around and meet people. I socialized as much as possible, trying to find the rhythm of East German higher education and its social norms. I wanted to fit in. Later I realized how naive that was. In contrast to the competitive atmosphere of American universities, students here were just passing time. Nothing was debated or discussed. The general life and pulse of the student body was the antithesis of the creative and new. Everybody was talking about getting by with the bare minimum, only doing the one required paper at the end of the semester and ignoring the teachers' book recommendations as if they were worthless.

I chalked it up as another experience and thought that it nevertheless might be good for me to visit Humboldt occasionally and see the changes from the other side too. So much of Berlin is like this. Institutions, culture, sports, infrastructure. Everything that was rebuilt following the War was done under opposing ideologies. Literally two countries were founded in one city. The Soviets had a clear goal in mind: convert everyone to communism and socialist ways. The ideological standoff between East and West was principally paid for by the aggressors of the War. Germany was torn. Hypothetical lines were drawn by the Allies, not with the idea of constructing barriers for the formation of different countries, but for practical, organizational reasons. The resulting standoff took Germany down two completely different roads of development.

While the first graders of Eastern Germany were marching in Soviet style military parades down Unter den Linden, singing "Brueder, zur Sonne, zur Freiheit" (Brother, to the sun, to freedom), students in West Berlin were playing "Yellow Submarine" during their lunch time recess. In East Germany the socialist indoctrination in the school curriculum was intense. Training, military exercises, socialism lessons, and, naturally, Russian language were mandatory.[6] This educational persuasion didn't stop until well through the university years. Now everything is in flux.

Berlin's university system was illustrative of the Cold War standoff of the past that characterized life in the German capital and the communist infiltration in East Germany's education. Today, it is illustrative of the dramatic institutional reorganizations occurring in Berlin and all of Germany to assimilate two separate social and political cultures. Curriculums, degrees, grades, and lecture schedules have been coordinated to meet a reunified German standard. Already, the Berlin government has begun to reduce the overlap of the same programs, e.g. medical school, within Berlin's higher education system.

Despite the obvious cost inefficiencies of Berlin's Universities, the system also has some advantages. A student at Humboldt can now take classes at either school. I had the chance to learn about different approaches and educational philosophies in my Berlin University life.

These differences create an unusual opportunity for exposure to the other side. The faculty at Humboldt has been under communist ideological indoctrination since the Soviet takeover. Their knowledge and background qualify their expertise in East European and Russian Studies. Their language skills and their perspectives on the arts, provide a whole new interpretation. What better place to participate in Eastern European Studies than at Humboldt University, next to Moscow University, the premiere university in the Socialist Bloc.

Conversely students accustomed to socialist education and thinking can now study at the Free University in West Berlin. The student body is as diverse as the species of animals one finds in a zoo. Humboldt University used to exclusively accept students from socialist countries, like Angola and Cuba. One result of this new composition is that a peculiar and dynamic struggle among the respective student cultures has taken root in Berlin's more than 150,000 student population. Established norms are questioned, anything is accepted, nothing is certain. The creative mind flourishes in this unstable and transitional environment. Exhibitions and exchange programs are multiplying and slowly bridges are being built between these unique and once autonomous systems.

This potential for educational diversity is intellectually inspiring and stimulating. Berlin's University system is a testing ground for the cultural revolution taking place in German society. If it can't take root with young and dynamic students, then how can it take root anywhere? And since it is working here, shouldn't there be more optimism that it will be forthcoming in the rest of Germany? Despite all of the negative aspects of Germany's division, perhaps one day West and East Germans will profit from their diversity and appreciation for other viewpoints. Maybe one day Berliners struggling to learn more about each other can use their diversity to bridge the prejudice in Europe between the West and East.

Notes

1 Including Berlin parliamentary president, Hanna-Renate Laurien.

2 Public money was given to help create the university every year from 1948 to 1963. From 1948 until 1963 the Ford Foundation provided over DM 12.7 million for guest professors, exchange programs, and construction work. Also, in the same time frame, American taxpayers subsidized over 22.8 million deutsche marks for the Free University. Source: Isabelle Tschierschk, "Bucher, Blumen, Bauwerke — Was die Amerikaner Berlin schenkten", Berliner Morgenpost, September 27, 1992

3 Berliner Morgenpost, "Pieroth sieht McNair-Kaserne als FU-Campus", September 14, 1992

4 Christine Richter, "Humboldt-Uni war fest im Griff der Stasi", October 10, 1992, Berliner Zeitung.

5 Berliner Morgenpost, "Gauck belastet Fink offentlich: Details zur Stasi-belastung des Rektors im Konzil der Humboldt-Uni aufgelistet", November 28, 1991

6 As an interesting sidenote, the Berlin Senator for School Development said in one committee hearing in 1991 that Russian should be the first foreign language taught in Berlin schools.

Chapter 12

The Allies' Withdrawal

In the backdrop of Germany's internal struggles to reunite, the allies are withdrawing from their strongholds on German soil for over 40 years. The days were not many between my discovery of Berlin's Tempelhof Airport and the day when the American flag at the main gate at Tempelhof Airport was drawn in and folded up. On January 29, 1993, the official withdrawal ceremonies for the United States Air Force from Tempelhof Airport took place. At the ceremony, the mayor paid tribute to the famous Berlin Airlift that saved Berlin with food and coal during the Soviet blockade of Berlin. In conclusion, Mayor Diepgen said, "Good-bye always means a new beginning."[1]

In addition to the American Air Force withdrawal from their Berlin sector's former air-field, the U.S. Army recently broke down their command post too. Checkpoint Charlie, the infamous U.S. Army 40th tank regiment of the Sixth Battalion is known most for their tank to tank standoff with the Soviet Army at Checkpoint Charlie in October 1961. They announced the beginning of their withdrawal from Berlin on May 27, 1992.[2]

Mayor Diepgen also thanked the regiment at their McNair Barrack going-home parade. Both the U.S. Army and U.S. Air Force withdrawal ceremonies from Berlin were just several of the many Allied occupying regiments withdrawing in the early 1990s.

In 1992, the four Allied military powers still characterize life in the German capital. They are everywhere. It is a curious aspect of life in Berlin that one is regularly confronted with the Allied military powers. On some days I will see a tank rolling down the streets flanked by police

Checkpoint Charlie, 1988, courtesy of the German Information Center

Checkpoint Charlie removed, 1990, courtesy of the German Information Center

escorts, on other days I will hear the shooting practice light up the peaceful street where I live, or I will see the military police patrol cars cruising their sectors, or I will be playing tennis and be buzzed by a fleet of U.S. Army helicopters.

One clear spring evening, with the full moon lighting up the entire night, I went for a walk on the shore of Gruenewaldsee with my German girlfriend. The lake is situated in the middle of a large forest. Although it is only five miles from the city center, one has the feeling of being in the middle of nature. There are no houses here other than the old 18th century hunting castle formerly used by the German King. The park is densely overgrown—with walking paths around the entire lake.

On this particularly balmy midnight stroll, mysterious shapes and shadows frightened my girlfriend somewhat. I put my arms around her to soothe her nervousness. Her imagination was set off by what I must admit were very fantastic trees half lit in the forest's darkness by the full moon overhead. I felt like the protective figure—reassuring even myself with my own apparent certainty and self-confidence. I thought it curious that we had not seen other walkers enjoying this exceptional spring evening—and we'd already been halfway around the circumference of the lake, I casually thought to myself.

Suddenly a rustle in the bushes drew me a couple of steps backward in a mixture of fear and surprise. Whatever was emerging from the shrubbery lake shore was no rabbit or even deer, it was standing upright! The full moon's ray only highlighted part of the ascending creature. I could just make out that it most definitely had human proportions. Meanwhile my girlfriend sent out a scream of alarm that rang across the sleepy lake like a car alarm in a parking garage. Then about five feet from the first approaching person, another appeared and with a deep convincing tone said, "U.S. Army," as the camouflaged armed soldiers revealed themselves with their flashlights.

I was caught somewhere between relief and terror while my girlfriend shied away in embarrassment and intimidation. In response, I provocatively asked the American soldiers what they were doing. The soldier explained in a calm and assured voice that this was just part of a normal series of night training sessions.

Shaking our heads and moving along, the tranquillity and peaceful atmosphere had long since vanished, as quickly as a drop of water evaporates in a hot desert. The mysterious flavor of the evening, the big Milky Way lighting up our path was spoiled for us. The feeling of occupation overcame me. My sympathy for my girlfriend, speechless and somewhat defensive following this surprising encounter, swelled like a big wave. Going to sleep that night, I empathized with Berliners. No wonder more people don't take evening walks.

Nevertheless, it is very peculiar and interesting to observe how Berliners adapt to this part of their city life. Yes, they are startled and taken back, but they curiously bury their discomfort and humbly accept their fate.

Some still welcome the Allies' presence and I have very rarely met someone who openly opposes the maneuvers. Conversely the former Soviet military presence is hardly so favorably regarded. Each time there is a departure of troops or forces it is positively reported about in the press. Despite the apparent dichotomy of regret and euphoria surrounding the Allies' departure, one thing is certain. Berliners are quick to point out that all the occupying forces are 'going home.' Some people say it would be nice if the Americans would stay and seem disappointed that they are leaving. This position is only to be heard from people under 50 years of age. The build-down of the Cold War forces is present in the hearts and minds of all Berliners.

But once again the ghosts of the past reappear. As soon as the mayor and Berlin's representatives start to gain momentum to move forward, start to talk of the vision of Berlin's future, and pay tribute to the Allies for making it all possible, they are thwarted by some horrific memory of the last time Berlin was the capital.

The Berlin paradox is out in full force in these post-reunification years. Berlin can't shelter itself from the fierce winds of history and ghosts of bye-gone days that periodically rule the streets. It is out of anyone's control. Whether it is in association with World War II or East Germany, they are united by their undying drive forward—and the bond seems to increase as the storm rages into another lull of the past. Within weeks of the mayor's farewell speech to the U.S. Army at Checkpoint Charlie, just blocks down the street from the former border crossing, city officials announced the discovery of parts of Hitler's underground air raid bunker. During the construction of underground train tracks on Potsdamer Platz, a construction crew discovered the remains of part of the former Nazi bunker system.

In response, Berlin's news media was filled with spectacular stories of whole intact rooms found with murals of Nazi mythology, kitchen utensils, and blankets. A public debate erupted as to what should be done with the bunkers. Some wanted them to be immediately destroyed while others wished for them to be put under monument protection, preserving the rooms in their original style. One thing was clear, no one wanted them to be triumphantly exploited or opened to the public, for fear of creating another meeting place for right-wing political extremists.

The discovery was spectacular in a number of ways. That the former Nazi regime still has leftover remains of the bunker where Hitler and Eva Braun killed themselves on April 30, 1945, is astonishing.[3] I assumed that after the capitulation in 1945, after years of continuous bombing, that all such structures were completely destroyed. It seemed reasonable to take for granted that the Allied powers had systematically investigated all such hiding places, especially considering the thoroughness of post-war city management and Nazi hate.

I pose the questions that ran through my mind as I read this in the press with astonishment. Didn't they even search, let alone destroy the bunkers found underneath the Nazi headquarters? During the hot point of the Cold War in 1961, including the building of the Berlin Wall straight through the middle of Potsdamer Platz, didn't the thorough East German border control search and destroy such possible refuge points or potential escapee bunkers? Over the course of years this area has been continually re-fortified with mines, fences and other barricades, didn't they ever look under the ground?

Again my consciousness is impressed with the terrible history this city lives. One gets so swept up in the fervor of planning the new German capital that it is easy to forget about "those days." The fact that my generation must consider what should be done with old World War II bunkers used by the Nazi regime is disturbing to me. I didn't want to be reminded that the older generation of German society is still composed of people who lived this history. Why don't they just blow it up and forget about his damm elaborate bunker system. Does it really have historical value? Will it have symbolic meaning or significance at the turn of the century? My German friends and I drank our way through the news, unable to fully comprehend, especially in light of the timing of the discovery and the hoopla surrounding the American Army's withdrawal ceremony.

The Russian Withdrawal

While the Western Allies were packing up and going home in style with big celebrations, the former Soviet troops were withdrawing secretly, like dogs with their tails between their legs. Dejected, defeated, and poor, they pulled out ahead of schedule.

I was now able to use my position working for the government to extract as much out of the city as I could. Often during party group meetings I learned of interesting developments and places. For instance, one day I was listening to the mayor tell the party group of his recent visit to Berlin's Lichtenberg District and the Museum of Capitulation at Karlshorst.

Sitting in the back row of the conference room, it was clear to me that no one was really interested in his report of his "short but friendly" meeting with the director of the Russian garrison. Representatives were excusing themselves, talking with their neighbors, and joking around. In contrast, I was fascinated, his comments inspired me to pay my own visit to the place where the Third Reich officially capitulated after the long and bloody years of World War II, which culminated in the Battle of Berlin.

Just getting to the isolated house in the East on that cold windy day proved difficult, despite the fact that the physical distance couldn't have been greater than seven miles. Berlin's transportation system was still so far from being reunited that it took me over an hour to make all of the transfers necessary and to find the place, not to mention the historical house itself. Only upon asking the fifth passerby for directions was someone able to point me in the right direction.

Underway on that gray wintry day, I noticed that the neighborhood was very quiet and that many of the houses were decrepit. It was a residential neighborhood, turning one corner to the next, I felt like I was walking in a ghost town, thrust back decades. The architecture was impressive, with a sprinkling of one or two mansions on every block, but they all had one thing in common. They were ill cared for, dilapidated, and rotting. Before World War II, Karlshorst was known to be one of the best neighborhoods in Berlin.

Now the old houses had been all but let go in the Berlin of 1992; some were still occupied by Russian officers and their families. After winding my way around a street, I saw the road coming to an end. On my left, there were two impressive houses that completed the block, on my right, a walled off area, from which I could see in the distance another large rooftop. Walking parallel to the wall, I noticed that it was decaying, with chips and pieces having already fallen to the ground. I approached the entrance without a gate. Walking into the compound, I immediately felt like I was in another world. A weight fell upon my shoulders.

My attention was suddenly drawn to the field on the right side of the house; old Soviet Army vehicles were lined up like at a used car lot: including an old truck, jeep, the Stalin Orgel (the famous Soviet rocket transport), and more. In contrast to the streets and sparse cars I had seen on my way, all of these vehicles were in tip-top shape and the house looked well cared for.

After gazing over the vehicles, my taste buds were salivating for the upcoming exhibition I could only fantasize about. What had I discovered? I could just imagine those artifacts driving across Poland, pushing the Germans back. Imagine that Stalin Orgel driving into Berlin in 1945. But as quickly as I began to glorify the results, a solemn and powerful realization came over me. The costs of war, the human sacrifice, the fight that must have gone on here, in this area, on the very ground I was standing on! The empty parking lot and the fact that I was the only person there increased my sense of foreboding. Then, as if I was being welcomed by the gatekeeper, a young soldier sitting on the footsteps of the house, casually smoking a cigarette, glanced away as I approached the house, climbed the doorsteps, pushed the heavy door open and entered.

The heavy door shut behind me. I began a journey back in time, back to a time that an exiting generation in our society lived and sacrificed for. Maybe I am too young to appreciate the events surrounding the history this place embodies and symbolizes for the Germans and the Allies alike. I was quiet, and scared of treading on this sacred ground, and of not being able to fully appreciate all that this place symbolized.

The solitude of the place overwhelmed me when I realized there was no one in the museum's welcoming booth where the sign asked for a two deutsche mark entry fee. I wondered when the last visitor came here. After five minutes of waiting patiently suddenly an older lady appeared from behind a curtain. She mumbled something to me in Russian, I gave her five marks, and turned the corner into the next room.

My first impression after quickly surveying the room was of being in a stranger's house. This stranger's house was full of suffering. Despite the fact that this museum had very strong ideological overtones of the "Great Victory of the Soviet Red Army," they were the ones who suffered most. In the last three weeks of the battle for Berlin, the Soviets lost over 300,000 soldiers.

The detailed exhibition to be discovered in these rooms allowed me to immerse myself into the grim details of the war. Personal biographies were in every showcase, as were very well illustrated maps and documentation. One special discovery was the battle map of the climactic Soviet invasion of Berlin. The Battle of Berlin was outlined on a huge board about the size of two pool tables. On the side, there was a big red button, and on the map, I could make out colored light bulbs that represented movements, troops, and points of battle. At first, I took a step back to regain my composure. Then, after taking a deep breath, I approached the battlefield and curiously pushed the button.

As quickly as a kite lifts off into the sky on a windy day with the pull on the string, I was lifted to a fantasy of troop movements as the board lit up like a pinball machine. That is where I live! I watched the orange arrow designating divisions sweep over my home district and a red flashing star blink on and off in the middle of Berlin. Staring at the bright red light blink on and off, I was somewhere lost inside of myself, it was eerie, it was seductive. Red stars filled my eyes as I observed the troop movements, anticipating the unfolding strategy. Blink, they are spreading out and surrounding the capital, flash, I could only see red, as I watched the arrow spread out: now it is surrounded, flash boom, as the squeaky speaker replayed the explosive recording over and over, like a broken record. Now they are attacking again, flash, they are coming from the south, boom, the whole board is flashing now as the sound of explosion keeps repeating itself.

Slowly I could feel my stomach rising in my throat, flash, boom, flash. Then, after the battlefield was consumed by one continuous blinking light of conflict, the invasion was apparently complete. From this point forward, the confrontation points were no longer on the city's edge. They were moving in, they were approaching the center. As quickly as I noticed this advance, unexpectedly the red blinkers were flashing in the city center. Is that the Reichstag? It was a big red blinker—noticeably bigger than all of the others. I shivered upon this recognition. The speaker volume hung on a monotone note, like the repeating noise at the end of a record. And the light stayed red. Then, after a five second pause, each feeling like a minute, there was silence and the all the lights went out. Although it was silent all around me, my heart was hitting my chest wall with a rapid tapping noise that reverberated in my ear drums. I stood there dripping sweat, I felt exhausted and drained. I pressed the red button three times before moving on. I felt hypnotized as I wandered through the rest of the exhibits, including the well-preserved room where the Soviet Marshal who captured Berlin, Georgi Zhukov, and the entire Allied high command witnessed the Nazi commander sign the Act of Military Surrender.

Taking the long train ride back to my comfortable West Berlin domicile in Schlachtensee, I closed my eyes and saw a flashing red star blinking on and off like the lights used in the board displaying the Battle of Berlin.

Changing trains at Friedrichstrasse, I was suddenly overcome with intense fatigue, like a fighter must feel after going 15 rounds. I slept until midday, but awoke from what seemed to be my deepest sleep in a year. For weeks walking on the streets of Berlin, every time I saw a light, my mind would wander to the blinking red light that consumed me at the museum.

What will happen to this museum now that the Soviets have withdrawn? Will it remain in its present form? Unfortunately not. A twelve member Russian-German commission was established by the German government to work out a concept for the former Soviet victory museum. In contrast to the present day one-sided interpretation of the war, a new exhibition tracing German and Soviet history will be erected. Berlin's Karlshorst museum will be the future home of German - Soviet Relations from 1917 to 1989.[4]

My visit to the Karlshorst museum illustrated how often one forgets about the former Soviet soldiers in Berlin. Living in the American sector, one can forget about how many other forces are here. Nevertheless, the former Soviet soldiers were a big part of Berlin's community. In 1993, there were small weekly newspaper announcements describing another departure of soldiers back to their respective countries in the Commonwealth of Independent States, predominantly Russia or the Ukraine. What a fate, after what their forebears did to just to get to Berlin, to battle in the streets of Berlin with Nazis tooth and nail!

But Berlin has been helping them too. Weeks after my visit to the Karlshorst museum, for example, I noted the irony when I read in the papers on November 10, 1991, that the Berlin government announced that the last shipment of the Senate's Reserve (actually meant to feed Berliners in case of another Soviet blockade) was being sent to the former Soviet Union in order to help them through a difficult winter. This campaign, begun by the Berlin Senate, had raised money and sent goods to help Soviet citizens through their difficult transition.[5]

Reading through the newspapers and listening to commentaries about helping the people of the former Soviet Union, I couldn't help but think that the war was won by the Nazis or ended in 1942. Now, everywhere one looks and whatever one hears about the Soviet Union, from the forces stationed in Berlin to the political and economic crises they are in, it is like speaking of an unwelcome orphanage. They have nothing and we need to help them, having no choice because if we didn't they would only become more problematic.

When the Germans talked of the tremendous efforts they were making and how much money they were giving, I for a moment imagined myself to be a Russian soldier in 1942. My wife would have died on the Nazi attack front near Kiev, and my mother and sister swept up in the Nazi tornado that ravaged our farm and town. With the II army corps, I would have helped defend Moscow during the bitter winter and push the Nazis back. Town for town we regained our homeland, unrecognizable after the Nazi *Verbrannte Erde* (devastation strategy). All the suffering and torment our nation went through, over 25 million dead, embittered us beyond description.

Attacking Berlin in spring of 1945 was the climax of our rage, destroying the machine of terror. Then I was a 23-year-old lieutenant, now I am a 70-year-old veteran, living in a state apartment with no heat and worthless meal stamps. I read in the *Moscow Times* today that maybe we will be getting some supplies from Germany. As my curiosity grows, I read in the finer print that the supplies were once stored in hideouts in Berlin, in case the Red Army besieged the city again.

I'm overcome with a foggy recollection of my younger days and our campaign for Berlin. Did we ever reach our final goal, its seems so unreal now? Or I imagine myself to be a sixteen-year-old private stationed outside Potsdam. Even after our lunch time meals we are still hungry, and in the evening we go to sleep with growling stomachs. We have no right to go outside of the compound without an officer escort and only for special approved occasions. Yesterday we all had to line up and watch the fire squad execution of two comrades who were caught in the city trying to apply for asylum. We should be going home soon, perhaps in a couple of days, perhaps a year. One thing is certain, everything is uncertain.

As alluded to by my visit to the Karlshorst museum in East Berlin, while the Western Allies are departing victorious in the true sense of the word, Russians are withdrawing dejected, defeated, and to a fragmented empire. Later, I experienced another trip that illustrates the dimensions of the problem. This became especially apparent, when I joined the North Atlantic Assembly at the Berlin Concert Hall, the *Schauspielhaus*. On that beautiful evening, I had little idea what the evening would bring.

After picking up Natasha, a Russian friend, at the secured Russian embassy entrance on Unter den Linden, we began our short walk toward the concert hall. I didn't know what music was going to be played, but I was looking forward to a nice evening. Walking into the market place and then into the playhouse, we were excited by all the people running to and fro, in the charged, pre-concert atmosphere. In order to avoid the crowds, I suggested to Natasha that we make our way up to the back balcony.

Arriving at the top where the Prussian king and queen used to sit, I was surprised to find that only the first two balcony rows were free. The back row aisles, meanwhile, were packed full with infantry-like boys dressed in dull green worn out fatigues that reminded me of M.A.S.H. uniforms. Whispering in my ear, Natasha told me that they were Russian soldiers. I felt a bit out of place in my formal tie. I was expecting to see other members of the delegation in their evening attire. At this party, we looked like we didn't belong.

Taking our seats in the second row, in the middle, I was aware of a unique atmosphere around me. I began to look around us and observe our fellow guests. Sitting behind us were Russian soldiers, noticeably younger and not very attentive, to the right of me on the side bank were American officers, who in contrast to the former were dressed in fancy green buttoned and ironed uniforms, looking very healthy and fit. On our left side were rows of German Bundeswehr soldiers, mixed in with some British and French officers as well, dressed in their best ceremonial uniforms.

I took a deep breath, in reflection, Berlin 1993 was a site to behold. Here we were, an American and Russian, sitting side by side in the balcony looking over the North Atlantic Assembly delegation and their guests, with the victorious Four Power Allied soldiers and officers sitting mixed in with the Bundeswehr officers. Where at one time the king and queen of Prussia sat, overlooking their concert hall, today the Allies peacefully sit side by side with reunified autonomous Germans. Who could have imagined this just five years ago? In her speech, the president of the Bundestag Dr. Rita Suessmuth, paid tribute to the Allied presence, recalling the important role they played.

As the French horn trio completed their solo with a triumphant crescendo, I began to contemplate what these different people around us were thinking. What a range of different ideas, concerns, and problems they all must have. While the Russians sitting behind me may have grumbling stomachs that are making them uneasy and restless, the Americans on the right seem controlled, formal, and in good posture. I imagine that they are all thinking somewhat about their future as the music continues to soothe me, and open me up, wondering what their futures will bring them, their returns back home, their respective departures which Suessmuth just referred to. The feeling of transition was omnipresent in the concert hall.

Walking down the stairs, I could see the Russian soldiers herded off to the waiting buses outside. Only the badge-carrying persons were allowed to the reception. The Berlin paradox reared in my gut again. My first reaction was that I wanted to leave too. The champagne, pastries and smiling faces were repulsive to me. Natasha and I wandered around the formal reception area for fifteen minutes, giving our regards to Berlin's Senator for Federal and European Affairs, Peter Radunski, and his wife. However, despite seeing familiar faces and some distinguished leaders of Berlin's government, I was feeling so overwhelmed by what we had just experienced.

I wondered to myself what the Russians soldiers' daily life was really like. How were they going about their withdrawal? After asking such probing questions of my boss and other friends, I was disillusioned to discover that no one really knew much about the Russians.

Indeed, average Germans have no knowledge of the magnitude of the Russian military withdrawal going on —nor did I—that is until I got to join the North Atlantic Assembly, in representation of the German delegation, on another interesting outing.

Arriving late to the Reichstag, I wasn't sure where the bus was going to take the North Atlantic Assembly's Scientific Committee, but it didn't make a difference to me. I was just happy to be with the group on the bus.

But as we pulled into Tempelhof Airport and proceeded to board the German border patrol helicopters, I knew this day was going to bring me more than I could have possibly expected. As the helicopters lifted off over this famous airfield, and ascended into the blue sky, I made my fellow passengers aware of the freeway-like building project zig-zagging below us. "That was where the Wall was," I said, as their faces lit up with excitement and they gazed out their windows, "now it is all being torn down and the land mines dug out of the ground."

In response to my remarks, a Portuguese delegate seated across from me jumped up from his seat, his face beaming with excitement. In the span of minutes, I think he snapped off an entire roll of film of the former no-man's-land strip. Later he told me that he was so curious to see where his former continent ended, and where today the new one is centered.

The hour-long flight to Koenigsbrueck, the former westernmost Soviet military headquarters, just above Dresden, was uneventful, except for our close-up tour of the strip mining in East Germany. It was appalling to see how the land was so raped. As the helicopters descended upon our landing at Koenigsbrueck, we were all curious and attentive to see where the Russians lived, what they had, and how they withdrew.

Exiting the windy landing fields, with the rotor blades slowly coming to a stop, we boarded the Bundeswehr trucks like traveling soldiers preparing for an overland journey. I laughed a little inside, thinking to myself that the German Army was going to put a show on for the well-respected NAA delegation, and take them in transport trucks with big, heavy-duty tires and roll bars. But my suspicion was quickly washed away, as we began to bump over pothole after pothole, on the dirt road of the military compound. As the jarring and jamming settled in, all eyes were attracted to the abandoned houses on the roadside. Between the road and the houses were piles of scrap, sinks, plumbing, and other junk. Everything was piled on the side of the road. "Those were former barracks," said our German Army host.

Nevertheless, I was still suspicious that the Bundeswehr was putting on a show for us, showing us the worst parts of the recently abandoned command post to make the impression stronger. But that was just the beginning, the road became bumpier, the obstacles greater, the littered roadside more cluttered. It was literally as if we were driving through a junkyard, with abandoned cars and other goodies stacked up as high as the truck. I had heard that the Soviets were abandoning their premises, but this was appalling.

As the car hit another jarring bump I began trying to converse with the German commander who was responsible for the whole area. "What are you going to do with this area?" I shouted above the jarring shocks and the high engine pitch in first gear. His answer was clear, as he met my eyes, "It must all be removed. The quantity is greater than we expected. It costs a lot of money. But believe me, what you see is nothing compared with what they have hidden under the rubble. We just recently found an eight meter deep car oil deposit in the ground, and that is nothing to say for what we've yet to find."[6]

As we rolled out of the more private areas, I asked him what the base behind us was, hidden behind a thinly covered patch of trees. "That is where twenty SS-20's were stationed, but they were taken away following the INF agreement." How long ago that seemed to me. But seeing this site and hearing his remarks painfully reminded me of the threat we all lived under and seem to have so casually forgotten. Suddenly, I began to appreciate the significance of the former command, and the magnitude of building down such an operation. My unjustified suspicions at the beginning left me bare and my guard was gone, I felt overwhelmed.

As we finally reached our first destination and disembarked on a hill overlooking a huge open field with nothing but shrubs, I covered my eyes as the wind was whipping off the field and the sun was blaring down on us. Everyone began to gather around our speaker, and I moved forward to hear. "Look over there," said the commander. "Do you see those ridges, the trenches, way off in the distance?" As the layers of land became somewhat apparent, I heard him raise his voice as everyone was looking, "that is where the Nazis practiced for the attack on the Maginot line. This was the main training grounds for the attack." I was suddenly taken back by the history of the place and the passage of time. "That old shack on the hill was where the officers used to observe the troops movements and such." I was amazed that such ghosts of the past were even there, as chills ran up my spine. Here, far away from the German capital, in the middle of some barren wind-blown field, I was again reminded of the past. Every place in Germany has mirrors of the country's history.[7]

I tried to imagine what life was like here, how they lived, how they celebrated, how they were rewarded. As much as I tried, the harder it seemed. Although the last Russian forces just withdrew three months ago, it was as if we were taking a tour of some distant culture from another time.

We made our way back to our starting point where the helicopters were waiting. The drive took us well over 15 minutes. The size of this compound was tremendous. My curiosity was brewing to find out more. However, realizing that our tour was coming to an end, I turned to the smart German Army commander and asked him a few final questions. "Do you know what life was like here other than observing the remains, sir, I mean, did the surrounding German community have regular contact with the Soviet command for food resources, exchanges, etc?" I asked.

The commander's face lit up in response to my question and I could tell this was a story he was waiting to answer, "I will answer any remaining questions back at the helicopters," he said. But as if he could not resist himself, he continued: "No," he said emphatically, "none at all, they were literally leaches of the land and surrounding community. They isolated themselves, on purpose. They were victorious military occupiers in the true sense of the word. Although there were over 15,000 personnel stationed here, over twice as many as the surrounding community, they were completely shut off and isolated from the German district. They had their own bakery over there, and that was their headquarters," he explained and pointed to a yellow, old-fashioned house with broken windows. From our vantage point in the bumpy army jeeps, it looked run down and abandoned. "And then one day they packed up and were gone," he said. "Everybody is happy," continued the commander, "It is not like the departing Western Allies in other parts of Germany. Everybody here is happy the Russians are gone. They were occupiers in the true sense of the word, you can believe me." As the commander was speaking, I realized that I had hit a sensitive nerve. In contrast to his other, "official" remarks, I noticed that this time he let his guard down a little, and was really speaking from his heart.

Then my mind wandered to the next frame, the withdrawal itself. I asked him about the logistics, how everything was transported, coordinated, etc. By the looks of the place they just literally picked up camp in a matter of days and were gone like the wind. "Moscow didn't supply them with anything for the move home. We provided them with the train locomotives, the cars and all of the necessary equipment to facilitate the move to the Russian border. We even supplied them bungee cords to secure the goods on the trains, it was amazing," continued the commander.

"Do you know where the withdrawing soldiers were going?" I asked, as my curiosity grew with each one of his insightful answers. "Do you know where they have been re-deployed to? Where did all of those soldiers, tanks, and units go?" "I'm not sure about all 15,000 troops," he said, "but the first tank division went to Siberia on the Chinese border and the other division went somewhere close to Kiev in the Ukraine," answered the commander. "I have no idea about the rest. You must understand, the Russian commanders wouldn't let us in on details of their withdrawal, let alone about where they were going. They were just as obstinate and stubborn as before," he said. "Even as the highest German Army commander responsible for observing and assisting the military withdrawal from Koenigsbrueck, I was only able to speak with one or two commanders, and they hardly even answered my questions. Nobody else would even talk to me — I'm sure they were not allowed to speak with me. Everything went on in some big secret time frame, which we were never informed of. As the last departing train left, I was handed over the keys and able to go where I wanted on the compound for the first time," as he laughed a little. "Nobody thought it would be this bad," as he pointed over the littered and abandoned fields.

"But now that they are gone, we have a lot to do, it will take us a long time to clean this place up." Without giving my well-informed host a break, I fired another question about the size of the base to him. "Isn't this one of the biggest bases in East Germany?" I asked him assuredly.

"No," he said. "Rather this was one of the smaller bases, one of the lesser third bases from over a thousand Soviet Army bases in East Germany.[8] In Brandenburg, you can drive over a 100 kilometers and still be on former Soviet bases," he said.

As our caravan approached the hovering helicopters, I asked him one final question. "If I were to come here in ten years, what do you imagine that this military complex will be?" "I hope that it will be a national park, that they will be able to clean up the place enough so that nature can repair itself and that people can come here and learn," he concluded.

From these two experiences with the North Atlantic Assembly, my attention was alerted even more to Russia's military presence in Germany and its withdrawal. Weeks later, breezing through another newspaper, I found a relevant announcement on April 24, 1993. The Russian West Group Forces Orchestra, from Wuensdorf, and the German Bundeswehr Orchestra from Bonn, played a benefit concert for the departing Russian military forces together. Upon reading this announcement, I couldn't help thinking to myself that there were probably still some members of the Russian orchestra who marched into Berlin in 1945. A year ago a trust fund was set up to support the returning soldiers' families, for example medical care for debt stricken families and such. Since its founding, the fund has supported over 40 cases, funding over 90,000 deutsche marks. Concluding the concert under the direction of the German Director, the Brandenburg state opera played "A Dedication to the Prussian King" from Mozart. Reading this announcement, I recalled an article that I read about Wuensdorf, a little town on the edge of Berlin.[9]

Like a parasite, this Brandenburg town of 2,500 has lived on the fur of the big Soviet bear. Wuensdorf was the headquarters for Soviet West Group troops stationed in Germany. It was the biggest Russian base in Germany, 6,000 acres of land and 560 acres of buildings. 70,000 people lived behind the walled city, including military personnel, locals, and family members.

Wuensdorf was the headquarters for the Russian withdrawal from Germany. But back in 1993, when Wuensdorf was the bustling depot of withdrawal, it was well-known that a black market had established itself as the command's goals changed. A bi-weekly market at the Wuensdorf military base featured everything from fake Adidas t-shirts to cars. The latter you could get for 2,000 or 3,000 deutsche marks, but not with any papers or license plates.[10]

But it was not only the common Soviet soldiers who pawned off their own shirts and belt buckles to make some hard currency before their return to the Soviet Union. Everybody was doing what they could in the final, hectic days, to make a dollar. For instance, even the Soviet General Matvei P. Burlakov, who commanded the Western Army Group in East Germany and their withdrawal, was involved. General Burlakov, along with other officers, was accused in the Russian press of illegal sales of millions of dollars of government property intended to be returned to Russia.[11]

Yuri Y. Boldyrev, a Member of the Russian Parliament, who formerly headed Russian President Boris Yeltsin's anti-corruption department in 1992, said in a newspaper interview that in a report he gave to Yeltsin in 1992, that Western Group generals made millions of dollars on illegal sales of arms, food, and real estate in which the goods were transported to Poland and Russia as military supplies and sold at the higher, free market prices for profit. Also, Russian generals sold oil and army electronics on the black market, in which the profits were deposited in banks in Switzerland, Finland, and the United States.[12] Under increasing pressure from the media as the investigation continued, Yeltsin dismissed deputy defense minister, General Burlakov, on November 1, 1994.

Nevertheless, the investigation into illegal sales of military property also had its victims. With such powerful people involved in illegally selling property, corruption was widespread. The stakes were heavily weighted against such information reaching the public. One tragic example of important investigative reporting was Dmitri Kholodov. Mr. Kholodov, a Russian reporter for the newspaper *Moskovsky Komsomolets*, was murdered in a terrorist act in October 1994. Mr. Kholodov had been investigating illegal sales of government property by the Western Group forces for over a year. In one report, Mr. Kholodov reported the purchase of two Mercedes sedans in connection with an illegal sale of army property.

And Wuensdorf was the center of it all. It had its own train station, with Moscow's daily train schedule posted on the bulletin board. Every night a sleeping train departed for Moscow, most of the passengers came from the surrounding bases in the rest of East Germany. Wuensdorf was the last Soviet base to close, and was to be evacuated on September 1, 1994.[13] The withdrawal was successfully completed on time.

In 1993, Wuensdorf was not open to the public. Nevertheless, on special occasions small groups were given brief tours: but the famous gigantic pictures and paintings from the Battle of Berlin in 1945 were strictly off limits. Supposedly, they will be opened to the German public for one year following their withdrawal, upon which time they will be returned to Moscow for the 50th anniversary victory over Germany.[14]

Speculation is flourishing about what will become of Wuensdorf now that the Soviets are gone. The Brandenburg state development agency already held two symposia, from which one proposal seemed to find positive echo, to make it an *Aussiedlerstadt* (emigrants town). The Russian Germans are known, in contrast to other foreigners, to be nice people, hard working and trustworthy.

After having followed the developments as much as possible from the newspapers and such, I knew that I was always receiving third party information. I knew no Russians and had previously only had contact with Americans. But all that changed as I made my way to the Russian Embassy for a meeting with their commercial division. There, I met Natasha, when I asked her for directions to the entrance of the monstrous embassy. (Helga and I separated six months after my arrival in Berlin, she had left for graduate studies in America.) Natasha and I became friends and soon I learned more about her and her family as we fell in love. Her father worked for the Russian embassy commercial division since Gorbachev had taken power, but since February, 1993 he had been given a permanent leave of absence.

Somehow he managed to hold onto his job until the middle of the summer of 1993. Then they packed up all of their things and had their big farewell party. All their friends came and they drank an amazing amount of vodka. Upon politely asking them if I could have a glass of water, they smiled and laughed good heartedly while filling my glass with more of this jet fuel.

Natasha and I both anxiously anticipated the big day of their departure six months after we first met. She told me that they would be gone on Thursday, then on Friday, then lastly she told me that they had to leave on Sunday. Despite the uncertainty, it didn't seem to bother her or be much of a surprise. Nor were here parents troubled, they seemed to be happy to live another day in Berlin. In the meantime her parents had Natasha collecting all their last minute shopping items as quickly and efficiently as possible. She was so busy that I didn't even get to see her weeks prior to the big day. Then Sunday finally came.

As I returned to my apartment and walked through the door, it looked like a tornado had hit. Like a spring storm, she had come and gone. Natasha's red, blue, and white duffel bags were strewn indiscriminately across the apartment. Expecting to see her that night, I waited and waited . . . in vain.

I didn't hear from her until Thursday the next week. Later I found out that as soon as they arrived in Moscow, her parents ordered separate taxis in order to transport all of their goods home. "They are planning on divorcing," said Natasha. "But apartments are so expensive, they are going to build a wall through the apartment and a new entrance door." Then she added with a perplexed look, "I'm not sure what they are going to do with the toilet." "And what will your mother do?" I asked. "Well, she still has deutsche marks for now, so everything is okay, but afterwards I don't know. She is still pressuring me to find her a way back to Germany and a job.[15] My father is off on vacation in his homeland, Siberia."

I finally learned of Natasha's whereabouts for the five days from the time she dropped off her bags at my apartment until she suddenly appeared on Thursday. As she came walking through the door on that late Thursday night, I was more concerned than upset. In fact, I had given up trying to find her, when even the Russian embassy refused to answer my inquiries, saying simply that Family Bolgov was gone. She looked haggard and exhausted.

"Everything was going according to plan when we packed all day Friday and Saturday," she said. "Sunday afternoon we drove to Wuensdorf airport, and the plane was to depart from the airport at 5:00 p.m. Arriving at three, we packed all of our things on board the airplane," said Natasha. "Believe me," she continued, "there were so many goods being transported for the 20 passengers, more than the luggage compartment could hold, that they finally took out around ten seats to make room for the rest. Then shortly before departure, the flight was canceled, no reason was given as to why. We made our way back to Wuensdorf, took a room, and waited for the re-scheduled departure on Tuesday morning at 7:00 a.m. Then Tuesday they told us the flight was once again canceled, because of a political crisis, they had no landing rights and that we should come back at three, when they would try again," she said. "What do you mean, political crisis," I interjected. "I haven't heard of any such crisis." "I don't know," she said casually.

Since I have known Natasha and her parents, it has always impressed me how they seem to take everything with a grain of salt — but I guess that is what you'd have to do after your empire crumbles and you are abandoned in the world without a guide.

She didn't even begin to address my questions, instead she continued with her story. . . . "Then the Wuensdorf airport told us that we should arrive back at three o'clock on Wednesday, but when we arrived at 2:30

there was no one there, just a note saying that they would try again the next morning. The next morning the plane left on time."

Summary

"There must be a qualitative and substantive difference in how we welcome the departure of the Western Allies and the Russians," stated Mayor Diepgen emphatically in the Committee for Federal and European Affairs. The day was April 29, 1993, another historic moment in post-reunification Germany. The Committee's honored guest was Brigadier General Freiherr von Uslar-Gleichen, the Bundeswehr's newly appointed Berlin City Commander—the first German city commander since reunification in Berlin. During the Cold War, Allied law forbade the presence of Bundeswehr officers or uniformed soldiers in Berlin.

In reply to the mayor's opening remarks about the Allies' departure, General von Uslar-Gleichen pointed out how honored he felt to be in Berlin. For three years, such an assignment to be in Berlin, reporting to the Committee on Federal and European Affairs was inconceivable to him. After this one minute dramatic introduction, everything quickly became businesslike. The Brigadier General sat erect and spoke clearly and precisely. He reported how the German Army and federal government plan to have a huge farewell celebration for the departing Allies on the final day of withdrawal.

Mayor Diepgen continued, saying that in his view World War II was now just ending. With the departure of the Allies the post-World War II history of Germany would begin. "There must be two programs to deal with their departures, since the Allies each played categorically different roles in post-war Berlin and Germany," he said.[16] In reply to an opposition representative's criticism that the mayor was not addressing the seriousness of the departure with clear plans and initiatives to preserve the relations which had made it possible to have such a good partnership with America, the mayor seemed to feel personally attacked. He responded with concrete plans for exchanges and of continuing programs begun by the Allies.

"The troops will be leaving, but that doesn't mean that the relations will change. Now we have to work harder, cultural exchanges, educational exchanges, economic and security partnerships, all have to be strengthened, and studied as to how they can be improved. Qualitatively there is a difference in what we are doing, but quantitatively not at all," said the mayor. Diepgen went yet further, "Of course every high German official will be on hand at the celebration, it will be an historic day. I don't know sometimes if you all see this, but history is being written every day." He then went on to coolly reproach the representative for implying that the withdrawal of the Western military forces was going to mean less attention to the friendship they had built up.

I had never seen the mayor address a subject with such passion as that day. I left impressed, but later looked upon the situation more realistically, and somewhat pessimistically. Although I do not doubt the mayor's sincerity, I felt it might be a natural conclusion after such a intense, lengthy, and mutually dependent relationship, that the two countries would drift apart.

Despite this topic dominating much of the meeting, many of the representatives were more interested in who would be receiving the property rights of the Allies. The Allies had as much property as the boroughs of Berlin' Kreuzberg and Neukoelln Districts respectively taken together. Now the debate between the federal government and Berlin about the use of these lands would come under debate. Most of the Allies' houses and apartments would be taken over by federal bureaucrats.

The Western Allies will all be leaving behind a strong legacy of friendship. There are countless examples of small memorabilia that will remain, including street names, school names, and more. That is not to mention the many war memorials that stand. In this department, the Soviets outdid the Western Allies.

Behind the museums and exhibitions that the Germans will erect to remember the Allies, each of the four powers have also undertaken steps to ensure they will be remembered.

World War II Soviet Memorial tanks will remain part of the Soviet Memorial in Tiergarten commemorating the fallen Russian soldiers in the Battle of Berlin, announced the German Federal Army. The tanks were allegedly some of the first to roll into Berlin. Under a friendship treaty between Germany and the Soviet Union shortly before the end of the Cold War, it was agreed that all existing memorials would be preserved in East Germany.[17]

Notes

1 Speech by the Mayor of Berlin, Ebehard Diepgen, at the farewell ceremony for the U.S. Air Force 7350 post at Tempelhof, January 29, 1993

2 Der Tagesspiegel, "US-Panzereinheit verlasst Berlin nach 34 Jahren", May 27, 1992

3 Rick Atkinson, "Should Berlin Preserve A Nazi-Era Bunker", The Washington Post, December 6, 1994

4 Christina Schultze "Historiker vor manchem Raetsel", Der Tagesspiegel, March 16, 1993

5 Sugar, dried potatoes, fruits and vegetables, and tuna fish accounted for over 75,000 tons and DM 130 million of the goods shipped. Also medical and hygienic supplies were included.

6 The Industrie-Betriebs-gesellschaft mbH (IABG), the prime contractor of the German government that inspects Soviet West Group properties for contamination said of the condition at Konigsbrueck: ". . . an initial assessment of the residual load situation has been carried out for the Koenigsbrueck property by means of intensive on-site inspections. In this process about 1,600 suspected residual load sites were discovered and documented. Their focal points are the firing range areas, in which, in addition to the expected ammunition and ammunition components, amounts of scrapped building waste have been found. Over the whole site, contaminations of spilled mineral oil were registered, severe in some places." (footnote: Determination of Suspected Residual Load Areas on the Properties of the West Group of the Soviet Troops (WGT), "Information for the Site Visit of the Former Soviet Military Property Koenigsbrueck Training Area", May 21, 1993

7 Ibid. And how of much it is the military. Said the IABG report: " In all, about 1 million hectares (1 hectare = 2.5 acres) of land are used for military purposes in the Federal Republic of Germany. This corresponds to a proportion of 2.8% of the total land area. Of that 1 million, about 250, 000 hectares were used by the West Group Troops . The Koenigsbrueck property was constructed as a training area and firing range for the Royal Saxonian Army in 1904. At the same time, the villages of Otterschutz, Zietsch and Quosdorf were settled. Later the area was used by the Reichswehr. In 1938, as part of its use by the Wehrmacht, came the completion of a second construction phase which included the development of the villages Krakau, Steinborn, Bohra, Sella and Rohna."

8 Ibid. In Brandenburg there were 324 properties, Sachsen-Anhalt 271 properties, Saxony 165 properties, Thuringa 128 properties, Mecklenburg West Pomerania 127 properties, and East Berlin 11 properties.

9 Peter Jochen Winters, "Fuer die Musiker ist die Blockade Geschichte", Frankfurter Allgemeine Zeitung, April 24, 1993

10   Jacqueline Henard, "Allerlei Ideen fuer die Zukunft Wunsdorfs", Frankfurter Allegemeine Zeitung, July 16, 1993

11   Steven Erlanger, "Scandals Put Russian Defense Chief on the Defensive", The New York Times, November 2, 1994

12   "Russia has become a country on the Take", The Washington Post, November 13, 1994, pg A36

13   Ibid.

14   Ibid.

15   According to the editor of a leading Russian newspaper in Berlin, 140,000 Russians reside in the German capital in 1995.

16   There were two separate departure ceremonies; one for the three Western Allies and one for the departing former Soviet armed services.

17   The two 85 millimeter T34 Soviet Tanks, belonging to some of the first to roll into Berlin in spring of 1945, stand guard at the impressive memorial on the June 17 Street only 200 meters away from the Brandenburg Gate.

Chapter 13

Culture Forms Politics:
Marlene Dietrich

Berlin's hosting of the first Central and East European Cultural Metropolis conference on April 25, 1992, was a good harbinger of spring. The lifting of the Iron Curtain was most obvious in Berlin, but Budapest, Moscow, Prague, Sofia, St. Petersburg, and Warsaw also showed signs of a cultural flowering.

These centers have historically been the source of ideas, creativity, impulses, and compassion. Contacts, informational programs, and exchanges have been established between these hubs of art and culture. Curiosity is high to make up for the years of isolation and separation. Only now can we fully appreciate how brutal and artificial the forced separation of these cultural metropolises was. The control formerly exercised over these traditional centers of commerce and culture was as precarious as the number of Lenin and Stalin monuments littered across their landscapes. Where communist headquarters were once located, cafes, art galleries, and discos are blossoming.

Berlin, with all of its East meets West connotations, is now laughing at those artificial days. Where life was once threatened, today the seed of new life, the birthplace and activity of the city center has re-emerged. The rhythm of the city, the meeting place of people, ideas and cultures is back. The once monotonous, abandoned gray streets in East Berlin are now decorated with colorful billboards and people with dyed red hair. Blues, reds, and oranges are bringing personality and life to this former no-man's-land. The new East Berlin is sometimes loud and hectic; one can often hear the noises bouncing off the dirty and run-down buildings. Unlike the days of the horrific East German suppression, there is nothing more about which one has to be silent. Quiet conversations are being replaced by blaring music, honking car horns, children playing, all mixed in with the hum of everyday life.

This became poignantly clear to me as I walked through the tunnel between trains at Friedrichstrasse train station in East Berlin. In this tunnel, West Germans used to cross the inner-German border separating East and West Berlin. Walking up the 10 degree inclined slope and reaching the top of the stairs, I was overcome with the sense of distance, enhanced by the length of the hall. With the end barely visible, it felt like emerging into something new. The white shining tiled walls gave the already cold draft a bitter welcome. A separation was being made and suddenly my eyes fixed joylessly on the orange wall I was approaching. The end was in sight. I was overcome with relief, with the feeling of refuge. But as my pace increased, the orange wall was no closer. The shallowness of the ceiling caused me to lose my perspective.

Today, in this tunnel where fear still bellows from the walls, Gypsy music is being played and people move about in a carefree way. Berlin has arisen from the ashes of the Wall's rubble, and it is again living like many never imagined it could. East Berlin is beginning to express its true face, it is full of contrast and confrontation, loud and quiet, with wide-ranging tempos. The city rhythm varies. The pulse of the city is often like agony screaming out, slow, intense, and hard. Graffiti is splattered everywhere, with the careless and random nature of this art. "Anarchy is Freedom," "The War is us," "We are all sitting in one boat just before shipwreck," "Nazis get out," "Asylum lies, foreigners get out," etc.

Businesses are setting up shop. Free enterprise and trade are now the main activities on Pariser Platz, the site of the Brandenburg Gate. Peddlers offer everything from Soviet military hats, Berlin souvenirs, coffee, tea and food. In a place where fear and anxiety once ruled, now there is a festive, lively and progressive nature to the place, with construction cranes in the background symbolizing the physical and spiritual rebuilding taking place. Bikers touring the former strip where the Wall was, laugh and joke, riding along as if it never existed.

This market atmosphere is a metaphor for the subtle, less tangible exchanges taking place in Berlin's cultural life. Philosophy, religion, and art are all meeting here. The city is being reborn, although the shape still remains amorphous. While East Berlin is undergoing this rapid metamorphosis, West Berlin is changing too. Despite the fact that West Berlin was already the cultural capital of West Germany, it was always haunted and influenced by the Wall, the division and the artificial influence it was subjected to. The energy and life of this cultural metropolis is taking root in the ashes of the regime which haunted their suppressed souls, sedating the natural and spontaneous formation of ideas, art, music—the fruits of freedom. Berlin's old street names, old names of squares and plazas that were replaced by the East German communist dictatorship, are now being restored to their traditional names, some already proudly marked on new signs. The identity crisis is gone, now that the city has been allowed to find and express itself. The contradictory tradition is back. East Berlin is no longer mute.

Even at Alexanderplatz, the church and the synagogue have re-opened again, whereas during the Cold War they were boarded up and used for storage rooms or laboratories.

One good indicator of what may be on the horizon for Berlin can be found in the Berlin's Prenzlauer Berg District, East Berlin's former cultural center. Prenzlauer Berg is the barometer by which we can read Berlin's emerging identity. The experimenting impulse of life and ideas can be seen in the tucked-away cafes, in the basement art galleries, in the run-down apartments where young groups are meeting.

Since reunification, Prenzlauer Berg has emerged as part of the Berlin scene, where late-night bands scream into the night, symbolizing the nature of the culture where dissatisfaction and frustration are juxtaposed with curiosity and interest. Here, unlike the rest of Germany, young Germans went East. Although originally stemming from an economic motivation (i.e., cheaper rent), the move is producing unforeseen social rewards. Consensus is being formed and an indescribable dynamic has taken root as a result of this precarious confrontation. The creativity and exchange are calling forth something new; they are confronting each other, grasping for understanding. These young, dynamic, frustrated people are the only ones meeting, the only ones who seem to be able to appreciate each other and overcome the walls in German society. East meets West is true of Berlin like no other city in Germany, but in Prenzlauer Berg, in contrast to other city districts, they live in synergy. Therefore, it seemed right that this first Central European cultural meeting was organized in Berlin: "the city destined to recapture from Paris the title of world cultural center," according to *The New York Times Magazine*.[1]

On May 6, 1992, one of Berlin's most famous actresses of this century, Marlene Dietrich, died in seclusion in Paris. Because Dietrich was probably Berlin's most famous movie star, her death, and the subsequent reception she received from Berlin, her birthplace, is indicative of Germany's identity crisis. Dietrich's death makes us confront Berlin's darker side again: the days for which this city will be best remembered in the 20th century, as the capital of the Third Reich.

Marlene Dietrich was a multi-talented performer, she was best known for her role in such films as the *Blue Angel.* Following the Nazi takeover, she left Germany and immigrated to the United States in 1937. From March 1943 until the end of the war, she was a USO troop showgirl. It was her own form of protest against the fascist dictatorship in her homeland. Following offers by the Nazi regime to return to Germany, she was so incensed by their gall at making her such an offer that she declared herself an anti-Fascist and a half-Jewish emigrant. Following the war she made her comeback in Billy Wilder's *A Foreign Affair.*[2] Today, some Germans still consider Marlene Dietrich a traitor because of her "disloyal" service in World War II.

Upon Dietrich's death, her funeral reception and burial have been the source of much public debate in Berlin and Germany. Her last wish was to be buried next to her mother in Berlin's Schoeneberg District. In response to the symbolism of her passing, the state of Brandenburg immediately named part of the Babelsberg Film Studio, where she used to work, after her. And what did the state of Berlin do to commemorate her passing? The Berlin government has yet to make any similar symbolic gesture marking the significance of this grand dame of the silver screen. There was some talk of changing the name of Wilhelm Pieck Strasse into Marlene Dietrich Strasse.

Although Berlin is the working model for the East-West thaw going on in the world, although Berlin is a cultural, economic, and political metropolis in the center of Europe, and although Berlin is re-emerging as the reunified Germany's capital, Berliners still couldn't muster the courage to properly pay their last respects to one of their most internationally acclaimed movie stars.

The lackadaisical way in which they have greeted her back home is disappointing. With little ceremony, she was quietly laid to rest in the Schoeneberg District, as she had wished. No recognition or special tribute was paid to her other than the usual salutations of government officials. This illustrates that Berliners cannot expect to be regarded as a world metropolis and European capital when they cannot properly recognize the life of one of their most internationally acclaimed. It points to provincial thinking on the part of the German metropolis, and especially some of its politicians. Berliners still have a way to go. Some just want to put the difficult past behind them. Why hadn't they made Marlene Dietrich a honorary citizen of the city long before?

The death of Dietrich and the subsequent public reaction illustrates another example of how Berliners handle their National Socialist history. I recall the varied Berlin newspaper headlines that announced her death. While some papers described her as a traitor, others described her as a heroine.

It is crucial that a consensus be reached on such important events, rather than one side's paper printing one story for one culture and the other its own story for its own culture. Figures like Marlene Dietrich are what people remember most, more so than a new train station or future government building. She is part of the culture that Berlin will inherit in the year 2000.

Notes

1   Paul Goldberger, "Reimagining Berlin", The New York Times Magazine,
    February 5, 1995
2   Munzinger-Archiv/Int. Biograph. Archiv 29-30/92, "Marlene DIETRICH"

Chapter 14

The Brandenburg Gate

Speaking at Berlin's Brandenburg Gate in July 1994, President Bill Clinton said: "Now, together, we can walk through that gateway [the Brandenburg Gate] to our destiny, to a Europe united, united in peace, united in freedom, united in progress. Nothing will stop us, everything is possible, Berlin is free."

The Brandenburg Gate, like much of the city, embodies the Berlin and German paradox. The gate was built in 1772 and symbolized German imperialism. After defeating Prussia in 1808, a crowned Napoleon led his troops through the gate in a horse-drawn carriage, holding a figure of the Goddess of Peace, who in turn is wielding an iron cross.[1] Later, the Prussian army returned to the Brandenburg Gate after defeating Napoleon at Waterloo. Much later, a torch light parade of National Socialists marched through the gate on January 30, 1933, to celebrate Adolf Hitler's election as German Chancellor. President Clinton, on July 12, 1994, called the Gate a "monument of conquest and tower of tyranny." Then on September 8, 1994, France, Britain, and the United States were given the highest military ceremony by the German Bundeswehr to commemorate the end of their 49-year presence in Germany with a torchlight parade through the Brandenburg Gate.

Before the fall of the Wall, the chariot on top of the Gate was turned around to face East out of provocation to West Berlin. Now it has been refurbished and turned around facing the traditional way, West. The victorious Soviets also took off the Prussian Eagle and iron cross. Both were later returned to the chariot in 1991.

During the years that I lived and worked in Berlin, the Brandenburg Gate came to symbolize the times. Back when I first visited Berlin in

1987, it was the symbol of division. Then I stood on the top of the observatory on the "other side," looking at the deserted Unter den Linden boulevard in East Berlin and the barren Pariser Platz. I was looking over the barricaded Wall into a ghost town. The place was mysterious, dark—in short, compelling.

Years later, in 1989, the Brandenburg Gate symbolized to the world the triumphant victory over the Wall and the beginning of the end of the Cold War. Now, the Brandenburg Gate symbolizes the rebirth of the German capital, and the meeting point of the New Europe without divisions.

My first view of the gate from the "other side" came in 1987. My girlfriend, Helga clearly did not share my enthusiasm for a trip to East Berlin. The same nervousness she exhibited at the border patrol presented itself in full on that rainy day. She repeatedly reviewed our travel procedures with her aunt.

As we separated at Adenauer Platz, I making my way towards Checkpoint Charlie, and she towards Friedrichstrasse, the concern and worry on her face were remarkable. She was most concerned I'd do something stupid. Because I was a citizen of one of the Allied powers in Berlin, I was obligated to cross into East Berlin and back to West Berlin through the Checkpoint Charlie crossing. Germans were only allowed to cross into East Berlin through the Friedrichstrasse train station checkpoint.

In contrast to her concern, I was excited and convinced that nothing could happen to me, for I was an American. After changing trains, I finally reached the famous Checkpoint. Was I disappointed! All that Cold War hype led me to imagine this place to be decorated with heavy machinery. Rather, as I walked through various mobile home-like offices, the most notable impression I had was that the East German guards were far from friendly. Regardless, I walked through Checkpoint Charlie with a carefree certainty as the guards brushed aside my smiles with cold glares.

Helga and I met at Friedrichstrasse. Her attentiveness and anxiety were heightened. First, she greeted me with a sigh of relief. Then in a serious tone, she insisted that we would spend this drab winter day only on the main street, Unter den Linden. The gray buildings and streets were colorless. Nevertheless, I was curious to see what was going on. This proved difficult. There was absolutely no life on the streets, no shoppers, no shops. Having each exchanged the mandatory 30 deutsche marks at the border crossing, we searched in vain for a place to spend it. After having a long lunch in the Grand Hotel, spooked by the absence of people, Helga insisted that we start to make our way home. Although reluctant, I consented because there was really nothing to do here and it would be getting dark soon.

Helga and I separated at the same place we met. With a kiss good-bye we parted. My walk back west toward Checkpoint Charlie was highlighted by a stopover at the Brandenburg Gate, the ultimate symbol of East-West division. As I came closer to the gate I observed life on that barren avenue called Unter den Linden.

The Brandenburg Gate, 1945, courtesy of the German Information Center

The Brandenburg Gate on the Wall, courtesy of the German Information Center

The Berlin Wall Falls, November 9, 1989, courtesy of the German Information Center

Bundeswehr ceremony at the Brandenburg Gate commemorating the Western
Allies withdrawal, September 8, 1994, courtesy of the German Information
Center.

At first I thought I was mistaken, but approaching further, I was
convinced that I saw people clustered on the street. Life! There was a
group of about 20 Soviet soldiers, aged about 14 to 16. I remember them
talking among themselves as I tried to speak to them. The only thing I
could understand from this brief charade was their wish for money, as they
kept pointing to the pocket where my wallet was. A strong feeling of pity
came over me.

The Wall dominates one's thinking when one is in its proximity.
Suddenly the barricades criss-crossing Pariser Platz came clearly into focus
and the Brandenburg Gate looked blocked by that Wall forever. With my
head down, I turned away from the soldiers and continued walking. Before
turning left at the Wall, making my way back through Checkpoint Charlie,

I was embarrassed and angry, remembering the arrogant way in which I so casually entered East Berlin. I left Berlin after one week, and was fascinated by the Brandenburg Gate, and even more so by the Wall.

Years later, after the fall of the Wall, and in the reunified Germany, I was sitting in a parliamentary session in which the fate of this ultimate symbol of German division and reunification was discussed. On that day, hot and heavy discussions were flying about whether the Brandenburg Gate should be opened again for vehicle traffic. The issue was discussed at all levels: in the parliamentary committees, then in the party group meeting, culminating with a decision by the Berlin government. But it was not just being debated in political circles—from the buses to the cafes, talk abounded about what would become of this great symbol in the German capital.

Then, unbeknownst to me, the decision was reached. Sitting in the back of the Rathaus Schoeneberg parliamentary hall, I heard the Senator responsible for Transportation being introduced by the parliamentary president out of the corner of my ear. As soon as the words of his decision to keep the gate closed were heard, the whole right side of the parliament erupted in protest; all of the representatives on the right side of the aisle hissed and booed the Senator for his decision, while the left side gallantly applauded him [the right side was the conservative parties and the left, the liberals]. Some representatives were looking at each other from across the aisle and taunting each other. Never before had I seen the otherwise formal, decorous sessions come to life with such passion.

Despite the decision at that time to keep the Brandenburg Gate closed, deeper forces were at work. Within six months of the Berlin government's decision to keep the gate closed, on May 26, 1992, the Brandenburg Gate was opened for through traffic, albeit taxis and buses. A feeling of awe filled me the first time I saw traffic moving through the gate. After much discussion and debate within the grand Social Democratic Party — Christian Democratic Union coalition, with the former having opposed opening the gate while the later was for its opening, the CDU finally won. This was a late but much-needed decision. Automobile traffic between East and West Berlin has become more and more congested and city officials have had limited options to ease this problem. When the Wall was erected, 75 street connections in the city were broken, and 28 still are.[2]

But it is much more than just a question of traffic congestion. Brandenburg Gate, having served as the symbol of the division of Europe, Germany and Berlin, has finally regained its original function and is again a major throughway linking East and West.

Following an official opening celebration with representatives from the Berlin government, left political extremists blocked traffic from traveling through the gate. Chaos erupted as police stormed the demonstrators carrying signs of protest against the reopening. A throng of protesters made a human wall to protest its opening for over eight hours before they were removed.

I couldn't help thinking to myself that the place was going to come back to life now that it had been reopened for traffic. Now my trips to the Reichstag, like the one in which I went to listen to the Federal Commission panel discuss the Stasi, when I stopped at the gate to reflect in peace and quiet on the symbol this place serves, will be much different.

The Brandenburg Gate's future is certain to be colorful as its history. Despite the opening of the gate, it took a long time for the reality of the decision to sink in. Weeks after the botched opening, as I was walking south on Unter den Linden, I suddenly stopped, half frozen out of shock and disbelief. Immediately it became clear to me that I was looking through the Brandenburg Gate, where cars were driving through the Roman gate pillars. I flashed back to where I was standing in the same place five years ago and I couldn't look through, the Wall had blocked any possible view of West Berlin. No one had been on the streets and the group of young Soviet soldiers had gathered under the linden trees. It was the only life present, five years ago, the same cold drab weather.

I try to imagine how this scene will look in five years. I can still see through the Brandenburg Gate, but everything else is new. On the left and right I see big buildings, dwarfing the former domineering gate. I can see the American flag blowing in the air on the building on the left and I think I make out the British and French flags on the buildings on the right. Further in the distance on the right side I see in the background the German Bundestag with a sky-light on top and a large German flag. Then I look to my left and am astonished by the beauty this one-time no-man's land has taken on. The buildings are big, however modest in comparison to American high-rises. The architecture is in good proportion and is aesthetically pleasing. Flashback: just five years ago, this was once nothing but an empty field, and five years before that I remember the Wall running down the middle of it with barbed wire and mushroom-shaped guard towers.

In short, it today is, as much as in history, the best place to watch and gauge the developments in Europe. It will likely be in the future too. President Clinton also said in July as he stood at the Brandenburg Gate: "The gate has been a symbol of the time . . . But in our own time, courageous

Berliners, have again made the Brandenburg what it was meant to be — a gateway. Now, together, we can walk through the gateway to our destiny, to a Europe united—united in peace, united in freedom, united in progress for the first time in history."

Notes

1   The Prussian Cross was established by Prussian King Friedrich Wilhelm III during the Napoleonic Wars. It was awarded to troops for their military service. Later, it was also used as a military award in the French-Prussian War of 1871, as well as also used by the National Socialists in World War II.
2   Rolf Liebold, "28 Strassen enden an der unsichtbaren Mauer", Berliner Zeitung, December 4, 1991

Chapter 15

Berlin's Economic Update

The first anniversary of the Bundestag's decision to move the capital from Bonn to Berlin offers a good chance to outline some of the socio-economic forces at work in the German capital. Not only will the legacy of the former East German culture influence the development of Europe's most powerful country, but so will the billions of dollars of financial investment.

After sitting through a year of committee hearings, I have caught the fever of the promise of the future. Despite the walls in Germany's social, political and cultural life that will take years to overcome, Berlin is on the wave of the future. The following is an article I wrote for *The Seattle Times*:

"Unified Berlin emerges as a key European center"

The world's Metropolis; Paris, Rome, London, New York, Berlin! Berlin is back. With the end of the Cold War, this famous city is re-emerging as one of the most important cities of the New Europe. A dynamic wave of activity has swept over this city of 3.5 million people since the fall of the Wall on November 9, 1989. Following weeks of celebrations, American initiated 2 plus 4 negotiations, and culminating in the reunification treaties, Berliners are finally able to plan the future of their city themselves. The state government, once burdened with free time during the Allied control, is now feverishly working to build one city out of two. Programs continue to be integrated. A common school system, transportation system, and waste program are already intact.

This time of transition is by no means easy. Many articles describing the insurmountable barriers present to the reunification of Germany and Berlin have been written. But how many have explained the progressive developments made? How can reunification be maturing so terribly when in Berlin, the epitome of the East meets West, everything is maturing so peacefully? What qualities characterize the people that proudly call themselves Berliners?

President John F. Kennedy adeptly recognized the unique Berliner character during his famous speech at West Berlin's Schoeneberg City Hall back in the spring of 1963: "I know of no town, no city that has been besieged for 18 years, that still lives with the vitality and the force and the determination of the city of West Berlin." These qualities, along with the never to be forgotten Allied support, have helped West Berliners survive over 40 years surrounded by the Red Army. Now they are the source of creative planning and optimism. Former East Berliners are adopting democratic Western ways and free enterprise remarkably well. With the help of their Western brothers and sisters they are both living better and gladly exercising their democratic rights.

The massive influx of Western lifestyle into East Berlin is transforming the once dull and monotonous streets. The street scene has come alive. Manifest in cafes and boutiques, a feeling of life and innovation abounds. The confrontation arising from the clash of cultures has produced a peculiar social environment. Culturally Berlin is almost unique. Three full operas, multiple theaters, and a Las Vegas-like show place Berlin right up there with Paris and London. A new national museum is planned and the increase in theater and opera activity is remarkable. The Berlin Philharmonic Symphony is world reknowned and many famous directors enjoy its modern acoustics.[1]

In every sector of the city a strong feeling of foreign influence is to be seen and felt. Foreign language ability illustrates just one pattern in the cultural mosaic of the re-emerging European metropolis. Russian was required from the first grade on in the former East Berlin, while every high school graduate in West Berlin commands either English or French.

Economic investment in Berlin is booming. Mercedes and Sony Europe are moving their headquarters to Berlin. Private investment has naturally followed suit. Rent prices are so out of control that the city had to step in to put a ceiling on them. Property costs have multiplied by over 50% in the last two years!

Also, Treuhand (the agency for privatization of former state run industries in East Germany), is centered in Berlin. After only two years in full operation, more than 90% (10,600 of the original 12,500) of East Germany's state industries have been sold.[2] The United States, through 1992, was the investment leader in the new German states, investing over DM 2.7 billion.[3] Appraising and selling former state industries is proving to be an invaluable experience for Berliner businessmen. While the majority of Western businesses are searching for clues to understand the dinosaur of communist industry, Berliners are forced to learn it, invest in it, and moreover, make it profitable.

Last summer the German government decided to move the capital from sleepy Bonn to bustling Berlin. This was a vote for the future. Berlin is historically and geographically attracted to Central and Eastern Europe. Situated in northern Central Europe, Berlin is only five hours by train to Prague and an hour to the Polish border. Contacts are flourishing with neighboring countries and city partnerships have already been made with Moscow, Warsaw, and Budapest.

At least $7 billion is being appropriated for the move from Bonn to Berlin. Appropriated for a wide range of infrastructure improvements, from a state-of-the-art metro system to the rebuilding of former East Berlin, this money is a breath of life for the city. Nationally Berlin as the capital promotes the *'Zusammenwaechsen'* process between the former East and West Germany. It affirms the united German commitment to improve national unity and economic parity.

Other political developments also make the German capital increasingly important. Special committees have been formed to promote *'Zusammenarbeit'* between the independent Berlin and Brandenburg states. While Berlin lies within Brandenburg, it is only logical to many that they also re-unite. Politically this would move Berlin and Brandenburg (Brandenburg is the historic state name for both) from the lightweight class up to a middle heavyweight.

Also, the German capital is a top contender for the summer Olympics in 2000. When President Reagan proposed the idea back in 1987 it was as much wishful thinking as Cold War rhetoric. Now Berlin is as serious a contender as either Sydney or Peking.

Whether one looks into culture, economics, or politics, Berlin is prepared for the geopolitical realities in Europe. From its dual nature since the collapse of communism, Berlin is a cosmopolitan of East and West living together. The capital of Germany has more hands-on experience, know how, and understanding for the transitions occurring in Central and Eastern European countries than any other city. Berliners are the first to admit that it is not easy and there are many problems, but with their 'determination and vitality', they are moving forward and making step-by-step incredible progress.

These promising developments lead many to believe Berlin will be the most important economic center in Europe between Paris and Moscow. Daimler Benz President Edzard Reuter thinks Berlin will be one of the biggest service industry centers on the continent.[4] Berlin's stock exchange manager, once the biggest on the continent, sees much potential for the exchange to become increasingly important, stating "within a time frame of ten years, I can imagine a very close partnership and cooperation with the stock exchanges to the East."[5]

Private investment is booming in Berlin too. For example, the Berlin government recently welcomed the opening of the American German Business Club. More than 200 American companies are currently operating in Berlin and the other new German states, with an investment volume from DM 6 billion and more than 42,000 jobs.

There are many examples, and the following will outline just a few of the bigger projects: Philip Morris invested over a DM 100 million to expand their operation in Berlin, Coca Cola over 100 million as well as 650 million in the other new German states. It is also mentioned that Kodak has moved back to their original plant in East Berlin, creating an additional 150 jobs.

On June 1, 1993, the Springer Publishing Company published their first Berlin edition of *Die Welt* newspaper. Publisher Claus Jacobi recalled that 18 years ago the famous international paper moved from Hamburg to Bonn because "we said that a national paper should be in the capital, and therefore we have now moved to Berlin." *Die Welt* now features a new section entitled "Hauptstadt Berlin" (Berlin, Capital City). Berlin also hosted the 1994 Conference of World Metropolises, at which the main subject was environmental issues.

A German silicon valley is being constructed in Berlin's Adlershof District out of the former East German Science Academy. 100-high tech companies have taken up offices there. Experts predict that within ten years and after DM 4 billion of public investment, 35,000 people will live there.[6]

In tandem with the promising private investment that is occurring in Berlin, Berlin officials are preparing the city for its future role as the German capital too.

For example, on June 10, 1993, the Berlin government announced their plans for a CIS International Trade Center on the Spree River. Their intended goal is to make Berlin the financial center for the CIS in Europe, where international banks and financial institutions will be located. Also, the government is encouraging educational reforms to meet future needs. Humboldt University has drafted a plan to begin a separate curriculum for a Western style business school, where leaders of the CIS countries can study.

The impulse of Europe's emerging metropolitan center can be seen in many economic indicators, but also on the streets. On May 21, 1993, the first ICE express train departed Berlin-Lichtenberg for Munich. The modern new train, which can reach a speed of up to 250 km/h, has now been put into service to Berlin. However, experts noted that the full potential of the train cannot be reached until 1997 because the tracks are in such bad condition.

Although one can easily be a skeptic about Berlin's chances of being the political capital of Germany before 1997, it is clear to see that their plans will be realized sooner or later. Berliners have a remarkable faith and connection to their city, one which only strengthens their ambition as the traces of communism disintegrate.

One example of Berlin's economic boom is the famous boulevard that runs through the center of the town: the Unter den Linden. Since my arrival in Berlin in 1990, Unter den Linden has grown in importance. It is Berlin's main avenue. The street lives history, the Prussian way. After the horrific destruction of the German capital in World War II in the Battle of Berlin, Unter den Linden had the chance to re-assume its Prussian character. If one walked through the Brandenburg Gate in 1950, one would have seen Schulte's Zeughaus on one side and the Knobelsdorff Koengliche Oper and the Kronprinzenpalais in the direction of the rest of the Hohenzollern castle.[7] It looked as if the city center had survived the war. As exhibitions took place in the Hohenzollern castle after the war, and food was served at the bombed-out Hotel Adlon on Pariser Platz before both were destroyed, the actual monarchical part of the Unter den Linden lived on.[8]

During the division of the city, West Berlin's Kuerfurstendamm took the place of Unter den Linden as much as possible. Berlin naturally gravitates around this grand boulevard. It is the only place in Berlin where one has the feeling that one is in the center: the breadth and spaciousness make one feel that this is where the important people and sights are. During the days of Soviet occupation it was mainly an embassy boulevard, with the Soviet Embassy dominating the Western end around the Brandenburg Gate. Socialist parades were regularly held on the grand boulevard, like the yearly military parade. Earlier, the Unter den Linden was also the site of the Nazi military parades.

In the 1990s construction is booming on Unter den Linden. Also, activity is burgeoning on the famous shopping street, Friedrichstrasse. Many embassies that formerly clustered in the center of the city have relocated because they cannot afford the explosive rents: new hotels, restaurants, and cafes are quickly moving in. Life is rushing back to the heart of Berlin with the removal of the 12 foot concrete dam.

Humboldt University has undergone a complete renovation from the outside and even looks impressive from the street. Further eastward on the same side of the street is the Zeughaus, which will be the future sight of the new German national museum. One of my favorite places on the street under the linden trees is the Lustgarden (leisure garden), where the national museum is. The size of the square and its openness gives one breathing space in the middle of a big crowded city. Recalling my first visit here in 1987, it is as if today the place is entirely new. The barrenness of those days is gone, now it is cluttered with ice cream stands, weekly flea markets, musicians, and many people are flowing in and out of museums and cafes.

Bright faces of college students walking around Humboldt light up the area and give the atmosphere a carefree feeling, especially during the long summer days. Recalling my visit here back in 1987, this place was deserted. I think we saw two or three people in the garden. The church was boarded up and let go, as if waiting for the demolition cranes. It showed how little care was given to such symbolic sites, although they began a reconstruction program in 1986.

There is the "museum island," where a variety of museums and the national gallery are situated. Just seeing these enormous architectural structures black with soot and literally on the verge of falling to the ground is sad. It looks as if they had been boarded up and left for scrap since the last bombs fell back in the spring of 1945.

But across the street from the Lustgarden is the biggest eyesore on this grand boulevard, der *Palast der Republik*, or the former East German parliament. In 1993, this asbestos-filled building was nothing more than an empty, costly, and ugly seventies-style building. Easterners and Westerners are divided as to what to do with the building. Some even want to erect the Hohenzollern Castle again in its place. Like the former East German Foreign Ministry across the big parking lot, the *Palast der Republik* is a constant reminder of the former communist regime. Their 1970s architecture doesn't seem to fit well into the plans I've reviewed for the new German Capital; they represent a different era, a different system.

Walking further East beyond the *Palast der Republik* the horizon is dominated by the towering television tower in the middle of Alexanderplatz. Now a 1950s style plaza with much concrete, the life and character have been all but completely sucked out of this historic square. It feels and looks so unnatural. It is not a place one visits in one's spare time. It is cold and impersonal. Despite the architectural abuse of this once famous area, there are still a few scents of its better days to be found. There is also an architectural contest taking place here. Without having much to work with, many hope that they can resurrect some of its former beauty.

Notes

1   As noted in Paul Goldberger's "Reimagining Berlin" (The New York Times Magazine, Feb. 5, 1995): Berlin is keeping them all. With an arts budget of roughly $800 million a year — more than four times the budget of the National Endowement for the Arts — Berlin is one of the most lavishly subsidized cultural communities in the world.

2   Sueddeutsche Zeitung, "Franzosen stehen in Ostdeutschland an der Spitze", December 30, 1992

3   Ibid.

4   "Von New York Lernen", Der Spiegel, February 20, 1995, pg. 43

5   Wolfgang Wack, "Berliner Boerse will wieder die Nummber eins werden", Volksblatt, November 6, 1991

6   "Von New York Lernen", Der Spiegel, February 20, 1995, pg. 42

7   Wold Jobst Siedler, "Der preussische Corso", Frankfurter Allegemeine Zeitung, April 30, 1993

8   For example, the Bouman Palais and Kronprinzenpalais with the Prinzenpalais next to it were all restored. source: Wold Jobst Siedler, "Der preussische Corso", Frankfurter Allegemeine Zeitung, April 30, 1993

Part Four

In Name of the
European Union

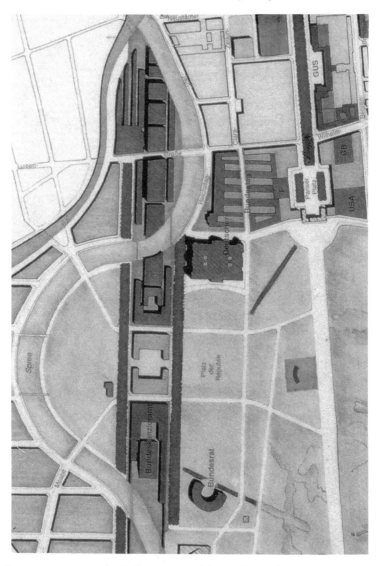

German government in 2000, courtesy of the public relations department of the Public Ministry for Urban Development and Environmental Protection, Berlin

Chapter 16

Rebuilding the Capital

A gainst the backdrop of the dramatic political and social developments occurring in Berlin, the city's capital plans continue to mature. The road is being paved for the move from Bonn. Many projects and announcements were made by the government to illustrate this dramatic trend.

My second winter working in the Berlin parliament started off with an appropriate example of Germany's focus shifting back to Berlin. On February 9, 1993, the biggest architectural competition in German history was completed for the Spreebogen. The Spreebogen is the area around the Reichstag where the German government will be moving to.[1]

All of the building for the German capital will be centered, paradoxically, at the heart of Europe's former dividing line. The entire area around the Reichstag will become the future site of the German government and everything apart from the Reichstag itself will have to be built from scratch. Formerly this was the site of the Wall, running right behind the Reichstag on the Western side of the Spree River. Now the entire area around the Reichstag, especially on the Southwestern side is barren landscape, also referred to as no-man's-land before the fall of the Wall.

This is the fifth attempt to reform this traditional place in this century. Nevertheless, the National Socialists were the first to really cause a wave of change here, moving their victory column over the French in 1871, *die Siegessaule*, down the street in order to make room for the fantastic Reich's Capital Germania plans.[2] The Battle of Berlin took care of the rest, for then. Now Berliners are undertaking a construction sight of such proportion here, that one has to wonder what it is about this place that is so symbolic to them. They don't give up easily.

There were many different ideas as to what should be done with this traditional area, but not surprisingly the judges selected a model resembling Berlin's historic appearance—at least for the Reichstag. The rest will be a high-tech state-of-the-art capital campus, complete with a national press center, parliamentary offices, and the Bundesrat.

Since the outset of the Spreebogen competition, Berlin had been heavily promoting the event and simultaneously pressuring Bonn to start packing. In the course of the week, the Berlin Senate repeatedly made public statements to the effect that Berlin is now ready for the move to begin, the buildings are ready, the Reichstag decision is made so let's make a deal and set concrete dates.

But at the same time, some German representatives in Bonn were dragging their feet and digging in their heels about moving back to Berlin. While Berliners had been pitching their sales pitch, opposition representatives in Bonn were saying that there was not enough money to move at that time and that they should delay until the country was once again financially stable.

However, what the opposition failed to see in the bigger picture was that the capital move was much more than just a question of money for Germany's leaders, it is a question of Germany's traditional center, from which Germany's future will be determined. No price was too high for the chance to move back home again, back to the country's historical roots.

Therefore, it was no surprise when the Bundestag officially approved the finances needed for the move, over DM 20 billion, and re-affirmed their commitment to be in Berlin between 1998 and 2000. The financing is for the construction and moving of 18 German federal ministries that will go to Berlin between 1998 and 2000.[3] Also, weeks later, on March 10, 1993, the federal Solidarity agreement for the new German states was approved. The total package represents an annual West-East transfer of more than DM 100 billion (about $60 billion).[4]

In response, Mayor Diepgen and the other German governors praised the billion dollar pact for German solidarity and for improving the discrepant living standards in East and West.

Also in his announcement, Mayor Diepgen congratulated the Federal and State Committee for Capital Planning on their recent decisions, including the location of all the Federal Ministries moving to Berlin. The impact and influence of both of these announcements is hard to imagine. In addition, the committee outlined the conditions for the architectural competition for the ministries on the Spreeinsel. The committee also announced an architectural contest for Marx Engels Platz, where a conference center, an international library, and the foreign ministry will be located.

During the intensive financial debates in Bonn about the costs of moving the capital the anti-Berlin coalition made their campaign official. Nevertheless, there is more building occurring in Bonn at this moment than in any other city in Germany. In response to this obvious contradiction, the Berlin CDU has called for a stop to the federal government's building projects, including a new national parliament, altogether costing some DM 2 billion.[5]

Ironically, efforts by some German Congressman to delay the move to Berlin, led especially by representatives from Rhineland-Palatinate, had the opposite effect. The federal commission's report on the location of federal ministries gave Berlin a strong impulse.

While record levels of government construction are occurring in Bonn, there is, paradoxically, on the cozy Rhine a contagious fever of interest in moving to Berlin. It is politically correct to be in favor of an accelerated move back to Berlin. Social Democrat party group chairman Bjoern Engholm announced shortly after this that the SPD's federal party group headquarters construction project in Berlin's Kreuzberg District would begin in May 1994. It should be completed in the summer of 1995, according to Engholm. The SPD wants to be the first German party group to create a Berlin-Bonn axis. This announcement was indicative of Germany's political parties aligning themselves for the 1994 campaign. Politicians were gearing up for the 1994 election year, and although it wasn't official, one could clearly see the trend that it was politically "in" to be for Berlin. It was no accident that all parties had jumped on the bandwagon. They all recognized that the East German states would be a decisive factor come election time.

One of Berlin's biggest supporters, Chancellor Kohl, announced on March 29, 1993, that he would be moving to Berlin beginning in 1995— i.e., after the Allies had completed their withdrawals. This is very significant. Previously Chancellor Kohl had been of the opinion that the government should move to Berlin only when all institutions could be located there. But he just couldn't wait to get back to the center himself, to oversee his grand project from the centerpiece of his plans.

Cabinet members of the German government are following Kohl's lead and have decided to move their offices sooner than the 1998-2000 time-frame outlined in the agreement. Riding the European wave back to the center, German Federal President Richard von Weizaecker announced in the winter of 1993 that he would be moving to Berlin before the end of the year.

Also, on June 9, 1993, Defense Minister Volker Ruehe announced that he wanted to open an office in Berlin as soon as possible. He has been quoted as saying that it would not just be a symbolic house, rather that he would work there. He planned to move into Bendlerblock am Landwehrkanal in Tiergarten in August 1993.

Bendlerblock am Landwehrkanal is a very historic building. It is where Adolf Hitler informed his generals of his political plans following his takeover of power. Also, Hitler's attempted assassin, Oberst Claus Graf Schenk von Stauffenberg, took the bomb intended to kill Hitler in his briefcase to Wofsschanze, detonated the timer on July 20, 1944, and returned to Berlin with a certain belief, that Hitler was dead. Later in the evening, he and three of his accomplices were taken into custody and executed shortly after midnight by a firing squad at the entrance of the building.

Ruhe plans to remind his future guests of this national memorial sight at the entrance upon which all officials will be received. On the 50th anniversary of the attempted assassination, the house was renamed the Stauffenberg-Block. On that day, Stauffenberg's attempted coup was honored by Chancellor Kohl in a national ceremony.[6] In addition, the more money Germans continue to sink into the new Eastern German states, the more important this area becomes. Already the move of the German capital from Bonn to Berlin is pulling interest eastward.

Although people in the German states of Bavaria and North Rhine-Westphalia would rather focus on their own regions and are not very interested in what goes on in Berlin, they have to be. It's their tax money, and according to their politicians, it's their future.[7] Billions and billions of deutsche marks are flowing from West to East. Yearly, over DM 180 billion are flowing from West to East and will for the next five years.[8] One should remember to that the six new German states' combined population is no more than the state of North Rhine-Westphalia. Traveling today in the older German states, one continually hears of the dramatic outlays of support they are giving to the Eastern states, of the high taxes they are paying, with a bit of reluctance and bitterness. Therefore, one must ask, what will West Germans want in return?

Meanwhile, while Germany's elected officials are bickering about money for their respective representational districts and states in Bonn, Berlin's horizon has been taking shape. The two physical worlds are becoming one. In a recent party group meeting the Senate distributed an inner city map to all the representatives outlining the area and buildings where the government will move to. The concentration of the government on the Spree River and around the Reichstag means that the whole area will be one big construction site. The center of the city will be the biggest construction site on the continent. 300 billion Deutsch marks is the benchmark cost for new construction alone. Already 250,000 people are working on the reconstruction of this profoundly wounded city.[9]

One doesn't need to stretch the imagination very far to consider what the building of a new German capital entails. Embassies need to be relocated and built, with the French, Americans, and British reclaiming their traditional properties on both sides of the Brandenburg Gate, in addition to the Adlon Hotel and the Berlin-Brandenburg Academy of Arts.[10] Berlin, already completely strapped for housing, has to build approximately 8,000 apartments to house the government bureaucrats by 1998.[11] All this is not even taking into consideration logistical difficulties like traffic and security. I wonder to myself sometimes if the city is prepared; if the people and government can improve the infrastructure and most of all psychologically deal with all the sacrifices necessary in order to realize their commitment.

Whereas the political preoccupation formerly was with the Wall, the forced division, and the relation with the Allies, now like a tidal wave the preoccupation is with the future, the plans for the country's new capital.

On top of the announcement for the Spreebogen, the Berlin Senate officially called for the construction of a new airport in the south of Berlin, stating that the capacity of the existing airports will not meet the future requirements.

Also in the spring of 1993, the architectural award for Alexanderplatz was decided upon. Alexanderplatz will be modernized to include high-rises. Berlin's Senator for Urban Development and Environmental Protection, Volker Hassemer, stated that in light of the current developments, Alexanderplatz will become Berlin's most important city center, with investors committing upwards of DM 7 billion.[12] For the sake of comparison, that is almost twice as much money as has been allocated for Potsdamer Platz, where high-rise construction was forbidden. Thus, Alexanderplatz will become Berlin's first high-rise center.

In another spur of spectacular developments, forecasting Berlin's horizon to be, the design for Lehrter train station was agreed upon. After months of intense debate between the state and federal government, as well as the German train department, it was agreed that Lehrter station will be Berlin's first central train station. Located directly across from the

Western side of the Spree, this station will be outfitted to handle the high speed German train.

The Berlin paradox continues. Today Lehrter train station is still a border station. There is very little life, with no shops, restaurants, or other tell-tale signs of civilization. It is the last station on the West side of Berlin. Like many other trains stations on the Wall, Lehrter station is in the middle of a wasteland. Exiting the station, there are empty fields littered with waste and construction equipment. The only way I know that this formerly was a place of significance is by the historic pictures found at the entrance.

But now it will be the center of Berlin's expansive railway system which radiates both East and West. In the future, Europeans will exit trains in the German capital center in what today is a barren expanse. Berlin's Lehrter train station will be the most important train station in Germany.[13]   Next to the Friedrichstadtpalast and Potsdamer Platz, Lehrter will be the second biggest construction project in Berlin. Building is scheduled to begin in 1995 and experts estimated that before 2002, up to 400 daily trains will be coming and going from Germany's new central train station.[14]

From the committee planning rooms, with long drawn-out discussions about the plans, I lose myself in fantasy, imagining it to be real. But where is it all headed? Riding the train through Lehrter train station, looking out the window toward the Spreebogen and Potsdamer Platz, as if I'm seeing double, the present and future in one picture before my eyes, in the middle just construction equipment.

And it is already underway. Construction cranes are springing up all around Berlin and they are especially noticeable in the middle of the city. I am struck by how many people complain about the lack of investment and the lengthy time frame it takes to get something done. Phillip Johnson, the architect for Mark Palmer's $800 million American Business Center at Checkpoint Charlie, commented: "I am excited to see how one can even get through the city with so much construction going on."

Today the entire Friedrichstrasse is one big construction site. I recall a recent visit to its train station. Squinting my eyes, I made my way through the busy station, on my way toward Humboldt University. The air was sandy, like a windstorm on the beach, and uncomfortable. I wiped my eyes; strange and sudden noises blared through the halls, swelling and receding like ocean waves.

Exhibits in the show windows alarm me, more so than the sledgehammers and ringing noises of the train station. They are unexpected and strikingly out of place. What used to be nothing has emerged into a modern flea market—from the main station running all the way to

Spreebogen Architectural Award, 1993, courtesy of Axel Schultes

Alexanderplatz, 1980s, courtesy of the German Information Center

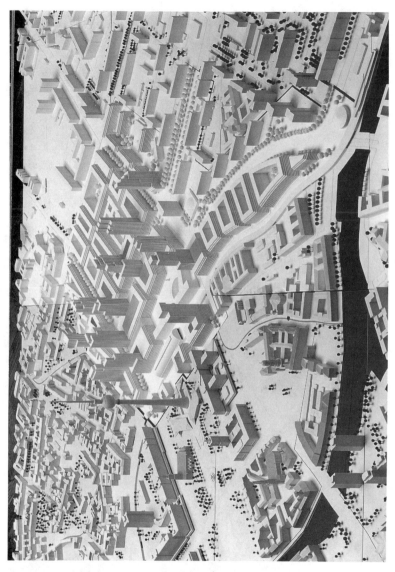

Alexanderplatz in 2000, courtesy of Uwe Rau

Lehrter Train Station, 1992, courtesy of the German Information Center

Berlin's Central Train Station in 2000

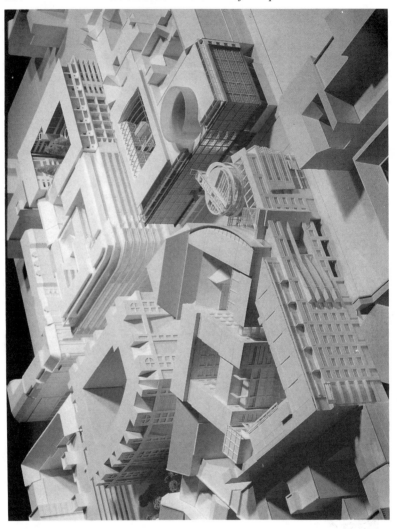

American Business Center at Checkpoint Charlie in 2000, courtesy of the
American Business Center GmbH and Co.

Humboldt University—with exclusive art shops, an Apple computer store, restaurants and bars—all Western style. It is so out of place here—accentuating the strong contradictions next to the run down and Eastern nature of the place and people.

The impact of the plans is hard to fathom. The landscape of Berlin and Europe are changing simultaneously. One is a function of the other. The center of Berlin will blossom out of the ashes of the Cold War rubble. While Europe is still awakening to the new possibilities and challenges of the New Europe, Germans are hard at work investing in Central Europe. Using their new states as a springboard, they are planning their future from Berlin across the continent. The building projects are just a metaphor for what is coming, in which the Reichstag, the whole Spreebogen, Lehrter train station, and Potsdamer Platz will be torn up.[15]

In line with the record amounts of construction, the Berlin government is returning to its traditional places of residence too. My first hint of the impact of these efforts began on February 19, 1993. My office was making a staff visit to the former Prussian parliament, where the Berlin parliament will supposedly move to in April 1993. As my assistant friend and I pulled out of the parking lot in front of Rathaus Schoeneberg, we both commented on the surreal announcement of the move. "I really don't want to move—it will be a fifteen minute longer drive for me to work," he said in all seriousness. After getting lost—we finally pulled into the muddy parking lot—surrounded by the construction crews' cars, motor homes, and heavy machinery.

After putting on our hard hats, we walked through the muddy field toward the scaffolding. We were all impressed with how much work still needed to done. No rooms were even close to being finished, although the entire parliament was supposed to move there in six weeks time. Heavy construction was still taking place all over, from the assembly room to the party conference rooms. But as is often the case, what one sees is not the reality. The whole region is in a state of transition and flux. Days later another plan was realized.

March 24, 1993, will go down in history as the close of another Cold War chapter for Europe and Berlin alike. As Berlin's parliamentary president passed the key to Berlin's Schoeneberg District mayor, I felt my pulse throbbing in my neck. Everyone seemed called to the moment, to the significance and meaning of what was taking place, what they had only dreamed of. This feeling was certainly different for West Berliners than for their newly found Eastern countrymen.

Exiting the train station on my way to work on that windy spring day, I was flooded with nostalgic feelings for Rathaus Schoeneberg. I saw the tower, the tower destroyed, I saw the rebuilt tower with the waving Berlin flag on top. Slowly my mind wandered and I saw the crane raising the American Liberty Bell up to the tower on October 24, 1950. Next I saw the motorcade parade of John F. Kennedy and Willy Brandt driving up to the packed square, then I saw a crowd of 500,000 people fill the square in protest for the division of the city on the August 8, 1961, and lastly the hissing and booing crowd as Chancellor Kohl and other German politicians sang the German national anthem on the steps of Rathaus Schoeneberg on the day after the Wall fell, November 10, 1989.

Like changing slides at a family gathering, suddenly a new collage of events appeared before my eyes, in this frame I saw many trucks moving the mayor's file cabinets out, in the next picture the Berlin Senate's. Everything was in flux. And in two weeks the moving trucks would be moving the entire parliament out.

Later in the day I had another vision as I became acutely aware of my office surroundings. Downstairs was the exhibition in tribute to the late Willy Brandt; across the long hallway in the Brandenburg Hall, the representatives were debating. The halls were active and alive with moving people during this, the last legislative session in Rathaus Schoeneberg. Nowhere was the dream, the sacrifice, the faith in the re-unity of their city and country greater. The provincial status of Berlin was, 44 years later, finally over.

Leaving this one-time beacon of democracy and domicile of freedom was hard for some. Many representatives and workers didn't even appear to be fully present, reflecting in relief, disbelief, and triumph for the heroic hours Berlin's democracy held strong in the middle of raging storms and communist threats. It was the climax of a dream that was over 40 years old.

The building is a metaphor for the progressive build-up of democracy and the foundation of freedom, faith and conviction. Understandably, some West Berliners do not want to leave their security. Like the young child does not want to leave his or her parents, many Berliners don't want to move out of their provincial city hall.

The goal is achieved, the city is united, but this once unremarkable city hall has become beloved and honorable. Now that the Cold War is over, some Berliners still want the Americans to stay. The Wall is down, but many Berliners still don't care to go to East Berlin. They seem afraid to take the step they have so eagerly worked for. Isn't this analogous to the attitudes in Europe too? Many prefer to just sit back and watch the developments from afar, on television. It is like setting a goal and dreaming of reaching that goal, but when it is realized, it is no longer desirable. Although the war was brutal, it provided clarity. It is over, for all the good and the bad it brought. Europe is awakening, but slower than some would like. The magnitude of the transition in Berlin, the East-West confrontations, the moves: although they are crass, hard, they promise to bring something new.

Notes

1   Most of the prize went to Berlin architects Axel Schultes and Charlotte Franke.
     There were over 835 proposals from 54 countries competing for the infamous
     Spreebogen design. source: Wolfgang Pehnt, "Die Seele des Spreebogens",
     Frankfurter Allegemeine Zeitung, March 16, 1993
2   Stephan Speicher, "Siegessaule fuer Germania", Frankfurter Allegemeine
     Zeitung, January 12, 1993
3   "Major Parties Agree on Framework for Move to Berlin", The Week in
     Germany, January 21, 1991
4   The Solidarity agreement provides for a transfer of DM 100 Billion, with an
     annual financial transfer of DM 56 billion (about $34.5 billion) for the five
     eastern states, as well as additional billions in credits and grants for housing
     construction, modernization of the infrastructure, environmental cleanup and
     business promotion. To cover the costs, since 1995, Germans pay a 7.5%
     "solidarity surcharge" on their income tax to help pay for the investment in
     the new German states. source: "'Solidarity Pact' approved by Bundestag
     and Bundesrat: DM 100 Billion West-East transfer Starting 1995", The Week
     in Germany, June 4, 1993
5   Frankfurter Allegemeine Zeitung, "Berliner Politiker fuer Baustopp im Bonner
     Regierungsviertel", June 19, 1993
6   Also, in conjunction with the ceremony in the German capital, an exhibition
     entitled "Against Hitler: German Resistance to National Socialism 1933-1945"
     opened in the capital of the United States, Washington, D.C.
7   In only seven years from 1991-1998, Berlin will increase its debt from DM
     21 billion to over DM 60 billion, or DM 18,000 per capita. source: "Von New
     York Lernen", Der Spiegel, Feb. 20, 1995, pg. 48
8   The Economist, "Germany's mezzogiorno", May 21, 1994, pg. 10
9   "Von New York Lernen", Der Spiegel, Feb. 20, 1995, pg. 43,46
10   Lothar Heinke, "Neue US Botschaft mit alter Adresse: Pariser Platz Nummer
     2, Anfang Januar wird auf dem Gelaende der amerikansiche Vertretung eine
     Tafel enthueillt, die auf die Vergangenheit und Zukunft des Areals verweist",
     Der Tagesspiegel, December 30, 1992
11   "Von New York Lernen", Der Spiegel, Feb. 20, 1995, pg. 48
12   Hertie, Gruener and Jahr, and Deutsch Inter Hotel are the main investors on
     the 30 acre square.
13   German Bundesbahn Chairman, Heinz Durr, also reported that Lehrter train
     station will entail an investment volume of over DM 700 million. source:
     Otto-Joerg Weis, "In Berlin wird der grosste ICE-Bahnhof gebaut", March 3,
     1993
14   Ibid.

15 On March 11, 1993, the government and the President of the German train company, announced that four tunnels will be constructed under 'the Spreebogen. A 3,5 km tunnel will be for high speed trains and regional trains traveling in a North-South direction, the second will be a 4, 5 km extension of the underground metro from Alexanderplatz to Lehrter train station, the third will be a new 2,0 km underground train line from Gleisdreick to Lehrter train station, and finally a 2,7 km street tunnel will be built under Tiergarten. The street tunnel is part of a ring traffic model with the following goals in mind: Free the inner city of traffic and establish a 4:1 ratio of public versus private transportation in the inner city, and avoid through-traffic in the government and parliament quarter. Construction contracts will be awarded between the summer of 1994 and early 1995, with the tunnel laying beginning for all four projects in the summer of 1995.   Officials estimate the cost of all four projects to be around DM 4.2 billion, from which DM 2.2 billion will finance the high speed and regional train tunnel costs. Construction is planned to begin in early 1995 and be completed in 2000.

Chapter 17

Brandenburg: The Prussian Center That Holds

The capital move from Bonn to Berlin and the move out of Rathaus Schoeneberg are indicative of Germany's shift back to a regional focus. There are many developments that have taken place since reunification, beginning with the decision to move the capital, that illustrate this. Another good example was when Mayor Diepgen formally announced Berlin and Brandenburg state's respective approvals of their plan to reunify. Owing to greater Brandenburg's importance in German history, this initiative showed Germany's leaders' pragmatic focus on the future with occasional, selective references to the regions' powerful tradition.

The announcement took me by surprise. Berlin and Brandenburg are both undergoing dramatic transitions. The last thing they need to have on their respective state parliamentary agendas is a future united state and all of the resources necessary to reach that. Where are their priorities? It seemed that the political priorities of Germany's leaders were well ahead of those shared by the society. Germans on both sides of the former divide are still coming to terms with national reunification. Is this regional tradition in the power center of the former Prussian state, in the Mark Brandenburg, Hohenzollern dynastic family tradition, something stronger, and more binding?

Traditions die hard, and the state of Brandenburg has strong historic roots. Under various auspices Berlin has for over 700 years been regarded as part of Brandenburg. Brandenburg was the center from which the Prussian state burgeoned. Only over the course of the last 45 years have these areas been separated. One large incentive for a unified state is that it would make a reunified Berlin and Brandenburg state the fifth largest state in Germany with approximately 6 to 8 million citizens. The champion of

German reunification, Helmut Kohl, also expressed his official support for the reunification of Berlin and Brandenburg on March 19, 1993.[1]

Chancellor Kohl and Berlin's Mayor Diepgen know the powerful historic traditions of Brandenburg and were likely reaching out to the Hohenzollern Prussian tradition as not only a regional unifying element in the new German states between West and East, but as a national reunifier too. By moving the capital back to its century-long Prussian roots, Germany's leaders were hoping to overcome the decades of forced national division that was inhibiting their successful reunification. Perhaps proponents of the states unification were also motivated by a hidden desire to show everyone that they were now able to do what for so long was hindered.[2]

The Prussian heritage (with Berlin its capital, Brandenburg its hub) is historically the most efficient and productive in all disciplines, from liberal arts to manufacturing.[3] Germany was founded on Prussian leadership. Imperial Germany spread its wings around Prussia and fought its wars. Around Prussia, Hitler dominated the continent, as he spread German influence from Paris to the edges of Moscow. Berlin was always the capital of Prussia, and now the capital of the reunified Germany is Berlin.

Prussia is a dynamic center that has stood the test of time, war, and division for centuries, and has been dormant since the Cold War. Berlin, after the founding of Humboldt University, was the center of philosophical reform in Germany after the French Revolution and the establishment of the English free trade system. After the defeat of Napoleon, Germans developed for the first time a national patriotism parallel to that of Prussia. This proved to be one of the critical forces that led to the founding of the German Reich.

The founding of the Reich in 1871 centered around Prussia. Even in the Reich, Prussia dominated economically, militarily, and culturally. The King of Prussia was the German emperor, Prussia provided the Reich Chancellor, and Prussia dominated the Bundesrat. Prussia also had the greatest number of members in the Reichstag and its military tradition became the model and core army in the Reich.[4] Domestic Prussian problems always affected the Reich (e.g., the cultural fight after 1871, *Sozialistengesetz, Ostmarkenpolitik*)—to such a degree that one could say that the history of Prussia is the history of Germany.

Prussia's influence subsided with the founding of the Reich, despite the firm hold that Bismarck tried to solidify. Upon German unification, the state grew too large and romantic ideas and imaginations of national opponents to Bismarck grew exponentially.[5] Prussia, in the Reich, became too large for itself.

With this historical background in mind, we can better judge the powerful tradition on which Germany's leaders are betting. There were many developments in post-reunified Germany that point to a resurgent Prussian regional tradition. A majority of Berlin and Brandenburg politicians are lobbying for the states to reunite. The prospect of a united Berlin-Brandenburg state offers the opportunity for making each state's vote stronger. It is also impractical and inefficient to have two fully autonomous state capitals, Potsdam and Berlin, only 12 miles apart. In addition to the practical reasons for fusing the two states, such a fusion serves as a model for the regional development taking place for Germany in a united Europe. Mayor Diepgen said: *"Die Entscheidung fuer ein gemeinsames Land ist ein vorbild fuer die europaische Wettbewerbsfahigkeit aller Region Deutschlands."* (The decision for a united state serves as a model for the European competitiveness for all of Germany's regions).[6]

Berlin and Brandenburg will most likely reunite before 2000. In 1999 there will be a united vote for state and local representatives. Levels of cooperation are increasing among state agencies in everything from environmental projects and economic development to cultural activities. Also, talk is rumbling in the parliament of the need to build a new state-of-the-art Berlin-Brandenburg international airport.

On June 6, 1993, representatives of Berlin and Brandenburg took their negotiations about the future site of the reunified state parliament public. Brandenburg's Governor, Manfred Stolpe, has protested heavily against opposition to Potsdam being the future capital. However, other leaders in the Brandenburg government expressed reservations about how Potsdam could be the capital of a united region.[7] To house the parliament requires the construction of a new parliament, which experts estimated would cost between DM 150 and 200 million. Opponents asked if it is sensible to make such an investment after Berlin has just completed its new parliament, which could accommodate the united parliament.

Also at issue is the name of the unified German state and what the flag will look like—in other words whether the red eagle of Brandenburg or the Berlin bear will prevail. While neither side is prepared to compromise, some are calling for the middle ground alternative; the black eagle, or even the flag of the former free state of Prussia.

In another paradoxical development, on May 24, 1993, an Emnid poll as to whether the German capital's move from Bonn should be postponed for 10 years, reported that over 75% of Germans said it should be postponed and only 25% are for a quick move. Also, a survey in *Der Spiegel* found a similar result, with 72% of Germans polled being in favor of a 10-year delay of the capital move. Also, only 51% of Germans think of Berlin as the capital of Germany.[8]

Why are the political parties pushing for an accelerated move? What forces of nature are compelling Germany's unwavering leader, Chancellor Kohl, to stand firm amid nervous neighbors and reunification blues, and unerringly push the country back to the former Prussian and German Reich capital? Why are Germany's leaders in consensus that Berlin, the region of Brandenburg, should be Germany's national focal point? What has led them to change their minds from the passionate debate in 1990 about moving back to Berlin, the historic and bitterly fought 321-316 victory?

It is not only because Berlin is a locomotive for the economic rebuilding of the new German states. And it is not only because the new German states offer room for much economic prosperity for the new, unexplored markets in Central and Eastern Europe.

There is perhaps a grander strategy. The return to the center of the Prussian tradition also has deeper strategic roots. Located in the heart of Central Europe, a Prussian regional resurgence from its Berlin capital has the opportunity to re-assert itself in what is otherwise a power vacuum, a kin to the defeat of Napoleon when Prussia stepped onto the European power stage with Russia, Austria, Britain, and France. Kohl knows that national interest is a dead-end for a torn Germany and that Germany's future lies in regional European development.

A powerful Brandenburg Prussian region would contribute to the stability of all of Central and Eastern Europe, and re-establishes Germany's traditional relations with Russia too. Chancellor Kohl arguably recognized this from the beginning, when the Wall first fell. Is that why it took him so long to consent possible German claims to the "lost territories" during the difficult reunification negotiations with Poland and to signing a "Reaffirmation of Existing Borders" treaty?[9]

Upon German reunification, some of the country's leaders, quite correctly, saw that Germany was again the center of Europe. Some interpreted this to mean that the success of Europe depended on Germany's ability to bridge Western and Eastern Europe together. Now, German politicians are following the nose that knows. The governing are leading the governed back to their roots.

Chancellor Kohl has long recognized that the success of German reunification rides on the successful integration of the new German states. How can only 23% of the country's population change the fate of the solidly grounded, prosperous West Germany?

The capital move from Bonn to Berlin, and Chancellor Kohl's unequivocal commitment to the new German states is the beginning of a new era. Germany is focusing on its Central European roots, and Europe is forced to follow, as we will see in coming chapters.

Europe is no longer divided. Germany is reunified, autonomous and free. It is no longer frozen in time, resting on the fate of others. Germany is now taking command of its own destiny: the security of its borders and the security of its neighbors. Brandenburg is the region from which Germany will build its resurgence in Central Europe. It is a region that holds in the middle of Europe and will into the year 2000—and beyond. Thus, it is clear that the Western-oriented Germany of the post-World War II from the Adenauer legacy to the present—will clearly be challenged by the traditional Central and Eastern European influences.

But while politicians in Berlin and Brandenburg are promoting the advantages of a reunited state, people in some other German states are not as enthusiastic. During a Berlin parliamentary delegation visit to Dresden to discuss the integration of East Germany's art and culture into the reunified Germany, in which I also participated, a Saxon whom I met shook his head when I told him of all the activity that is going on between Berlin and Brandenburg to promote a unified state. His eyes took on the look of a rival as he reflected on the re-emergence of the former Prussian state despite its reduced size. In response, he took me on a tour of Dresden, Saxony's capital city, and proudly showed me all the things they are rebuilding too. Everyone is focusing on their regional traditions since reunification because that is the only solid tradition they have.

On the heels of the chancellor's support for Berlin and Brandenburg reuniting, a 200-point action program for a united Berlin and Brandenburg was agreed upon by the two respective governments. Although a public referendum scheduled for 1999 will ultimately decide whether the two autonomous states will be reunited, they are cooperating in many areas to promote contacts and reduce unnecessary double costs.

Mayor Diepgen correctly reminded his supporters that Berlin was the locomotive of the idea from the beginning and that a majority of the initiatives are from the Berlin Senate. A few of Berlin's proposals include a unified court system and a unified state development agency. Brandenburg proposes creating a unified land use agency, a unified traffic agency, and a unified museum for early history.

As the two states negotiate, Berlin is pushing hard to accelerate the fusion—eager to increase its territorial range and federal influence with a bigger voting block. With their big banks, know-how, and demand that has been pent-up for over 40 years, Berliners are anxious to get their hands on Brandenburg property rights and development plans.

In the sometimes difficult negotiations, Berlin officials have warned the Brandenburg government against stalling the negotiations. Many in Brandenburg fear being overtaken by the bigger, more experienced, Western-controlled Berlin. After having watched what has happened to their former East German capital, they fear being overwhelmed by big money and lofty promises from West Berliners. Berliners are quick to retort with their own reproaches, criticizing Brandenburg for living in the dark ages, and not properly addressing their receding economy, lack of investment, and loss of jobs, where bureaucracy and red tape linger on.

It is also a question of the current political majorities in their respective states. Brandenburg's Governor, Manfred Stolpe, is a SPD left-wing democrat, while Berlin's mayor and acting governor is a CDU conservative. The respective state cabinets are encountering difficulties working together and they both are working for better positions to strengthen their respective party blocks.

Brandenburg is often accused of being one of the most bureaucratic and historically damaged states in the former GDR. Rumor has it that following the collapse of the Wall and the sudden evaporation of the government, many Honecker regime bureaucrats fled to the neighboring Brandenburg. Stolpe himself has been repeatedly called on resign by many respected politicians, private citizens, and church officials for his association with the Stasi. To some degree it has been proven that he worked as an unofficial worker for the Stasi during his time as chief lawyer of the Protestant church. The church was the only large public institution not directly controlled by the government of the former East Germany.[10] Nevertheless, proof is very hard to come by and many accusations are being countered by others, claiming to be witnesses. Unlike East Germany's first and last non-communist Prime Minister, Lothar de Maiziere, who immediately resigned from his special ministerial role in Bonn when public pressure mounted against his earlier functions in East Germany, Stolpe has fought like a fox. Despite widespread calls for his resignation, he has skillfully held onto power.

As a result, some Berliners are apprehensive about cooperating with the current state government in Brandenburg. They would prefer to wait until the next election to try to unseat this dinosaur of East German politics. Also, the Brandenburg CDU is still having a hard time building a constituency. The Berlin CDU doesn't want to reunite with Brandenburg until they can be assured their party has developed popular support. Nevertheless, Germany is focusing its efforts and energies on rebuilding the new German states, with Berlin being the center of the action. Germany is moving east.

It seems as if everyone feels the shift of interest and momentum towards Germany. Germany is regarded as the motor of the unified Europe. Whether the solidarity agreement or the capital move, Berlin and the new German states are receiving the lion's share of attention and priority in Germany. And the Berlin-Brandenburg reunification negotiations are raising people's eyebrows too.

President Clinton also notices the shift in power. Without President George Bush and President Gorbachev, there never would have been a reunited Germany as we know it today. There also wouldn't be an American president giving Germany the green light for "the full range of Germany's capacities to lead," as Clinton said. Perhaps Clinton recognizes the importance of stabilizing the region, of letting Germany re-establish itself and its strength in the center of Europe. He possibly also realizes that it is a center that, depending on the era, either holds Europe together or breaks it apart.

Notes

1   Der Tagesspiegel, "Kohl unterstutzt Fusion von Berlin und Brandenburg", March 29, 1993

2   In 1947, the Allied Control Council abolished what used be the state of Prussia and all its agencies.

3   Originally Prussia was the name of a small Baltic people who later became Christianized by the Order of the Teutonic Knights. Ironically, the conquerors later adopted the Baltic people's name. The two northern-eastern provinces of the German Reich were known as West and East Prussia into the twentieth-century. After 1701, the Hohenzollern family dynasty named their state Prussia, which entailed not only West and East Prussians, but also Pommerians, Brandenburgers, Silesia, as well as Rhineland and Westphalia. Like many family dynasties, the Hohenzollerns were looking to expand their wealth and territory. The Hohenzollern family, originally from the south of Germany, received the Magravate of Brandenburg from the German Emperor in 1415 and came to settle in Berlin and Potsdam with much success. Relative to the surrounding states, the Magravate of Brandenburg was more modern, colonization, however brutal, had progressed quicker as in Pommerania and Silesia. Through power politics and centuries of dynastic marriages, the Hohenzollerns were also able to attain the rights to East and West Prussia, and thus the Hohenzollern House was now a composite of Brandenburg and Prussia, governed from where the Hohenzollerns first resided, in Berlin and Potsdam. Further down the river of history, Prussia was a tolerant, powerful empire that was able to govern various elements of tribes and history into one loosely organized state. After the Treaty of Westphalia, Prussia joined France, Britain, Russia, and Austria as the most powerful states in Europe. In the 19th Century, Prussia reached its pinnacle of power after the industrialization and increased in strength, it eventually challenged Austria for control of the German principalities and won, and afterward challenged France to forge the first successful unified Germany in 1871. For more information, see Sebastian Haffner's *The Rise and Fall of Prussia* Weidenfeld and Nicolson Press, 1980.

4   *The Rise and Fall of Prussia* Sebastian Haffner, Weidenfeld and Nicolson, 1980.

5   Chancellor Otto von Bismarck was the champion of the old order based on the idea of the monarchical state, and he was not attracted either by the "larger Germany" ideals of the ardent nationalists or by the worldly aspirations of the romantic imperialists. Bismarck was anything but a romanticist, and he had no use for these words and fantastic dreams of political romanticism. After Bismarck successfully balanced Germany's geo-political interest in the center of Europe, until his resignation in the early days of the pugnacious

Kaiser Wilhelm II, the Reich pursued the dangerous path of nationalism and territorial expansion. With the onset of Kaiser Wilhelm II's romantic vision of a German 'world policy' and a German 'place in the sun,' the 19th century Prussian tradition of tolerance and regional focus was over. Nevertheless, many point out that Bismarck was to blame for the forthcoming chaos that dominated his beloved Prussia and the German Reich because he did not develop or nurture an educated political class or political base, rather he just focused on being their dominant leader.

6   Der Tagesspiegel, "Der Umzug regte eine Debatte ueber Politikverdrossenheit an", April 30, 1993

7   Brandenburg's SPD Party Group Chairman, Wolfgang Birthler, June 15, 1993.

8   Michael Mueller, "Berlin-jeder zweite denkt dabei an Hauptstadt und Regierungssitz", Berliner Morgenpost, February 25, 1993

9   Opposition parties criticized Kohl's decision for not inviting the Polish leader to Germany's commemoration of the end of the WWII on May 8, 1995 in Berlin. source: The New York Times, March 25, 1995, pg. 4

10   The Economist, "Germany's mezzogiorno", May 21, 1994

Chapter 18

The Reawakening

Not only are the spectacular construction awards for Berlin 2000 and the plan to reunite Berlin and Brandenburg an affirmation of the support for the region but the reunification of the city itself stirs up memories of the Prussian heritage that are still strong. One example is the Berlin parliament's move back to the center of the city. Deep symbolic forces are at work that remind one of the re-emergence of the former united region and its power over all of Europe.

Since the Berlin parliament moved back to the bustling, torn-up streets of Berlin's city center, construction workers have been busy with the preparations for the grand opening in the former Prussian parliament. The area surrounding the powerful building was the center of transition and incongruity. It was paradoxically a beautiful building, but it was surrounded by dust and barren fields. It is another landmark of Europe's rebirth and renewal. The building itself is a temple of German history; for decades it was forgotten in the shadow of the Wall. Now, it is rising up as reunified Berlin's parliament.

As I was descending the freshly laid red carpet on the grand staircase after leaving my new office on the fifth floor, workers were putting on the final touches for the next day's big opening. Walking through the filled parking lot, where round-the-clock construction crews live in their cars and campers, I thought back to how much they had accomplished in the last two weeks, how this dirt road had been paved, how the men hammering the little stones on the sidewalk had completed their job in a single day.

Inside, for days the crews have been working until almost midnight. The foreign cleaning ladies had polished every corner, washed every window, and cleaned every floor. Tonight they had off, tomorrow would be the day when the guests would be filing in, when the cameras would be showing Germans and Europeans that Berlin's parliament had moved home. They would show the glimmer and glare that was a toast to the hours of construction and planning that had gone on here.

Walking around this evening as it is still quiet, I am overcome with feelings of a reawakening. Maybe by looking back, to what this place used to be, we can discover an indication of what is perhaps on the horizon for the region.

Downstairs, in the parliamentary hall, Prussian Governor Goering gave an eerie speech on May 18, 1933. From somewhere, I can still hear the echo of that time. It is quiet, and I am approaching the parliamentary hall. Goering said on his inaugural speech as Prussian Governor:

> . . . For the first time the government has the opportunity to present to parliament its plans for a new beginning of Prussia. . . The Chancellor will lead in close association with Prussia, whereby the just and important interests of Prussia as the largest German state shall always be preserved. . .(Applause)! . . . The Chancellor assigned me, in the interest of Prussia, to protect what is Prussian. Under no circumstances will I tolerate that Prussian territory be divided from Prussia . . . (loud applause). . . . The Chancellor wants Prussia, Prussian politics and Prussian administration to be the basis of the Fatherland today and forever. He wants the daily, practical experience of Prussia to be the basis of its law. Thus, as in centuries past, Prussia has the important mission of building the foundation of the German Fatherland. . . .[1]

With these words ringing through my ears, I stumble a little down the staircase. As I pushed open the heavy front doors of the parliament, a weight fell from my shoulders.

On the eve of the opening parliamentary session, the crescent moon illuminates the edges and corners of the powerful new building. I look back at the Berlin flag waving overhead. Put up yesterday, the raising of the flag symbolizes preparedness for the party to be held the next day, April 18, 1993—opening day. I could not help but stand in awe of how much Berliners had accomplished with this building in two years. It is all coming true, just what the party group leaders had said countless times in committee meetings: the reconstruction, investment, the return to tradition. And in a year the Prussian Landtag will be receiving brothers and sisters, a hole will be dug and the building will begin for Sony Europe and Daimler-Benz.

But the building deserves more. It should perhaps house the Bundestag.[2] It is far above being just a state parliament, seems to call to each that walk through its door, it is grander, more extravagant, and deserving. Will the parliamentarians, as a result of being back in this traditional place, also have grander ideas? Or will they remain humble?

As the keynote speaker, Professor August Everding, methodically makes his way to the podium for his speech commemorating the opening, the atmosphere is bubbling with intensity. Not a seat is free; I stand at the back wall and observe the ceremony. Everding started off by joking about the fact that the Berlin parliamentary president invited a Bavarian to speak at this tremendous opening, and the intensity seemed to settle down somewhat.[3]

Then he reminded the audience of the historic nature of this gathering. He mentioned the debates in Berlin academic circles in 1965, where the question of the day was "what is history good for?"

Today I am speaking on a podium from which I was never before allowed to speak. It is a podium that was created by a surreal history, from our crazy history. This place shows what history can form, destroy, and rebuild. Across the street stands the Gropius Building, with its art and politics, a few meters further are pieces of the Wall, and across from those concrete slabs is the former *Reichslüftfahrtministerium* (Air Force Ministry).

This place is a lasting example of the history of our country. Here Goering was Prussian Governor. In the banquet hall upstairs Rosa Luxemburg founded the German communist party, in this room the Weimar Republik governed, here was the Supreme Court, here was the lower German parliament house under Grothewohl, here the city administration planned a new post-war city, and later on the biggest spy antenna in Berlin stood on top of this building. And today the parliament is moving in from all of Berlin.

Here out of the ruins of a city and country, the connection between old and new is still found, behind the renovation work we can recognize the old walls of this room. On this podium where I speak today, where art, terror, politics, lies and truth were practiced, I speak in one city — the capital of our country.

The place was silent, his robust voice, his intonation was superb. He was moving the crowd with his presence and his deep and soothing voice.

After his allusion to the history of the building opened our eyes to what had taken place here, he spoke to us about the importance of culture:

> On March 25, 1931, with 213 votes from the rightist party, the Kroll Opera was closed. Thus, under the auspices of saving money, an artistic voice was stilled. The Kroll Opera became the Reichstag of the Nazis. A music theater with its own orchestra was closed as then Representative Koch stated "die juedisch negroide Epoche der preußischen Kunst zu beenden" (to end the black Jewish epoch of Prussian Art). Another representative, Herr Koeppen, is quoted as stating that the parliament is the worst forum to handle cultural questions. After the meeting, the director of the opera was attacked by a group of Nazis while walking home.

Then came the hammer. We were all shirking our shoulders, sitting a little more humbly, no smiling faces, no small talk. We were completely quiet. He went on:

> I believe that politics that avoids art ultimately fails freedom. The artist elucidates like the politician. Both carry the torchlight. Culture is a vision, a power of the fantasy, a pioneer, an economist, a politician. We are all living with the vision of a better world, a free and peaceful world.

> Today one thinks twice before saying that politics and culture also have something to do with happiness, to create and renew, happiness to be happy. We must be careful that a culture doesn't develop in which every anti-rational, politically correct spirit fails to find opposition. One must sometimes scream in order to be heard. *Wir alle sind Verlautbarer* (We are all reporters). We must have a open and democratic cultural life—in this house and all.

As the applause rang through the room, I was moved. The congratulatory statements were made, champagne was being poured. We all seemed to leave the main hall like one leaves a church or other religious building, inspired and more in focus.

Back on Berlin's bustling streets on my way back home, I felt far removed from all of the ceremonial enthusiasm. Later my friend Ulf called me and told me about his terrible day at work. "The mood is always so solemn," he said "everybody is really nervous because their Gauck Authority evaluations are arriving at the end of the week. It's like walking on pins and needles around there," he continued, "everyone is on edge. I am going to start to look for another job, working over here [East Berlin] is much different." I went to sleep thinking about how far the politicians are from their constituents.

The next day I awoke with a splitting headache. Ulf's phone call had derailed me from the government's dream train. Berlin's parliamentary president, Dr. Hanna-Renate Laurien, commented on the new glass pyramid-shaped rooftop in her opening remarks at yesterday's ceremony, saying that it was meant to "shine the light of the day."

Yet in respect to the light that shown through the same glass pyramid in past years, why wouldn't she be a little more careful with such words? From Berlin's new seat of parliament, won't new ideas develop too? The people are changing. The seat of the government has changed. Couldn't a dark cloud be on the horizon again? What about all of the plans to reunite with Brandenburg? Will the government even be in Berlin when that day arrives?

At this time of reduced parliamentary representation, saving money and promoting efficiency, isn't it going directly against what Professor Everding eloquently stated? Or the majority vote debate which the major parties alluded to in their leader's opening remarks. Is there a trend in the Berlin parliament toward more or less democracy? Or how about the Maastricht debate in Germany: is the treaty being supported by German politicians or at the grassroots?

Many of the same representatives who seemed to speak so fondly of his speech at the reception — of the importance of opposition and different opinions, in politics and culture, were themselves proponents of cutting the number of representatives in half, for a quick reunification with Brandenburg, and increasing the powers of the Senate next to the parliament.

Stumbling through the hallway of Berlin's new parliament, *Das neue Abgeordnetenhaus* (NAH), where a handful of construction workers are fastening on a door, I made my way to a lecture at Humboldt University. Descending the grandiose staircase I was filled with reflections about history. I experienced similar feelings walking down the staircase in Rathaus Schoeneberg, but the two emotions really can't be compared. There is so much more history and tradition in the NAH. Only then did the provincial status of Rathaus Schoeneberg begin to sink in. I looked back on our stay there as something necessary before we were allowed to progress further.

Walking out of the main entrance and through the construction gates I looked back at the building, an impressive building (the building that once housed the Prussian parliament, with representatives from almost two-thirds of present-day Germany). It has so much history behind it, despite the fact that all of the furniture has not been delivered, that our fax machines are not completely wired and that the smell of paint and waves of dust engulf the room. The tradition is here. It is not a new and remodeled building, but rather it has a long history that embodies the paradoxes of Berlin.

Looking to my left, I see a bustling of activity, construction workers and trucks are moving as though programmed, bustling to and fro with everything from copy machines to windows. From the outside it looked like an ant hill, everyone was busy doing something. In front of me the Martin Gropius building stood quietly, with not a person in sight. It was strangely and sleepily present in the background of the frantic and constant activity around the NAH. To the left side, the back side of the Treuhand. In front of that, like a straight arrow, a bumpy dirt road is bordered by a long sector of the Wall still. These three apparitions, the construction workers, the Wall and the Treuhand, are like a spectrum of time, a metaphor of Germany's future, present, and past.

I began to cross the desolate field to the left of the Gropius building. I came to the middle of a field, about the size of a soccer field. To my left was the Wall, now clearly in sight with its graffiti, straight ahead I can make out buildings, to my far right is the Martin Gropius building and the Topography of Terror exhibition. A mound of dirt suddenly stopped my progress. I looked down at my dirt-covered shoes and stopped for a moment to consider where I was. I am in the center of Berlin.

Before me I could make out Checkpoint Charlie. Coming closer and closer, I couldn't help but reflect on what it was once like and what has happened to the famous border crossing. It was very much the same. I made my way through the peddlers selling souvenirs. The triangular square was empty, but the architecture of the buildings gives one the chance to see clearly where the Wall reigned.

As I struggled with my reflections of Berlin past and present, I found myself in front of a huge sign: "Future site of the American Business Center." I looked around me, but I was unable to find a construction site of any kind. The place was dead except for the normal tourist activity bustling around the former East German guard tower. Walking further East on Friedrichstrasse, my puzzlement was replaced with awe as I saw a huge gaping hole — a tremendous construction sight — across from the Schauspielhaus on Gendarmenmarkt. Arriving finally at Humboldt University, I dusted off my jacket but consented to let my dirty shoes be.

Later, when I returned to the new parliamentary house, I made my way through the huge construction site. The hammering isn't as loud as it was six weeks ago, but it is still annoyingly present. From the fifth story I take a look over the land again, over that area that is so treasured, so precisely planned for, and discussed. But it looks so worthless. Looking through the scaffolding on the fifth story of the new parliament, out onto Potsdamer Platz, the only apparent symbol of interest is the German flag blowing on top of the Reichstag in the distance, everything else is an eyesore. Then my face cringes upon recognizing an old East German guard tower and bunker in close proximity to the house, a perplexing sight. Why are these apparitions of the East German dictatorship there? The air is unclear and the space in between is so unattractive. Why is the place that is so worshipped and glorified in the press cared for as if it were an unwelcome orphanage? Some of the highlights that perplex the mind in addition to the old East German guard tower, include a MIG jet fighter skeleton, run-down pieces of the Wall, and dirt and junk gathered together and fenced off.

Much like when the Wall split the sandy field, it is disturbing to be there; it is still a dividing point. I have recalled my visits and crossing as the Wall was still standing, as if those days are far behind us, as if it is all over, as if Daimler-Benz and Sony will be moving there tomorrow. But today it looks as if it was all a joke, I am moved with feelings of rejection and deception from both the investors and politicians. Perhaps they are so caught up in their plans and projects, like many Germans claim them to be, that they don't objectively see the reality of what actually is?

The resurrection of the Prussian heritage appeared again on March 23, 1993, when the German Foreign Minister Klaus Kinkel, and Mayor Diepgen began publicly debating the future location of Germany's Foreign Ministry. Rumors were circulating that Kinkel and other federal politicians were for the demolition of East Germany's former congress hall, the *Palast der Republik*, while Diepgen wanted to use the existing building.

As if the decision divinely fell from above, overnight the announcement to demolish the former East German parliament was made. *The Palast der Republik* stands on the sight of the former Hohenzollern castle. The campaign to rebuild Berlin's Hohenzollern castle immediately gained momentum. Many conservative members of the Berlin parliament are pushing strongly for the re-emergence of all that is related to Prussia. Representatives have repeatedly taken me aside and told me how proud they are of Prussia's acceptance of persecuted Jews and Catholics in the 19th century, as well as other more favorable tenets of Prussian history.

The debate surrounding the rebuilding of the Berlin Castle is a good example of the efforts to re-establish Germany's traditions and roots in the greater Brandenburg. Many conservative members are for the rebuilding of the war-damaged castle that was blown up by the East German communist leader, Walter Ulbricht, in 1951, recalling the tradition and Prussian heritage this building had.

I recall a 1993 CDU party group meeting in which representatives heavily debated the issue of rebuilding the castle. They were splintered on the issue. Mayor Diepgen and Senator Hassemer were outspokenly against any plans to rebuild the castle. Their opposition was that it would cost a lot of money and that public interest wasn't great. "Don't listen to them," said one representative to me after a heated round debating the castle, "they have no vision at all." Opponents, led by the conservative CDU party group cultural speaker, Dr. Uwe LehMann-Brauns, were passionately for the rebuilding and consideration of this part of the city's history, complaining that the communists cannot be allowed to succeed in destroying this important landmark. The forces of history, and the momentum of the drive back to Germany's center that holds, lies with the conservatives.

The outcome of this debate is still uncertain. However, the fact that the Spreeinsel architecture competition for the area will include proposals using reconstructed castle models leads me to believe that the debate will intensify.

On the other side of the coin, within days of the announcement that the *Palast der Republik* would be torn down, protesters in the East organized themselves around the Spreeinsel initiative. I'm sure that many West Germans have been dreaming for decades for the day when they would have a chance to tear down this symbol of everything Eastern. Many East Germans feel that the decisions about their new capital are going right over their heads, and that they are being taken over. The group's first meeting a week after the decision was well represented, with a range of persons from all walks of life, gathered together to express their opposition and vent their frustration. One young man at the gathering said that he believed politicians, with their decisions, were speculating on the inexperience of Germans in the new states. He went on to complain that East Germans paid a lot of money for this building with their taxes, and now as unified Germans they are supposed to pay for its replacement, including the demolition of the *Palast der Republik*. But the protest against the powerful decision makers is not just coming from citizens of Germany's new states. One protester came from Munich, and said that she had never imagined that so much emotion was tied up in this building and that she had been so far unsuccessful in gathering this much energy to go to anti-racist parades, concluding, perhaps here we can turn the tide, whereas in the past one was always defeated by powerful politicians. [4]

Then, one month later, Germany's man of the century, their leader, Chancellor Kohl, arrived in the wake of the decision to analyze his plans to unite his people around the center that holds, the Prussian tradition. After taking a detailed tour of the Spreebogen, and Unter den Linden on his surprise unannounced visit, he expressed his interest in speeding up the bureaucratic details and to begin building as soon as possible. He concluded his visit by telling reporters: "This will be the most beautiful government center in the world" and "Soon I will be here permanently."[5]

Although the protesters to the demolition were justified in their complaints and have much public support, in retrospect it is clear to see that upon German reunification the German train moving back to its traditions has left the station. There is no turning back. Kohl was and still is the conductor. Kohl also looked at the *Palast der Republik* and gave the go ahead for the demolition "to begin as soon as possible." The replacement, regardless of the architectural design, would be an international congressional center. Chancellor Kohl also said on his visit that he has an "emotional relationship to Berlin."[6] In the opinion of University of Bonn historian Tilmann Buddensieg: "The Chancellor belongs in the castle."[7]

Within five months of the decision, supporters for the rebuilding of the castle began erecting a model of the castle from the *Palast der Republik*.

Once the model was completed, the Berlin CDU organized another excursion. I was as curious and eager as many of the party group members to take a look. As the procession of cars pulled out of the parking lot at the former Prussian parliament and we turned onto Unter den Linden, I was all eyes and ears. There it was. What formerly was nothing but an empty, vacuum-like end of this grand boulevard, was today alive, and filled with what looked to be the castle itself. Indeed I had seen pictures before, but this was on the verge of being indescribable. It looked like a gingerbread house that one could eat. As my assistant friend's car pulled closer, we were commenting on the unifying factor, the one missing link that was now in place. We were eager to get out and take in the castle, just to stand on the complete Unter den Linden again.

We stood in awe while other party group members and representatives pulled up to the castle. They all shared one thing in common. As they approached us at the castle entrance where everyone was gathering, a look of astonishment, relief and joy radiated from their smiling faces. Hardly anyone could believe that this had been so successful, the rebuilding of this model of the castle and the impression it gave, the hole it filled in their city. For a good ten minutes, what is otherwise a group of serious and sullen representatives, was like a high school team returning back to their school after a Friday night football victory. Smiles, laughs and jokes were characteristic of the unusual festive mood. There was an overall sense of relief in the air, as if they were thinking to themselves, after all these years, Berlin is finally Berlin again. A fever was running through the group in anticipation of the upcoming tour.

Once the party group chairman pulled up and exited his big silver Mercedes—beaming with excitement and pride, as if he lived there—the tour began. The conservative politicians seemed to become more and more convinced with each passing minute. Seeing is believing. Our guide traced us back through the history of the castle, the traditions, the arts, etc. I stood back and just took it all in, took in these castle supporters upon their first visit and tour of the former Hohenzollern Prussian castle.

Indeed, the history embodied in this building is a mirror of the history of the city, the Prussian dynasty, and the fate of Germany. "Look here," said one familiar face to me, "Old Fritz's wife used to spend time here preferable to his Sancoucci castle in Potsdam. While he was interested in hunting and his dogs, she wanted to be in the city life, where things were happening."

The short tour ended in good German style—we were served a huge buffet with everything you can imagine, all of the meat and drink imaginable, and of course a delicious tray of German pastries. The atmosphere was jovial and warm, people were excited, the skeptics whom I had watched over the course of years whenever it came to a debate about the castle, were warmly enjoying being in the center of Berlin, looking out the window and seeing the model tiles of the castle, which to them seemed to lose all of its imaginary character, and was now tasting like true plasterboard, to them as sweet as gingerbread. In their minds it was becoming realized, although few recognized it at the time.

Then, the Chairman of the party group, Klaus Landowsky stood up and introduced the man who was responsible for organizing this event and making the construction of the model possible, a businessman from Hamburg, Wilhelm von Boddien. But before the introduction, Landowsky shared his impression with his colleagues: "I am sure when the Chancellor takes a look at this next week on his visit here, that you will have gained another supporter for the rebuilding of the castle." The place erupted into applause. He also spoke of the impact this visit had on him personally as well as other Berlin representatives and that the project turned out much better than expected and that he wished them all success. He offered to assist in any way possible. After having observed the party group for over two years at this point, this was the most optimistic and united front I had ever seen about an issue. Upon returning from my second visit to the wonderful dessert buffet, I felt compelled to go. The over-optimism was infectious. The whole feeling of power and pride that radiated from this middle point of the city was getting to be too much.

Normally when Landowsky spoke at the end of other 'special' party group excursions, the representatives were champing at the bit to go home to their families or back to their offices. Yet after over an hour and a half, the place was still two-thirds full; the beer continued to flow profusely. Upon exiting, and walking away from the castle, by Humboldt University on my right toward the Friedrichstrasse train station, I paused and turned around to look back at the model. It was truly impressive. Every city revolves around its architectural symbols and places, Paris has the Louvre, Moscow has the Kremlin— it became clear to me that this has been the city's missing link. No wonder everyone was so relieved and joyful. Berlin is becoming Berlin again and Germany is well on its way to being reunited with its traditions. Weeks after that special party group excursion, the once divided party group expressed their united support for rebuilding the castle facade.[8]

Other neighboring symbols of East Berlin are reawakening too. The former East Berlin is coming alive in more than just its famous districts as, for example Prenzlauer Berg. In contrast to the castle, other cultural symbols of the East have been under renovation for years. Two of East Berlin's cultural symbols, the Jewish Synagogue on Oranienburgstrasse and the Protestant Cathedral in the Lustgarden, have been under renovation since way before the fall of the Wall in 1989. The former Prussian Kaiser church had its ceremonial reopening on June 2, 1993, while the synagogue will be reopened on the fiftieth anniversary of the end of World War 2, May 8, 1995.[9] Both will be in full swing by the time the German capital is in Berlin at the turn of the millennium. Both, however, are poignant symbols of how badly things went wrong last time Berlin was the capital.

The synagogue was set ablaze on *Reichskristallnacht* in 1938, and then used as a uniform depot by the Wehrmacht until it was bombed out in 1943.[10] It stood as a ruin until 1988, when Honecker permitted its long called-for reconstruction, more for foreign policy image purposes than anything else. Most of the funding necessary for the rebuilding is and has been donated by foreigners, including West Germans. Although it is still a year away from being completed, the Star of David is easily recognizable when one is in the area; it is the one source of brightness and hope on the otherwise gray streets of East Berlin. When it is opened, it will be used for religious services but will also serve as an archive, document center, and museum.[11]

The Protestant Kaiser's cathedral was also destroyed by the bombing in World War II. The way the Jewish Synagogue's destruction by the Nazis reminds us of the horrific past, the cathedral reminds us more of a time before the Nazis, of the center that holds in Germany, of Prussia. Unlike the remains of the Hohenzollern castle that were destroyed by the communists after the War, this temple of Prussia was allowed to remain bombed out until 1974, when Honecker decided to allow West Germans to restore it.

Craig R. Whitney of *The New York Times* said it best: "To visit its vast, neo-Baroque interior today, with wooded paneling, statuary, and numerous putti and cherubim restored to their original fin de siecle state, is to have an inkling of the equally vast political ambitions of the Wilhemine Germans who built it."[12] The place is filled with remembrances of the royal family, including the sarcophagi of many Hohenzollern royal family members and other Prussians who had been living in Berlin since the 15th century. The late construction in 1905 was the Hohenzollern family's attempt to build a cathedral to match the glory of Westminister Abbey and St. Paul's.[13] A question presents itself today, however: What about the political ambitions of the West Germans who have funded its rebuilding, including the government?

And guess who attended the opening ceremony of the Kaiser's cathedral? Eighteen years after the renovations began, the public had to stay home and watch the distinguished special invitation guests, including the Hohenzollern relatives, and Chancellor Kohl take part in the opening ceremony on June 2, 1993, on TV. Interestingly enough, back when the cathedral was originally opened, there were critical press reports of a "pompous affair without the public."[14] Ironically the same thing happened 88 years later.

With all of these ideas circling inside me, I was in the right frame of mind for the odyssey of the next days. A week and two days following the grand opening, the CDU party group staff members were shown the newly completed film introducing the new Berlin parliament to the public in rehearsal for the May 8, 1993, public open house celebration. At the end of the film, they showed a rapid historical review of the parliamentary room. The screen flashed pictures from the original construction site, then the Weimar Republik, and the elimination of parliament with a Nazi representatives leading the parliament with the *"Sieg Heil"* sign. Next the remodeled parliamentary room was shown as a festival room for parties, with pictures from Goering's wedding and Hitler's Christmas party flashing across the screen. In each scene, the room looked entirely different, not to mention the different actors on stage. Then the frame showed the hall to be a storage facility in the final years of East Germany. Finally, there was a picture of the Wall splitting both sides of the Niederkirchnerstrasse with a guard tower directly in the middle of the two buildings. As I saw that picture I wondered to myself, is that the same tower that is standing in the field at the foot of the parliament? More encouraging pictures of the construction just completed were shown at the end of the film, concluding with pictures from the festive opening session of parliament.

All of the ten Berlin CDU staffers seemed satisfied as we left the little theater — but I was disappointed. The film was good, very well done, but the director left out a gaping hole, where was the question mark for the future? It was as if the history was over. But no one seems to talk about the future; it is more certain and sure to talk about the past, it is done, it is clear and tangible, in contrast with the today and the idea of tomorrow, or next year. Why is it that most find it more real to talk about yesterday, and not tomorrow, aren't they both as unrealizable as the other, and where the one only offers the possibly of reflection, doesn't the other offer the possibility of action, of creativity, of change?

And then came May 8, 1993. But it didn't all hit me until later, at the end of the day, when I was alone and sitting in my rooftop office looking up through my skylight window. As I was reflecting back on the past days and all of the events I have participated in, everything that I have seen and felt regarding the past, Frederick the Great, Chancellor Kohl, Berlin and Brandenburg, the move back into the former Prussian parliament, the Maginot Line, the Allies' withdraw, the Russian soldiers sitting behind me and Natasha, the Battle of Berlin . . . lightning flashes through my rooftop window, and the loud thunder seems to be calling me, with the rain pounding on the glass, stirring inside of me as if it were rumbling from my stomach, I look up at my reflection in the window. I couldn't help meditating on the parliamentary president's remark during the opening celebration, *"Das Licht des Tages Beleuctung"* (To reflect the light of the day).

Today was the first open house for Berlin's new parliament. But as the beer and festive music were flowing in a jovial atmosphere, and sausages were handed out like their was no tomorrow, I wonder to myself how many guests reflected back on the unconditional surrender at Berlin-Karlshorst 48 years ago today?

It is late, and I am one of the only people in the former Prussian parliament. In a dreamy, but very conscious state of mind, with scenes of history, of today, and of the future floating across my mind, I reflect back on the prescreening of the film we were shown about the history of this building.

Ideas of the present, the past and the future have been running through my mind. Before my eyes I am seeing pictures of the parliamentary room decorated by the Nazis (Goering made it into a Nazi officers' club). In a festive style, the room was highlighted with light colors and paintings. In this premonition I am seeing Goering celebrating his wedding reception, with all of those brown uniformed people around him. Did they come across the street after work to enjoy the ceremonies, I curiously asked myself. Suddenly I became very conscious of the present. Today is only 48 years marking the end of that terror regime, what is a year, how time flies, how we forget. Hitler was here just 50 years ago celebrating his Christmas Party. My Dad is well over 50!

I had no idea that it was used for such purposes. How can we ensure that we will remember? My time is flying by, I will be leaving shortly; new actors will be here.

More questions continued to come to mind, provocative and curious. Who will be sitting in this room fifty years from today? Will it even be a historic day in another fifty years? And how will they look back on today? Like many Germans have reminded me, look at how the French regard Napoleon today as if he were one of the greatest national heroes. Will this also be the case for Germans and Hitler?

Suddenly my neck strains my head upward and I'm staring at myself in the window, I feel so much younger than I look, I think that can't be, I am surprised, I think I am floating now up with the clouds above, up where the cold air is meeting the warm air, where the moment is being symbolized by a spark of electricity, it is now, but it is gone as quickly as I think about it. I feel just like that, like a spark that is going, dissipating and leaving. I am dying to know what will be going on, thinking back on all of the change, all of the history of this place, all of the history that has happened in the last century, climaxing with the rage of Nazism and being destroyed by the bombers.

What will be happening here in another fifty years? As the thunder seems to shake my chair, I feel called upward, I want to look, but the moment is gone, as the rain continues to hammer on the window. In less than 100 days I will be leaving this place, less than 2,000 days ago Hitler and Goering were leaving this place for good. Who will be leaving here in another 1000?

The reflections and probing questions about a Brandenburg Prussian regional resurgence rose within me again when weeks later, on April 29, 1993, Potsdam celebrated its 1,000th anniversary.[15] The reawakening is local, regional, national; it is pan-European. Potsdam was formerly the Prussian military headquarters, where the Prussian garrison was located. Two weeks before the end of World War II, much of the Prussian residential city was left in ashes and soot after the Allies dumped over 1,750 tons of explosives on the city.[16] It was reported in Berlin's papers, that even Berliners were amazed at the amount of shelling Potsdam experienced that night.

Potsdam is not only Brandenburg's state capital, but also the cultural center of Brandenburg. Being the state's traditional capital and the home of the Prussian King's summer palace, it is highlighted by its historical sites and quaint size. Sanssouci Castle is a main attraction in this otherwise run-down city. Frederick the Great spent much of his time here and modeled the castle after Versailles. With a sweeping garden and well-preserved rooms, touring the castle gives one a look into the life of this famous Prussian King and the Prussian lifestyle.

Potsdam in itself has transformed greatly since the fall of the Wall. Life today is much better in Potsdam than during the Cold War. Despite the precarious nature of meeting young Soviet soldiers walking through town, improvements continue to be seen. Two years ago the buildings were completely run down, and the streets were lifeless. Now the central market street, Poststrasse, is blooming. Many stores have opened up and renovations have smoothed out the otherwise cold nature of many run-down buildings and torn up streets. Slowly improvements are being made and with every visit I see another new shop, renovated building, or new traffic constellation in place.

Many are already asking themselves when Potsdam will be the home of the reunited Brandenburg and Berlin state government. While Potsdam has traditionally been the capital of Brandenburg, it is only logical to many that it will regain this role. Also, with Berlin being overwhelmed as the federal capital, it is only appropriate that Potsdam will return as the capital for the region of Brandenburg.

The Berlin government presented a gift for Potsdam's 1,000th anniversary, a Gothic Library at the Sanssouci castle.[17] The building, constructed in 1794, has been left in ruins since it was destroyed in 1945.

Potsdam's anniversary reminded me of another visit that I made to Potsdam. In 1992 the grave of Frederick the Great, taken to West Germany as the Soviets marched into town in the spring of 1945, was returned to his willful place of burial at the Sanssouci castle. In a spectacular ceremony the Hohenzollern family planned an extravagant old German train ride into Potsdam carrying the casket. Prince Louis Ferdinand, the chief of the Hohenzollern family, even invited the Bundeswehr to take part in the ceremony.[18] A horse-drawn carriage carried the casket from the locomotive steamer from the last century to the castle in a haunting parade.

I was there for the whole show—I felt compelled to get up early on that drizzly Saturday morning just for the chance to live another historic day in the New Europe. As the well-organized parade turned the corner, I stood there watching the mixed crowd along with right-wing skinheads and leftist opposition groups. An eerie wind whipped around the corner just as the parade came into sight. In solemn procession, we all followed it to the castle. That was as far at the general public could go. In a private burial ceremony, of which Chancellor Kohl quietly took part upon the invitation of the Hohenzollern family, Frederick the Great was laid to rest next to his hunting dogs on the left side of the castle.

Days later, I felt obligated to go back and see for myself. I took the train to Potsdam again. Then I found myself standing on the elevated hill of the Sanssouci castle, looking over Potsdam's daunting landscape, and then looking down at the freshly turned soil of the burial site. It was the grave of *der alter Preusser* (the old Prussian), Frederick the Great. Looking up, I gazed over the castle park in full bloom. Somehow the burial of this Prussian legend seemed to symbolize something much greater, it symbolized the completion of one era, and yet, at the same time, paradoxically the beginning of a new one. It symbolized the rebirth of the region. Everybody is coming back to their traditional places since the end of the Cold War. Families long separated by the Wall are reuniting in the Center of Europe, cities and regions are reuniting, capitals and metropolises are re-emerging, while rejuvenated leaders, like Helmut Kohl, are paving the future of the freed Europe.

The Prussian Parliament on the Wall, 1990, courtesy of the German Information Center

The Prussian Parliament reawakens, 1993, courtesy of the German Information
Center

Open House at Berlin's new parliament, courtesy of the German Information Center

Western view from my office window onto Potsdamer Platz, 1993

The Berlin Castle, 1913, courtesy of the German Information Center

Notes

1   Erklaerung des Staatsministeriums, Sitzungsberichte des Preussischen Landtages, 5. Wahlperiode, 2. Sitzung, May 18, 1993, page 18. "Zu diesem Zweck ist heute der Preussische Landtag von seinem Praesidenten einberufen worden. Damit ist der Staatsregierung zum erstenmal die Gelegenheit gegeben, sich ihrerseits dem Landtag vorzustellen und ihre Ziele und Absichten ueber den Nueaufbau Preussens dem Landtage vorzulegen...Hieraus folgt, dass Preussen seine Politik in Zukunft im engsten Einvernehmen mit dem Reiche und nach den Richtlinien seines Kanzlers fuehren wird, wobei nach dem festen Willens des Kanzlers die berechtigen und wichtigen Interessen Preussen als grossten deutschen Landes in vollem Umfange gewahrt bleiben werden...Bravo!

...Der Kanzler hat mich zum gueter Preussens bestellt um mich besonders beauftragt, zu wahren, was Preussens ist. Unter keinem Umstanden werde ich daher dulden koennen, dass preussischer Besitz von Preussen getrennt wird...(Lebhafter Beifall)

...Der Kanzler will, dass Preussen und die peussische Politik und preussische Verwaltung auf alle Zeiten die Grundlage des Reiches bilden. Die taeglichen practischen Erfahrungen Preussens sollen fuer das Reich die Unterlage seiner Gestzgebung bilden. So faellt Preussen die wichtigste Mission zu, wie es diese im vorigen Jahrhundret auch gehabt hat, das Fundament des Deutschen Reiches zu bilden..."
Unofficial translation provided by the author.

2   Indeed Berlin did offer the renovated building to the Bundestag in order that they could move to Berlin sooner and not wait for the Reichstag to be renovated. The offer was not taken up at that time. Matthias Lambrecht, "Hauptstadt bietet Bonn Preussischen Landtag an", Berliner Morgenpost, March 2, 1993. Nevertheless, in 1995, Chancellor Kohl and other leading conservative politicians have expressed an interest in meeting in the Prussian Parliament when the Bundestag periodically meets in Berlin until the Reichstag is renovated.

3   For over a year before the opening, Berlin parliamentary President, Hanna-Renate Laurien, appealed on all Berliners to find the Prussian seal for the parliament and the statues symbolizing the establishment of law, order, and privilege that were removed by the National Socialists in 1936.

4   Jan Ross, "Harmonie der Empoerung", Frankfurter Allgemeine Zeitung, April 8, 1993

5   Matthias Lambrecht, "Kohl will Kanzler-Amt von 1994 an bauen lassen", Berliner Zeitung, May 6, 1993

6   Der Tagesspiegel, "Spree-Spaziergang inkognito, Bundeskanzler Kohl in Berlin: Palast 'moeglichst rasch' abreissen", May 6, 1993

7 Christian van Lessen, "Der Kanzler gehoert and die Stelles des Schlosses", Der Tagesspiegel, January 29, 1992

8 Christian Bahr, "Stadtschloss: CDU bekraeftigt Entschluss fuer Wiederaufbau", Berliner Morgenpost, June 16, 1993

9 Der Tagesspiegel, "Neue Synagogue wird 1995 als Centrum Judaicum uebergeben", May 16, 1992

10 Craig R. Whitney, "Renewing Berlin's Spiritual Symbols", The New York Times, February 20, 1994

11 Helmut Caspar, "Juedische Gemeinde will sich in das Leben der Stadt einbringen", Neue Zeit, September 5, 1991

12 Craig R. Whitney, "Renewing Berlin's Spiritual Symbols", The New York Times", February 20, 1994

13 Ibid.

14 Kurt Geisler, "Geschlossene Gesellschaft", Berliner Morgenpost, June 3, 1993

15 Der Tagesspiegel, "Ab 29. April wird in Potsdam gefeiert", March 10, 1993

16 Berliner Landespressedienst, "DIEPGEN: 'POTSDAM UND BERLIN SOLLEN SICH MIT IHREN UNTERSCHIEDLICHEN VORZUGEN AUCH KUNFTIG ERGAENZEN'", April 16, 1993, pg 3.

17 Ibid.

18 Potsdamer Neueste Nachrichten, "Hohenzollern-Prinz lud die Bundeswehr ein", August 7, 1991

Chapter 19

Berlin's Champion:
Helmut Kohl's 1994

Nineteen-ninety-four was a major year in German history. In addition to a record 19 elections (local, state, federal, European), the Allies completed their withdrawal — ending 49 years of occupation and defense of the European heartland. Chancellor Kohl is a champion of Berlin's destiny to be the reunited German capital and Germany's return to its powerful regional tradition in Brandenburg. This is important to understand because Kohl continues to play such a critical role in shaping his country's European future. The 1994 super-election year also offers a look into what type of a leader he is.

When the smoke cleared after a year of election hype in October 1994, Kohl's commanding lead over the Germans shone brighter than ever. The Allies were gone, including the last Russians, and Kohl was re-elected to his fourth four-year chancellorship, however small the majority. Indeed, it will be a tough governing session for Kohl because his coalition only has a ten-seat majority.

But Kohl's chancellory is not as unstable as some would want us to believe. Unlike in a parliamentary system where a vote of no confidence or a majority opposition to a specific policy can unseat the prime minister, the chancellor in Germany can only be replaced by a majority vote for a successor. Some speculate that the FDP could later decide that its future could be better preserved in a liberal coalition government. This is in the short term highly unlikely, especially considering how much the Chancellor did to help FDP make it into the Bundestag through his unrelenting campaigning. Perhaps SPD opposition candidate Scharping summed it up best: "It doesn't make a difference if it is a one, two, or three vote difference, it is still a losing coalition."[1]

It wasn't just that Kohl won the Chancellorship for a fourth consecutive time, step by step he won the Germans back to his side throughout the historic year. At the beginning of 1994, much of the world predicted Chancellor Kohl would topple. After President Clinton's ascendancy to power on the theme of change, combined with his youthful enthusiasm, pollsters agreed the time had come for the "iron" chancellor to step aside. Opposition SPD candidate Rudolf Scharping took Clinton's lead as much as possible. But somehow in the end the Germans marched alongside Kohl. How was Kohl able to squeak out the victory in the October 16, 1994, Bundestag elections?[2]

Back in 1993, as Germany's economy was in the deepest recession since the founding of the Federal Republic, Kohl responded to much public criticism with his own strategy. The Chancellor rose one day in parliament and lambasted Germany's economy and social net, one he presided over for the last ten years, calling it a *"Freizeitpark"* (an amusement park). That was arguably the beginning of his re-directing his course. It was his only choice. Echoes from the American presidential election and the theme of "it's the economy stupid" was on his mind, and he rightfully learned from his "good friend George [Bush]," who had nine months previously lost largely because of that.

Or was it something more than the economy? By reviewing the election year, beginning with the first election in May, perhaps further insight into Kohl's success formula can be discovered.

First Kohl dug himself into a hole. By selecting a controversial candidate, Steffan Heitmann, for Federal President, he failed to gain coalition support. After Heitmann repeatedly made politically inept statements about women, and drawing a line in Germany's WWII history, Kohl embarrassingly withdrew his candidate. Up to the election, Kohl was split with his coalition partners about which candidate to select. Finally, after much power playing, Kohl convinced his junior coalition partner, the FDP, to drop their own candidate before the decisive third voting round and support his new conservative candidate, Roman Herzog, to succeed Richard von Weizaecker. On that fateful day in the Reichstag, Kohl stood victorious after his candidate had won. The SPD leadership was furious. SPD Chancellor candidate Rudolf Scharping was quoted as saying afterward that the election didn't reflect the will of the people, but rather power and majority.[3]

In the end, Kohl made sure that Germany's symbolic presidency for the next six years would be CDU-conservative, and perhaps more significantly his FDP center-left coalition partners at his side. The effect of the Federal President's election was immediately felt in June's European Parliament's election. After much campaigning effort by all parties, the CDU gained 15 seats compared to the SPD's 10 seat gain, and more importantly a majority 47-seat CDU/CSU European Parliamentary representation compared to the SPD's 40-seat representation.

Nevertheless, the long election year was still taking shape. The CDU lost a number of state elections in the new German states, which they had dominated in the 1990 election, including the loss of control in Mecklenburg- Western Pomerania, Thuringia, and Sachsen-Anhalt.

And despite the setbacks in the state elections, Kohl got a lucky chance to discredit the opposition SPD as supporters of the former communists. After the Sachsen-Anhalt state election, in which no clear coalition majority resulted, the SPD decided to join a coalition government with the PDS. Kohl immediately jumped on the opportunity to criticize. Kohl said: "The Social Democrats want to be coalition partners with the communists [PDS] because they cannot make it on their own power. Those who decide to join forces with the PDS are not eligible for office." He went on to say: "I don't believe a word of the SPD's diversionary tactics."[4] He concluded his boisterous criticism of the SPD leadership by calling for traditional SPD voters, disenfranchised by their party, to re-consider their vote.

Kohl campaigned vigorously and non-stop, reminiscent of Clinton's successes in embracing the people and moving in the crowds. From the beginning of September 1994 to the end of the campaign, Kohl made 102 campaign appearances.[5]

Kohl made the campaign a referendum on himself personally. Said Germany's most-read newspaper, *Sueddeutsche Zeitung*, of Chancellor Kohl's campaign strategy: "The chancellor-campaign, just as Kohl demanded, portrayed the chancellor as larger than life, a chancellor without a team or rivals. The chancellor was shown as the longest active head of state in the world, as well as a friend of all blessings. It also showed the chancellor in his solitude. This strategy was designed to give the insecure voters faced with massive change a clear orientation point: the chancellor."[6] Billboards portrayed the chancellor's healthy 6 feet 4 inch stature big and bright. *The International Herald Tribune* called Chancellor Kohl's campaign: a "shameless cult of the personality."[7]

Kohl's diligent campaigning and attention to details earned him respect from the German voters, if only subtly. For example, he scheduled many of his own appointments and decided all the places that he would speak at and when. His staff diligently carried out his orders.

He also used the luck that came his way to his advantage with the rebounding industrial economies. Germany's recession happened to end right in the middle of the campaign. The myth of Kohl continued when some suggested that Chancellor Kohl timed the economic recovery out of the recession perfectly with the election cycle.

Up to the Bundestag elections, economic indicators continued to release promising forecasts.[8]   According to the Bundesbank, in the first half of 1994, the gross domestic product in West and East Germany was almost three-percent higher than a year before.[9]   Manufacturing output increased, building permits and housing construction increased, and the second quarter labor market increased for the first time in East Germany since reunification. At the same time unemployment decreased slightly in West Germany. The new German states experienced an economic growth spurt of 9% in the first six months of 1994, more than any other region in Europe.[10]   An atmosphere of economic normalization was taking hold. Special economic programs established to assist the new German states ceased in 1994, including funds through the German Unity Fund and the Treuhand agency. The Bundesbank stated in September 1994: "All in all, it appears likely that the necessary budgetary consolidation will make noticeable progress in 1995—a trend which will also be fostered by the economic upswing."[11]   As if it had been fine-tuned by a master, the recession ended almost simultaneously with the withdrawal of the allies.

And of course Kohl also took some credit for 500 billion deutsche marks that the government transferred to the former East Germany in what he described as "an unprecedented achievement in the world's modern economic history."[12]

Which brings us to the key part of Kohl's election year strategy: his image. Often referred to as the nephew of Konrad Adenauer, he certainly used this stereotype to his advantage. Germany's Finance Minister, Theo Waigel, called Kohl: "the most successful German Chancellor since [the founding of the Federal Republic of Germany] 1949." Also, Kohl reinforced his image as commander and chief. As the German Defense Minister Volker Ruhe and Germany's Foreign Minister Klaus Kinkel, publicly got in a dispute about Germany's position on NATO expansion, Kohl brought them into line and publicly said that cabinet members should rather reserve their discussion for cabinet meetings, stating: "Otherwise I will be forced to have difficult telephone conversations with President Yeltsin and others."[13]

In light of the tumultuous changes Germans have experienced since reunification, Chancellor Kohl wisely was self-critical of some of his decisions. His pass-key was his orientation to the average Germans. An editor of the weekly magazine *FOCUS* wrote: "Kohl's like a lot of his voters in the way he eats and the fact that he has gone to the same place on holiday for the past 25 years. He's one of millions, just more determined. They don't love him, but they trust him."[14] He could talk the small talk, sit and eat German pastries with the people.

Kohl went down to the lowest common denominator that we all share: regrets and mistakes. It started with words every German knows. Said Kohl: "Forty years of division are much deeper than many thought, including myself." Then down to the personal level: "My signature is on some laws that we had preferably rather not made. My main character flaw is that in the time of quick decision making, I don't think things through thoroughly. I accept criticism because a Federal Chancellor doesn't stand on a monument's pedestal."[15] He even went so far as to say that had he been born in the East, he probably would also had "have found a niche" or "somehow fit in."[16]

And Kohl paid critical attention to his media image. He appeared all over the television airwaves at the end of his campaign. And he played his comeback to his advantage as much as possible in the eyes of the public, ridiculing the German press for portraying him as the biggest idiot in the country and then at the end of the campaign as a power monger.[17]

In addition, Kohl also used the historic year in Germany to arrange for foreign visitors to come and support his campaign effort. Kohl was everywhere. He not only helped arrange the time and place of the visits, but he went out of his way to play up the publicity when he had the chance to show off his international reputation. To name a few, the Spanish President, Fellippe Gonzalez visited Chancellor Kohl in Rostock, Kohl's good friend, French President Francois Mitterrand visited him in Heidelberg, and Bill Clinton and President Yeltsin, within one month of each other, visited him in Berlin on occasion of the Allied withdrawal. He just happened to coordinate the withdrawal four months ahead of the December 31, 1994, deadline date, and a good six weeks prior to the election! Kohl's foreign policy campaign climaxed in the minds of Germans on August 31, 1994, truly a significant day for European history, as the last Russian soldiers withdrew from Germany.

Kohl also managed to get an invitation from Mitterrand to invite German soldiers to drive their armored cars down the Champs Elysées on the French Bastille Military parade on June 14, 1994, in conjunction with the European Eurocorps. The pictures of German armored cars driving down the Champs Elysées for the first time since WWII went on world press wires and television screens, the same day. Altogether, the image of Kohl's leadership and stature undoubtedly increased greatly after his well-calculated performances on the international stage during the election campaign.

And he appealed to German's love of their homeland and tradition, as well as the successes they have achieved under his leadership with words like: "When one puts it all in perspective, than the last ten years are probably the happiest decade in German history."[18] Kohl was often welcomed at campaign rallies by a noisy brass band with "Prussia's Glory."[19] *Die Welt* newspaper described him to be in the pose of the ever present Bismarck.[20]

And of course Kohl reminded his people that he is Berlin's champion. Said Chancellor Kohl:

> Our Berlin capital should be the business card of the united Germany. It is not just a question of details, rather, and ahead of everything else, Berlin's spiritual and cultural radiance is symbolic for the vitality of our democracy. The completion of the domestic reunification of our Fatherland is proven in exemplary fashion in Berlin.[21]

Henry Kissinger said of Chancellor Kohl after the 1994 election victory:

> I consider Kohl one of the seminal leaders of our period. He has been a guarantee of Germany's Atlantic and European orientation and a shield against the nationalistic or romantic temptations from which his people have suffered through much of modern history.
>
> . . . He [Kohl] has managed the NATO missile deployment, the unification of Germany and the integration of Europe with such matter-of-factness that few remember how precarious these processes were at every step along the way. . . . It is important, for whatever happens, America and Europe will not soon find so reliable and so courageous a partner as Chancellor Kohl.[22]

But then his shining image was tarnished, when in a brief moment of relaxation at the end of a long campaign day, when the Chancellor let the reporters hear what many had long suspected, when he said: "I'm an old wise guy."[23]

Chancellor Kohl may retire from office, handing over the CDU chancellorship to CDU Parliamentary Chairman Wolfgang Schaeuble on January 1, 1997. That would solidify Chancellor Kohl's place in history as the longest running chancellor in post-WWII Germany. Succeeding the pillar of German democracy, Konrad Adenauer, who governed for 14 years, Chancellor Kohl will thus have achieved his goal, perhaps completing the job of post-WWII Germany. Whereas Adenauer was key in linking Germany to the West and Europe, Kohl was responsible for leading a united Germany back into the center of a widening and vibrant European Union in which Germany is the most powerful country. Kohl will likely go down in history as perhaps Germany's most famous leader in this century, for not only did he achieve his objectives, but along the way he got some leaders to believe his objectives were in their best interest too.

Perhaps Berlin should incorporate into its mammoth construction plans a place for a statue of its champion to be located in the future. Also, perhaps Brandenburg should reserve a plot for Kohl at Sanssouci Castle.

Chancellor Helmut Kohl campaigning, 1994, courtesy of the German
Information Center

Notes

1   Quote of the Day, New York Times, October 17, 1994
2   The CDU/CSU's wining voting percentage was the smallest since West Germany's founding in 1949.
3   "Nach der Wahl des neuen Bundespraesident, Grummeln in der SPD", Frankfurter Allgemeine Zeitung, May 27, 1994.
4   Ibid.
5   Hans Ulrich Kempski, "Der Kanzler kaempft mit aller Kraft", Die Sueddeutsche Zeitung, October 13, 1994
6   Nina Grunenberg,"Ich bin ein uralter Fuchs", Die Zeit, October 21, 1994
7   Rick Atkinson, "Is Kohl Sinkable? Maybe, but for Now he's on a Steady Course", International Herald Tribune, October 7, 1994
8   Germany's trade surplus rose to DM 21.5 billion in the second quarter of 1994, a 6.5 billion increase from the first quarter and a DM 5.5 billion increase from the second quarter of 1993. The investment climate followed the promising economic upswing. Between April and July, 1994, 4.5% more domestic orders were booked by domestic producers of capital goods than in the first quarter of 1994, and orders rose by 3% in real terms compared to the second quarter of 1993. In the first six months of 1994, Germany's government incurred a deficit of DM 5.5 billion compared with 20.5 billion a year before. Net borrowing was estimated for fiscal 1994 to be DM 150 billion, down from the approximately DM 200 billion in 1993.
9   Deutsche Bundesbank, "Monthly Report September 1994", Vol 46, No. 9, pg. 6
10 "Kohl nennt Debatten ueber die Dauer seiner Amtszeit unsinnig", Frankfurter Allgemeine Zeitung, October 8, 1994, pg. 2
11 Ibid, pg. 39
12 Hans-Joachim Noack, "Bismark mit Strickjacke", Der Spiegel, October 10, 1994, page 47
13 "Kohl nennt Debatten ueber die Dauer seiner Amtszeit unsinnig", Frankfurter Allgemine Zeitung, October 8, 1994
14 Rick Atkinson, "Is Kohl Sinkable? Maybe, but for Now he's on a Steady Course", International Herald Tribune, October 7, 1994
15 Hans Ulrich Kempski, "Der Kanzler kaempft mit aller Kraft", Die Sueddeutsche Zeitung, October 13, 1994
16 Hans-Joachim Noack, "Bismark mit Strickjacke", Der Spiegel, October 10, 1994, page 40
17 Nina Grunenberg, "Ich bin ein uralter Fuchs", Die Zeit, October 21, 1994
18 Hans Ulrich Kempski, "Der Kanzler kaempft mit aller Kraft", Die Sueddeutsche Zeitung, October 13, 1994
19 Hans-Joachim Noack, "Bismark mit Strickjacke", Der Spiegel, October 10, 1994, page 45

20 Ibid, page 43
21 Dr. Helmut Kohl, "Berlin — Haupstadt des vereinten Deutschland", Berliner Morgenpost, April 30, 1993
22 Henry Kissinger, "Beginning of the End of the Kohl Era", The Washington Post, October 20, 1994
23 Nina Grunenberg, "Ich bin ein uralter Fuchs", Die Zeit, October 21, 1994

Chapter 20

Berlin and Poland

One Berlin representative friend, Klaus, and I were meeting for coffee one morning. Discussing the daily news, suddenly, out of the blue, he asked me: have you ever been to what is today Poland? In response, I chuckled a little and said no. "Would you like to come with me to see where my family comes from, where my grandparents were raised?" he asked. He seemed to notice my personal deliberation, and continued: "It would certainly be educational for an American to see, we could leave in the morning and come back late that night. Besides, I need to go there anyway to see some old friends."

As we rolled through the streets of the German capital in his flashy BMW, heading East, scenes of a different world already filled my eyes as we crossed over the former Wall zone. The streets were quiet and relatively empty compared to West Berlin. Pedestrians were few and far between. Then, turning a corner, we were suddenly on a monstrous boulevard, flanked by colorless buildings on both sides.

The street's width immediately impressed me. "This is German Reich's street number one," he said with a touch of pride. "Once you could drive from here to Koenigsberg. This will have to be rebuilt too. That is right, straight ahead is East Prussia." With those words settling in my mind, I had a premonition that this little friendly excursion to the East was going to be different than I expected.

The deeper and deeper we drove, the further I felt from home, and all of the security that brings. Stopped at a traffic light, suddenly a Russian military officer's Jeep pulled alongside us. As I glanced over at the uniformed officer, a shiver ran up my spine. I reassured myself that the days of occupation were over. Looking at the uniformed Russian officer

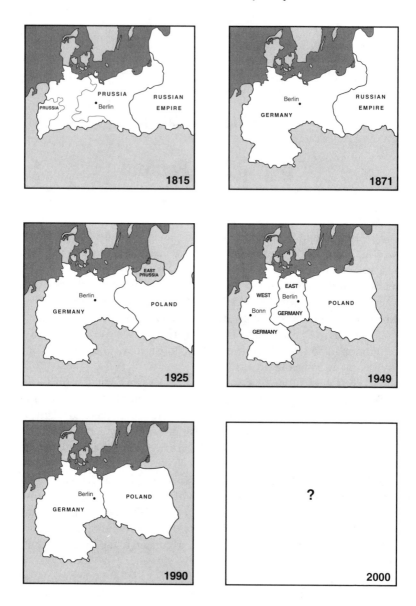

in his patrol jeep, I think we both needed a break. We pulled over to get gas at the next stop, to fuel up before our journey into the unknown world ahead of us.

The road to Frankfurt on the Oder River, a German border town to Poland, reminded me of the transit highway on which I first came to Berlin in 1987. Potholes were everywhere and we didn't drive faster than 60 miles per hour, difficult for my hard-driving German friend. But that wasn't the focus of my thoughts. Rather, as I was gazing over the empty fields that characterize the landscape from the outskirts of Berlin to the Oder River, I was reflecting on the Battle of Berlin. Gazing over those barren, windblown fields, I imagined seeing scores of retreating Nazis fighting off the Soviets. [1]

This battleground area that I was viewing through the car window, like the Civil War memorials to be found in the Virginia countryside, is sacred. Nevertheless, one distinguishing difference between this countryside and Virginia's is that there is nothing commemorating the carnage that took place here. There are no special turnoffs or lookout sights. There are no memorials nor even signs to point to the sacrifice that took place on those barren, naked fields in the new German state of Brandenburg.

While I was dreaming about the day that Europe would reach that point in history, when exhibits rightfully pay respect to the lives lost here and the sacrifices made, Klaus continued to complain about road conditions. This time the former communists running the state government in Brandenburg were responsible for not having repaired this "important highway" sooner. It wasn't just that. His whole person—his posture, his jaw—seemed to tighten as we went East. I should say that Klaus hardly ever traveled away from his apartment block in West Berlin. And maybe this journey, this coming back home, if you will, was unsettling him. I was just taking in the scenery and reflecting back on the war.

The next thing I knew we were in and out of that little border town, Frankfurt on the Oder, quicker than I remember. All along the bumpy road, I kept counting the kilometers on the signs in expectation of this town which, like many, is a mirror of war and the division of Europe. From what I did see, it was small, unimpressive, and barren. The only significant thing was the short river traversing. You could look downstream, where Soviet soldiers once crossed after the retreating Nazis destroyed the bridges in an effort to stall them as they invaded. In 1992, Klaus angrily pointed out: "Refugees cross there at nightfall, get to the other side, and apply for asylum. Don't you see those people down on the beach, I bet they are just waiting for nightfall, when they will swim across." He was becoming increasingly confrontational. As I gazed over the bridge at the group he was speaking of, I saw someone fishing.

Also, because we were just crossing the divide into Poland, I imagined that it was going to get worse. I sat back and resigned myself to making the best of it by not standing in the line of fire of his loaded remarks. He was, like a nervous fighter, looking for a fight. It was as if the only way for him to release his own discomfort and frustration was to take it out on someone else.

Once we crossed into Poland, the roads were worse, the place very poor, much poorer than the other side. Indeed the conditions were worse. Nevertheless, I couldn't help asking myself, why this disturbed him so much. It was as if he thought it was his, whereas I felt worlds away from Berlin.

As we approached our intended destination, Klaus became increasingly agitated. He was a little lost, anxious and nervous that he wouldn't be able to find the little village. Then, with a burst of energy, he sat up in his seat and said: "We didn't come all this way in the middle of nowhere not to succeed." And with a look of pride, he pulled up on the lake shore of the intended place. "We're here," he said triumphantly. "That is where my parents' friend lives, the man who used to hold me as I child." Looking across the street at the white house with a garden, I immediately noticed that it was better-kept than most of the houses, and more aesthetically inviting. "I'll wait," I said, "while you go see if he is home." Before exiting the car, Klaus tightened his tie, combed his hair, and then stepped out into Poland.

"Finally," I said to myself, "a little peace." After that stuffy and nervous ride, I was relieved to exit the car, sit by the lake shore and watch the ducks playing in the still water. But to no avail. As I was leaning my head down, suddenly Klaus reappeared. "David, stand up, this is Herr Mueller, my parents' best friend. Herr Mueller, a true Prussian from Berlin, lives in Poland now. But it doesn't make a difference because Pomerania will be Germany's 17th state soon," he said, while they both smiled a crooked smile at each other. The idea shocked me, and my body language showed it. In response to my obvious, though silent, demurral, Klaus turned to Herr Mueller. I overheard him say: "He is an American, he doesn't understand."

Upon hearing these words, I wanted to go. I was dependent on my host. Klaus asked his friend to take him to the burial site of his grandparents. "Okay," he said reluctantly, "but I haven't been up there for a while. If you want, it is up around that corner of the lake, back in the woods on the hill." Klaus was delighted, despite Herr Mueller's reserve, and he led the way along the pristine lake shore, most impressive because of its lack of inhabitants.

I trailed behind while the old friends chatted. Turning the corner, we saw a dirt road leading off the lake's shore back into the woods. Klaus immediately directed us there. He seemed to be attracted like a hunting dog following a scent, oblivious to anything and everything except the trail he was pursuing. His excited expectation and apparent victory were a switch from the nervous and belligerent tone he had used up to this point. He was suddenly lighthearted, with a serene joy radiating from him.

The old man was having trouble keeping up, and as we approached the dirt road, he became clearly more and more reluctant. He pointed up the hill to the right, seeming to tell Klaus that he should continue the rest of the way alone. But Klaus was so immersed in the joy of being here, of being able to visit this place, in a free Europe, that he didn't see the man's reservation, and excitedly took him by the arm up the dirt road. Tension was building, and it was obvious that the man knew better, had some good reason for being reluctant. Nevertheless, I must admit that I was also curious to see the cause for Herr Mueller's reservation. My wish was realized shortly thereafter.

As the old man pointed to the right, off the track, into the trees, I could see the rest of the fence that used to protect the compound had fallen, the area fully overgrown with shrubbery and fallen branches from the trees overhead. Klaus' face turned to stone, and his stiff jaw returned. Walking into the overgrown area, I saw him standing over something, pointing at it, and then, as if Klaus were to fall, he put his hand on the ground to support his apparent weakness.

There, between the grass blades, and tipped to one side, was a charred gravestone. It was uprooted and turned over, face down. In response to this sight, Klaus' movements intensified. He quickly took off his leather gloves and reached his hands into the soil to turn the gravestone over. After five minutes of intense digging, he succeeded in flipping it. The result was worse. There was no name, nor date—just a defaced gravestone.

As if he were boxed in a corner, Klaus quickly surveyed the rest of the former graveyard. His eyes beamed fire. Everything was disheveled, stones were either tipped over or in multiple pieces strewn over the graveyard. Even for me, there was a sense of tragedy.

As we stepped back onto the path, the old man's face hung low, he didn't want to look at his countryman's face. The way back to the car was solemn. Klaus' German picked up a notch in accent, as I heard him complaining, and in his complaint, seeming to inquire whether his friend knew the fate of this sacred place.

"Back in the 1980s a group of youngsters from out of town were here, and from what I heard, when they found out that it was a German cemetery, they destroyed it," said Herr Mueller. "I used to go every week to put flowers next to the resting place of those I knew, but as you can see, I am an old man now, and it's a long walk for me, and it obviously needs a lot of work. The problem is, I'm the only one still alive out here who even cares about it." "Otherwise," he continued, "I would go and clean it up, turn the stones upright, and try to correct this tragedy." As the old man was telling this story, I could see Klaus' face tighten, his eyes squint, as if he were flinching.

In response to Herr Mueller's story, Klaus calmed the man, who had obviously been keeping his feelings to himself about this place for a long time. "I will come and help you, I will come here with some friends one weekend and together we will put this place in order," Klaus said.

Then, the next thing I knew, we were in the car, headed back to the German capital, and in a hurry. From the time we departed the lake shore, Klaus became eerie and fatalistic. He passed slower moving Polish autos while rising in his seat and cocking his head back just at the point of overcoming the other car, culminating with a deep sigh of triumph. He seemed eager for the next chance to pass as we rallied home. Klaus was somber. I saw dark circles under his eyes, like he hadn't slept for days. As the car jolted on hitting another pothole at the excessive speed in which we were rallying, Klaus didn't even flinch. He was in his own world.

Later, I found out that Klaus also took part in an annual conference on September 2, 1992, in Berlin called *Tag der Heimat* (Day of the Homeland). The conference was organized by the Union of Expellees (*Bund der Vertriebene, BdV*), an interest group whose members compose the right spectrum of the German party system. Most Union of Expellee members come from the former German territories lost in the Second World War. Following the capitulation of Germany, over 3.5 million Germans were expelled in the name of ethnic homogeneity from former German territories.[2] The majority of Germans were displaced westward into West Germany and these lands became part of Poland in accordance with the Potsdam agreements.

Others stayed in Poland, like Herr Mueller, and adopted Polish citizenship on occasion of the occupied Germany. Since the founding of the Federal Republic of Germany, debate has flourished about how many Germans were in Poland and has been a major source of contention with Poland. Patricia Davis writes in "Ethnic Germans in Poland: Bridge Builders or a New Source of Conflict":

In the name of ethnic homogeneity, the communist government in post-World War II Poland denied the existence of any Germans . . . as late as September 1989 they claimed that the number of Germans in Poland were a mere 2,500. Figures from proponents of ethnic Germans range wildly in the other direction: the Union of Expellees gives a figure of 1.1 million: the German Red Cross sets the number at 750,000. Most current estimates place the German population in Poland between 250,000 and 400,000.[3]

As the above story and these facts illustrate, it was and still is no easy separation for Germans from their traditional homeland and people. In Pomerania, Posen, Silesia and other parts of Poland, there are many traditional German cities and townships. In addition to the tumultuous post-World War II years in which millions of people were displaced, a mistrust and resentment has developed between Germans and Poles over the latter's occupation of what many consider the former's property. Generations of family history and ethnicity issues continue to characterize the Polish-German border in the reunified Europe. Questions that have been smothered by the Cold War are resurfacing. This is directly relevant to what Berlin will be in 2000, because the German capital is less than 80 kilometers away from the Polish border. Berlin's contacts with Poland have increased since the fall of the Wall. The two countries play a critical role in each other's political agenda.

During the Cold War, German-Polish reconciliation went from ice cold to tepid. Timothy Garton Ash describes in detail in his book *In Europe's Name* the evolution of German-Polish relations and the central role played by German minorities. One tenant of Germany's Ostpolitik was to improve the condition of German minorities in the East. Writes Ash:

> All Bonn governments, from Adenauer to Kohl, made it their business to help these Germans in the East. Socialists, liberals and conservatives agreed that this was a national duty: to help the Germans who were still suffering the most from the consequences of the war and the 'Yalta' division of Europe. . . . German minorities became, like so many aspects of German Ostpolitik, simultaneously an issue of domestic and foreign policy.[4]

The importance of both the lost territory to Germans and the German minorities in Poland has in large part characterized German-Polish relations since WWII. During the German reunification treaty negotiations, Germany's dispute of the Oder-Neisse border was a critical question. In response to Germany's equivocation, the Allied Powers insisted upon recognition of the border before German reunification. Chancellor Kohl subsequently called the loss of the Oder-Neisse region the "price of unification" and thereupon recognized the existing borders as fixed and permanent in a November 4, 1990, Polish-German Friendship "Reaffirmation of Existing borders" treaty.

Nevertheless, it took Kohl a long time in the reunification negotiations to concede the former region, which concerned many. For example, Margaret Thatcher said: "Chancellor Kohl had managed to convey the worst possible impression by his unwillingness to have a proper treaty to settle Germany's border with Poland. Finally after much pressure, Chancellor Kohl did agree to settle Germany's border with Poland with a special treaty in November, 1990."[5]

One opposition group to the "Reaffirmation of Existing borders" is the Union of Expellees. To this day, many Germans still deny these lands belong to Poland. Many Germans were displaced from towns like Koenigsberg, where, like Klaus their families lived and where they were perhaps born. The history they learned from their parents instructed them that these territories are German. Many just want to be able to visit burial grounds of their relatives or the houses where generations of their families lived.

However, many of the concerned expellee interest groups are not angelic. Most Union of Expellee members, for example, want to expel the current Polish population from these territories. Some German expellee organizations are actively involved in supporting the German-Polish minorities' calls for autonomy. During the *Tag der Heimat* conference there was much protest over this very issue. When Dr. Wolfgang Schaueble, Parliamentary Chairman of the CDU-CSU Bundestag party group, said to the group that the existing borders are *"endgueltig"* (final), he was practically booed off the stage and never recovered his audience's full attention.

Polish-German relations that have been frozen or held at bay behind the barrier of the Wall are now a urgent priority. Justice is also a question. With the end of the Cold War, only now are we beginning to understand the crimes committed against German citizens and soldiers by the Soviet occupation forces. On November 1, 1994, an article appearing in *The New York Times* by Craig R. Whitney observed:

> For nearly 50 years, the fate of the millions of ethnic Germans rounded
> up and expelled by the victorious communists from the eastern provinces

of the Reich and western Poland at the end of World War II has been passed over in silence by most of the rest of world. Little distinction was drawn between members of Hitler's armed SS legions and ordinary Germans whose families had lived for centuries in places like Silesia, West Prussia and Pomerania that were wrested from German control by the wartime allies in 1945. About seven million fled communist retribution or were shipped out in cattle cars, and an estimated two million perished.[6]

Some Germans are calling for justice for crimes committed against them in post-WWII. For example, Polish authorities are investigating the case against Solomen Morel, a Polish Jew who was put in charge of the Nazi concentration camp near Katowice in the spring of 1945. Dorota Boreczek, a Polish woman imprisoned in a Nazi prison camp at Swietocholowice in February 1945 with her German mother, said, "I was only 13 years old, and I saw people dying like animals there." She now lives in Germany and is trying to raise money for a monument to the camp's victims. "We never got an explanation [of] why we were taken to the camp," she said.[7]

In addition, examples abound of Germans demanding a re-evaluation of the post-World War II concentration camps, such as Buchenwald, where the communists, including Polish citizens, interned thousands of Germans in forced labor camps.

From the highest levels of government down to various interest groups and individual citizens, Germany's border with Poland will continue to be a contentious issue, from which one can draw the only plausible solution: as long as people cannot reside, work, and live where their families come from, tensions will grow. The Polish-German border will become an even more important subject as Berlin re-emerges as Germany's working capital.

Ethnic conflict and nationalism are reappearing throughout the continent, from the rise of right-wing extremism in Germany to the rise in Russia of Zhirinovsky, who has suggested that Germany and Russia split up Poland. And the scenes of war, rape, and carnage from the former Yugoslavia are a poignant reminder to all of the possible consequences.

In response, politicians are taking steps today to defuse the source of contention and bitterness between Poles and Germans. They realize that the future of Europe rides on overcoming past prejudices and working together. The German-Polish Friendship Treaty, for example, addresses for the first time the German minority in Poland according to the norms of international law, including the right of each government to consult with the minority organization and their representatives located in the other country.[8]

And in the spirit of making the Oder-Neisse border more reflective of the people living on both sides, the German and Polish governments have increased their cooperation. For example, on May 7, 1992, German Environmental Minister Klaus Toepfer and his Polish colleague, Stefan Kozlowski, agreed to create a Polish-German national park on their Lower Oder River valley border region (on the Oder River). Kozlowski also offered to work on developing a water route to Koenigsberg for German tourists through Stettin, and spoke of this offering a "great possibility" for the growing together process between Germany and Poland.[9]

Days later, in a Berlin CDU Federal and European Affairs Committee meeting, representatives discussed the upcoming visit to the future German-Polish National Park on the Oder River, as well as our side excursion to the capital of the Polish province of Wojoewodztwo, Stettin. No one was interested in staying very long. The three-day planned weekend was cut to a day and a half, and everyone seemed satisfied. One day is enough time to spend in Poland, remarked another. The excuses started, the list was passed around. So when we boarded the bus in front of the new Berlin parliament on a stormy spring day, it didn't surprise me that around only half of the representatives showed up. The representative from the Senate couldn't fit it into his schedule.

Arriving at our first destination, Schwedt, a small town on the German side of the Oder River, was a real eye opener. Visiting little towns in the new German states is often depressing and a disappointment. Everything is progressing so much quicker in Berlin and its immediate surroundings that it is good to remind oneself of the other side by traveling outwards. The towns are usually oriented around a former 'cultural' center—where good socialist theater and discussions were held. There is always something precariously missing on these squares, like half a painting, or a missing arm on a sculpture. After searching hopelessly for the missing piece, it finally came to me, this was where the Lenin monument was.

The surrounding apartment buildings were uniform fifties-style architecture. There was no one in the streets except for the occasional bicycle rider. The stores looked quiet, the people dazed. Just finding the hotel proved to be hard. We all know that hotels are exceptions in small towns, but you can always ask the locals to point you in the right direction. But only upon asking the third passerby was our bus driver able to find the right way. We ended up right where we started. "That must be it," said our driver. Our hotel happened to be in the same grotesque building that we had just critically analyzed. The sixteenth and seventeenth floors of the twenty-story apartment house had been transformed into a hotel. Walking into the apartment lobby, my companions joked and laughed. Many recalled the adventurous days when they used to travel under hard conditions. And hard they were—for a floor with over 30 rooms there was just one shared toilet and shower. We all put our things in our rooms and vowed not to come back until the hour was late and we had had a few drinks—and a few more.

Then the fun began. The carriage drive through the national park to be was very refreshing. The threatening clouds which had just stood over us had dissipated and the sun was shining across the fields, where birds were singing. It was such a change of atmosphere that we all enjoyed ourselves thoroughly. The landscape was beautiful, I almost thought I was somewhere else, until I looked behind us and saw a huge steel factory plant bellowing junk out of its gigantic smoke stacks.

Our local guide told us that the cleft along the river was dug out by the Nazis to dock all of the barges of traffic traveling to Berlin. "It was never completed," he said, "there wasn't enough time." He told us how his father had worked on the project and he described to us in detail how the project would have turned out, just like his father used to show and tell him.

Winding around the corner shaded by the trees above, the horse-drawn carriage jerked up an incline, and suddenly, a panoramic view of a town with red brick houses and the traditional church steeple was before us. It was so pristine looking, the town was built up on the hill on the river's side, it was old, very old, and one representative rightly said "it looks like a town from one of Grimm's stories has come to life." We were all captivated by its charm and quality.

We lost ourselves, in thrall to the place, with the wet houses shining in the sun from the recent rainfall. But as we came closer, we saw the black, red, and yellow painted post in the ground designating German territory, then the edge and water. A deep feeling of disappointment swayed through the carriage, as we all looked at each other with empty faces; it was on the other side of the river. The beauty was literally breathtaking. As the sun shone on the hillside across from us and we walked along the still river side, everyone couldn't help but be attracted to the sight.

"It's definitely German," said one passenger. Everyone shook there heads in agreement. "Look," said my neighbor, "they clearly took the best part, where the rolling hills begin and the town is." "Oh, that's right," said one to the other. Then the discussion started about how the Poles managed to draw the border in such a way as to come so far to the West, to take

Stettin and the mouth of the river. "Legally, that could be disputed still," said another, "the border was supposed to be in the middle of the river, they took the whole of the river and more," he said with a shuffle in his carriage seat and a look of indignation. I sat quietly and dropped my head in reflection.

After a fine dinner at a local restaurant, we made our way back to the dread hotel. No one wanted to go upstairs, so we gathered around the lobby desk and ordered beer after beer and talked about the day.

Waking up early the next morning in our uncomfortable beds, we swallowed a quick breakfast and made our way to the bus. Today we were going to the other side, but we wouldn't be staying overnight. We had a special police escort to help get us through the border more quickly and escort us into Stettin. Within twenty minutes we were in the middle of a very big port town, the harbor was tremendous, it was like the shipping operations I was used to at home, in Seattle. The contrast between Schwedt and my home town were overwhelming. We were clearly in a foreign country, the language was incomprehensible to me, nothing looked familiar. I was so impressed by the magnitude and size of the place.

We pulled up in front of a very old rich looking red brick house that looked over the port from high on top of the city's edge. Now I knew we were in Poland. The people, the signs, the furniture, everything was different. Walking up the corridors, we were welcomed by the consulate general.

The most tell-tale sign of all proved to be my visit to the bathroom. The lights barely illuminated the space. After giving one deutsche mark to the woman out front, I noted that the toilet paper was thinner than a sheet of paper. Then I recalled the look of pain and dread some seemed to have as we debated the overnight stay in Stettin during the last committee meeting. Now I understood better.

And when our host opened the floor for discussion, the majority of the questions related to general German-Polish relations, although the purpose of our visit was to discuss the future Oder Thal national park. My boss asked the representative questions about the border problems, kindly the first time, harder the second and then he brushed him away as if he were not of any interest anymore. He dodged the questions like a skilled bullfighter. There was clear animosity and difference of opinion. I had the impression that they were not speaking to each other, rather around each other. It made for a very artificial atmosphere and it was clear we were all feeling uncomfortable. The next thing I knew we were in the bus again and being given a tour by a German minority in Stettin.

The short drive back to Berlin took no more than an hour and a half and made a strong impression on me: That a port as big as Stettin was so close, yet so far. After listening to Germans and Poles, it is no wonder that it is taking so long to re-establish these natural geographical ties.

Rounding the corner near Anhalter train station back toward the Berlin parliament, we all took another deep breath, like the one everyone took as we crossed back into Germany. Two prominent politicians laughed and joked, recalling their internship years in the *Europahaus* on Stressemanstrasse where they recalled it was like the end of the world, it was so far off and isolated. Times have certainly changed. Where do they think the end is today, I thought to myself?

This regional talk is everywhere it seems. Days later, the mayor stated during his visit to the Polish capital that the German-Polish border delays (average wait is currently 12 hours for cars and 24-36 for trucks) is a "terribly unsatisfactory condition" and called for a quick improvement to the problem.

I was curious to hear the representatives discuss the issue. And what a discussion it was. As one conservative representative aggressively stated, Poland will likely sell what he called the "lost territories" back to Germany, I turned and asked the other representatives if they agreed. I was initially shocked as they nodded their heads in agreement. But later I reconsidered my position. Why should it surprise me: everything is possible these days.

Notes

1   For the final assault on Berlin, the Soviets had massed 192 divisions — 2.5 million troops, 42,000 artillery tubes, 6,250 tanks — on the east side of the Oder and Neisse Rivers. In contrast, the German army was down to its last reserves. Army Group Vistula on the eastern front was down to 250,000 troops and 850 tanks, while Berlin itself was defended by 100,000 soldiers. "Berlin's defenses were organized in concentric rings around Sector Z — for Zitadelle — where the Reich's government quarter stood." (source: Rick Atkinson, "Victory Rose from Berlin's Rubble", The Washington Post, May 7, 1995, pg. A30

2   Patricia Davis, "Ethnic Germans in Poland: Bridge Builders or a New Source of Conflict?", German Politics and Society, Issue 31, Spring 1994, pg. 37

3   Ibid, pg. 37

4   *In Europe's Name* Timonthy Garton Ash, Vintage Books, 1993, pg. 233

5   *The Downing Street Years* Margaret Thatcher, HarperCollins, 1993, pg. 789

6   Craig R. Whitney, "Poles Review Post-war Treatment of Germans", The New York Times, November 1, 1994

7   Ibid.

8   Patricia Davis, "Ethnic Germans in Poland: Bridge Builders or a New Source of Conflict?", German Politics and Society, Issue 31, Spring 1994, pg. 37

9   Der Tagesspiegel, "Deutsch-polnisches Schutzgebiet 'Unteres Odertal' beschlossen", May 8, 1992

The Center of Europe

Chapter 21

After Maastricht

Two weeks before the French referendum on the European treaty signed on February 7, 1992, in Maastricht, Belgium, by European Community ministers, I asked the Berlin Senator for Federal and European Affairs what he thought about the referendum's passage. His answer was symbolic of the mood both in the Berlin parliament and on the streets. Chuckling and looking at me with a sense of certainty, he said: "The French won't pass it, I have studied French history and the French always reject public referendums," with a slight note of contempt at the idea that Francois Mitterrand even put it to a public vote.

The European Union Treaty, often referred to as Maastricht, provides the institutional framework for forging unity and cooperation among the peoples and nations of Europe. It is a new stage in a process begun in the 1950s with the creation of the three original European communities, which came to be known collectively as the European Community (E.C.).[1] Originally, the E.C. was created to help rebuild Western Europe and facilitate French-German reconciliation after the devastation of two world wars. It was created both as a barrier against the imperialism of Stalin and to integrate the Federal Republic of Germany in the European community. With the former now history, the latter is still important. Even after reunification, the argument continued to be made by Germans: The E.C. was needed to save Germany from itself. As we will see, the E.C. is not only saving Germans from themselves, it is also the bedrock from which Germany's influence is secured.

Some of the provisions outlined in the treaty include: the establishment of a European currency by 1999, European Union citizenship, increased powers for the European Community and for the European Parliament, as well as the introduction of a common foreign and security policy.[2] Despite the magnitude and impact of the French referendum on Maastricht, few Berliners had been closely following the debate. While European politicians called for a unified Europe, their countries' respective citizens seemed uninterested. In 1992 everything was hanging in balance in Germany. From the perspective of the Berlin parliament, it was far from being the number one priority. Although Berlin was the first German state parliament to announce its support for the French to vote yes on the treaty, the capital move from Bonn to Berlin dominated Berlin's agenda.

Summer 1992 was a time of change and rising national tensions. In response to the horrific violence at Rostock against foreign refugees, talk of German nationalism and Nazism flashed across Europe. I couldn't help think the reports were from a historical war film being flashed across my television. Some French anti-Maastricht politicians portrayed Germany as an overpowering bully in Europe and warned of a rising Fourth Reich.

Maastricht's provision for a united European currency also came under attack in the French referendum. The strength of the deutsche mark illustrates Germany's economic dominance in Europe, and high German interest rates showed the country's economic influence on both European and world economics.

Due to the high costs of reunification, Germany's Bundesbank set very high interest rates. Because Germany's economy is the locomotive for the European continent, and the deutsche mark the strongest currency, Germany's higher interest rates forced the weaker currencies in the European exchange system to raise their rates too. In this regard, Germany managed to spread the cost of German reunification throughout the European Community.

One week before the French public referendum on the Maastricht treaty, the exchange system came down hard on the E.C.'s weaker currencies. The losses experienced by Britain and Italy forced them to take their currencies off the market. As the financial markets went haywire, everyone blamed Germany. Coming only four days before the vote in France, these developments were a big strike against Maastricht. On the heels of the Danish vote against Maastricht and the favorable vote in Ireland, the fate of the Maastricht Treaty looked grim. And opponents of Maastricht stepped up their campaign. Said former French Defense Minister Jean-Pierre

Chevenement: "We are running into the danger [with Maastricht] of giving German banks the keys to French industry." Neo-Gaullist Marie-Francoise Garaud went even further, saying that "Maastricht organizes the predominance of Germany."[3]

For weeks various opinion polls had placed the chances for the referendum at fifty-fifty. French President Mitterrand put his job on the line if the referendum didn't pass. And what a storm of political and economic turmoil Captain Mitterrand's ship sailed through to reach Maastricht!

Then, weeks before Germany's national holiday, Europe saved itself from possible chaos. On September 21, 1992, the pro-Maastricht lobby gained a majority in France. As the news of positive results of the French referendum broke, it seemed as if everyone in Europe took a deep breath. This historic vote for the Maastricht Treaty will carry the forces of European integration quickly forward, pulling the British along, whether they like it or not. And if the British do not join the bandwagon, Germany and France will pull the rest of Europe along with them.

Nevertheless, the social and political landscape in Europe is still in flux. The trends occurring make a united Europe difficult to imagine. There are many competing influences at work in 1992. Many walls in Europe still need to be overcome, provoking the question: Are the chief architects of Maastricht (Mitterrand, Kohl, Delors) blowing against the wind while their ship uncontrollably drifts toward the rocks? Who really wants Maastricht? Pass all the treaties and agreements in the world, but if no one supports them how can it be expected to hold?

German politicians followed the French public referendum by subsequently passing the Maastricht Treaty, it did not, however, go to a public referendum. Rather, it was carefully guided through Germany's parliament. Thus, after decades of reconciliation, at least the two arch-enemies, France and Germany, are united by their interest in pursuing a more unified continent through Maastricht.

Nevertheless, not enough attention was given to what would have happened if the French referendum on Maastricht had not passed. Nationalism probably would have flared even more. The European Community President, Jacques Delors, Chancellor Kohl, and Francois Mitterrand likely would have lost their jobs; new federal coalitions would have formed, with predominantly national interests ruling. The French Socialist presidential candidate, Michel Rocard, warned that if the

Maastricht Treaty didn't pass the French referendum: "Germany would [then] re-discover its historical and geographical inclinations, and supported by its triumphant deutsche mark would turn East."[4]

During the Cold War, Germany undertook much effort to foster relations with Central and Eastern Europe that were forcibly blocked by the communists. Germany's Ostpolitik successfully prepared Germany for its dominant role in Central Europe decades before the Wall fell. Writes Timonthy Garton Ash in, *In Europe's Name*:

> It was not only economic ties that the Federal Republic of Germany endeavored to forge with the Soviet Union and Eastern Europe. The Bonn government declared itself interested in developing almost every possible sort of tie: political, social, cultural, touristic, sporting, academic, technological, scientific, environmental, road or rail, animal, vegetable or mineral. The stated objective was to create a whole *Netz* or *Geflecht* —a net, network, mesh or web—of ties between Eastern and Western Europe. This idea of *Verflechtung* or *Vernetzung*—interlacing, networking, weaving— was another leitmotif of German *Ostpolitik* in the 1970s and 1980s. . . . How did the actual West German 'net' compare in quantity and quality with those of France, Britain, Italy or the U.S.? The short answer is it was the thickest. Starting from the position far behind its Western partners in everything except trade, the Federal Republic had by 1989, through the intensity and consistency of its efforts, built a more dense network of ties with all Eastern European countries than any other country. In all forms of economic ties, the Federal Republic outstripped its main Western partners.[5]

Germany has stepped up its efforts in Central and Eastern Europe since reunification. On August 13, 1991, Berlin signed its first city partnership since reunification with Warsaw. Months later they also signed a city partnership with Moscow. Warsaw's mayor, Stanislaw Wyganowski, called the signing "An important step to reconciliation." He also said: "The art of memory doesn't always mean just recalling the injustices and skepticism that exists between young Poles and Germans, rather the best means to remove such barriers is through meeting each other . . . I myself have drastically changed my opinion about Germans. We actually have a similar mentality."[6]

But unfortunately, not all Poles and Germans feel this way. And politics is often mixed with rhetoric. Germans have historically long ties to North Central Europe, dating back to the days before the booming Hanseantic

League on the Baltic Sea in the 13th Century. The forces of history are strong, sometimes stronger than we want to recognize. The Union of Expellees' national chairman Herbert Czaja stated at their national conference weeks after the Warsaw city partnership with Berlin was signed: "The amputation of one quarter of Germany that remained after Versailles is not covered up in the self-determination of the German people."[7] He went on to demand a "right to return to the homelands."

Speaking afterward, Berlin's mayor reiterated that the goal is not to change the borders, the solution lies rather in the future, in a Europe of regions, where everyone should be able to live, where "he/she feels at home," said Mayor Diepgen.[8] He went on to say that Europe's borders should become "as permeable as possible" and that a Europe of regions should know "no national barriers."[9]

But as shown above, the road is long and hard. Deep prejudices and stereotypes within the European community need to be overcome, not to mention the stereotypes in Central and East European countries that have been smothered by the Cold War. And examples can be found throughout Europe's former dividing line. In May 1994 German representatives, including Foreign Minister Klaus Kinkel, called on the Czech government to enter into direct talks with representatives of the Sudeten German community, who mainly reside in Bavaria. Over three million ethnic Germans were expelled from Czechoslovakia after WWII and their property taken under the so-called Benes decrees. Czech leaders have declined to respond to German entreaties, calling the issue a 'closed chapter'.[10]

As the last two examples illustrate, it is urgent that the Maastricht Treaty take hold in a Europe full of uncertainty and insecurity. On this basis Germany's Eastern neighbors need to be integrated with the E.U. as soon as possible. The daily horrors of the former Yugoslavia are a poignant reminder of how thin the veil of society and freedom is.

The European Union is on Berlin's side too. On April 27, 1992, the European Commission President, Jacques Delors, approved Berlin's application to receive the E.C.'s highest economic priority for East Berlin.[11] The Berlin government called this one of its biggest successes: "Especially in the competitive developmental politics (in the E.C.) we are always having to compete against the misconception that Berlin, as the capital of the richest European Community country, doesn't need European Community assistance."[12]

With all of this European skepticism in my mind, I was delighted to receive an invitation from my boss, Klaus Rettel, on October 21, 1992, to go see the final Last Tattoo in Berlin. How did the conservative British respond to the dramatic campaign on the Maastricht referendum in France? The Last Tattoo was the famous British military ceremony given every year for the British troops stationed in Berlin. I am not one to take after military tradition, perhaps because I've never been in the military and have had no reason to applaud the military force, outside of the symbolic role it serves for peace and such. Herr Rettel told me it would be an historic occasion; the Queen would be in attendance.

Arriving at the stadium, Herr Rettel and I were expecting some sort of national British military parade. Traditional stereotypes were in vogue in 1992. Is this a function of the uncertainty and insecurity about the future, a return to nationalism and the conventional stereotypes?

To my surprise we had front-row seats for the program and many important figures were on hand, like the German Foreign Minister Klaus Kinkel, and his British counterpart Douglas Hurd. As the distinguished guests took their special box seats about five rows above us, my attention was riveted.

Why were the foreign ministers present? Tensions between Britain and Germany had recently flared as Britain was forced to withdraw its currency from the European currency exchange system. As a symbolic gesture of goodwill between the two countries, I imagined that Foreign Minister Kinkel felt it necessary to welcome the Queen on this, the symbolic Last Tattoo in Berlin. Perhaps he felt it necessary to show thanks and respect to the withdrawing British soldiers.

As the show began, the surprises continued. Instead of the nationalistic military parade, it was a spectacular tribute to the European Community. The well-executed show paid tribute to each E.C. member country with a short movie presentation against the backdrop of the British marching band playing each nations' respective anthem. I was very impressed. I had so much expected to see something out of touch with current realities that this greatly impressed me. The program was arranged to promote the individuality of each member nation within the context of the E.C.

I, like many, was pessimistic about a united Europe—despite the historic vote in Paris the previous month (already it seemed like ages ago by then). Many Germans, including this American guest, were finding themselves at the bottom of another popularity cycle—rooted in the nationalistic uprisings of violence in Germany and economic conflicts with other E.C. member countries. The German public at large seemed uninterested in such fantasies—they had other, more pressing, concerns: Germany first.

Yet the program was seductive—with the combination of the music and the marching soldiers playing the German national anthem. That Britain, of all the countries hit hard at this time of economic downturn and high-interest rates would organize such a show, speaks for itself. Or was the program a sign of something else to come in the future, something ironic? My boss and I, and others I'm sure, left thinking not about the day's headlines of E.C. conflict but about the future political landscape of the continent and its differing peoples and cultures. We were on a seductive road, forgetting about the actual difficulties and problems plaguing Europe now, losing ourselves in the idealistic and dreamy idea of a unified Europe. Or perhaps it is working: After all, hadn't I just witnessed the British army singing the German national anthem in Berlin?

Two Years Later

Since I attended the Last Tattoo, European integration has been progressing politically, economically, and in terms of collective security. Each success for the E.U. enhances Berlin's role as the center of Europe.

Politically, the European Union was realized on November 1, 1993, with the passage of the Maastricht Treaty by all European Community countries.[13] Thus, the second step of the European integration process has been achieved. In 1996, a treaty will be prepared at an intergovernmental conference of E.U. members to revise the Maastricht agreement.

By outlining the planned goals of the political, economic, and security policies of the E.U., perhaps we can envision what the likely outcome will be. First, imagine a United States of Europe, with a single currency and open borders for its peoples and goods. That is what Europeans are constructing before the beginning of the next millennium.

In the meantime, leaders are undertaking the difficult work of deepening and expanding European Union institutions. The European Union introduces significant rights to its 345 million citizens, including the right to reside in any member state and the right to vote in a E.U. country other than their own, as well as the right to run for municipal and European elections.

Based on sovereign agreements by member countries, the E.U. does not have a constitution. Member states, while retaining their national character, give up some of their national sovereignty to create a supranational state in a federal system. The E.U. is granted subsidiary jurisdiction on those issues which cannot be effectively handled at the local, regional, or national level.

The European Union's executive branch is the European Commission. The Commission is responsible for ensuring that treaties and agreements are properly implemented. It also proposes legislation. It is composed of 17 elected commissioners, two each from Germany, Italy, Spain, Britain, and France, and one from the remaining seven members. The European commissioners are elected to a five-year term. Also, a Commission President is appointed by agreement among the member countries in consultation with the European Parliament.

The European Union Council of Ministers is composed of ministers from the various member states. Ministers attend Council meetings related to their specialty— e.g., foreign ministers meet on issues related to the E.U.'s foreign relations. Acting under the Commission, the E.U. Council considers laws proposed by the Commission. Every E.U. member country assumes a six-month rotational presidency of the E.U. Council.

The European Parliament, a 567-member body with the 12 current members, is elected by universal suffrage for a five-year term. It can approve, block, or amend legislation introduced by the Commission through consultation with the E.U. Council and the E.U. Commission.

The E.U. also has a high court. The Council of Justice is responsible for interpreting and insuring the implementation of treaties agreed upon by E.U. members. It is composed of 13 justices, one from each member state and one elected presidential justice; they serve renewable six-year terms.

Another level of the European Union's government, which probably gives us the best indication of what Berlin in the year 2000 will be like, is the E.U.'s Committee of the Regions. European regions are key to the success of the supranational E.U. In the Committee of the Regions, a representative from each region represents that region in concert with the European Parliament. Some hope that the Committee of the Regions will form a second chamber in the European Parliament.

In 1994, there are 222 member regions from 15 countries. Liberated from their national boundaries, Europe's regions are booming. Traditionally influential regions in Europe, like Catalonia in Spain, Normandy in France, and Brandenburg in Germany, are surging forward. "The fact that a united Europe exists gives more hope to the likelihood of self-government," said Pasqual Maragall, the Barcelona mayor and vice chairman of the E.U.'s Committee of the Regions. According to the *Wall Street Journal*:

"Germany, with its 16 *laender*, is the model for Europe's regions. They control most social policy, including education, and they even have a say in international affairs."[14]

United Germany's identity crisis, built on the shaky foundations of German nationhood, is precisely its advantage in the European Union. Germany didn't evolve into a nation state like Britain and France. As noted by Marc Fisher in his book, *After the Wall*:

> Rather, the German lands were long divided between Catholic and Protestant principalities.... Germany remained stuck in feudalism, its land divided among warring princes and barons. There was no colonial empire where soaring myths of national destiny could be developed. Until 1871, the Germans were bound not by nationhood in the modern sense, but by far more slippery ties, of language and culture, literature and tribal roots. Germans came from all over: French Huguenots hoping for a better life, Poles looking for work, Jews seeking tolerance. They found a place considerably more diverse than later proponents of a German "race" or ethnicity would ever admit. That diversity left Germany in search of a definition.

A supranational Europe eases Germans insecure sense of common purpose. In contrast to Britain and France, Germany doesn't need to overcome a long-standing nation state in order to transcend into the supranational E.U.

In addition to reducing national tensions in Europe, the E.U., through its regional focus, is attempting to open and deflate the importance of Germany's Eastern border, as was done over decades with Germany's Western border. From Bavaria, Saxony, Brandenburg to Mecklenburg-Western Pomerania, these regions are leading Europe's regional efforts to overcome the former East-West divide. These regions are cooperating with their neighboring regions in the Czech Republic and Poland in everything from economics, environmental issues to school exchanges. The E.U.'s centralization of national policies, coupled with the decentralization of regional policies, returns power to the people at the local level.

As pointed out at the outset of this chapter, the final stage for the European Economic and Monetary Union (EMU) is planned to start at the beginning of 1999 at the latest. European Union member states have agreed to a three-point plan for the EMU. The first step, begun in 1990, involved the easing of large-scale restrictions on capital movements and closer economic policy coordination. The second stage, begun in 1994, entailed the creation of a European Monetary Institute and the closer cooperation on economic policies of E.U. members. The final stage envisions the establishment of a European Central Bank responsible for monetary policy.[15] European Union member countries, who meet specific economic targets, e.g., rate of inflation, budget deficit as percentage of GDP, and debt percentage of total GDP, in addition to other economic criteria, will be able to take part in a common European Union currency.

Once the above conditions are fulfilled and a solid E.U. monetary policy is established from the Central Bank, a unified currency will greatly benefit the European Union. The elimination of exchange rates will contribute substantially to fostering European unity through economic competition. Maastricht is first of all a political quest and secondly an economic quest. This parallel can also be seen in German history, monetary union leads to political union. Nevertheless, reservations exist about the idea of a unified European currency. Like many European countries, Germany is sensitive to the prospect of losing its national currency.

In addition to the political and economic measures since 1992 that are propelling the prospect of a united Europe, the security plans for the West are being integrated with those of the leading democracies of Central Europe. The European Union's Western European Union (WEU) a mutual assistance security pact formed after WWII, is to become the defense arm of the European Union. In cooperation with NATO, the WEU will formulate and implement the defense policies of the E.U. The WEU has developed an associate membership program for Central European countries. The WEU continues to gain standing in the international community. William Perry, United States Secretary of Defense, called the WEU the "Atlantic pillar of NATO."

Europe's future, unequivocally intertwined with Germany's, rides on the successful integration and stability of the East. Germany, through its reunification and the lessons learned from the integrating of the new German states, is the model country for the E.U. in their dealings with former Warsaw Pact countries that are in transition to Western style economics and politics.

As we saw in chapter 17, Germany is reaping the rewards of its reunification and betting its future on Europe and the re-establishment of its close ties to Central and Eastern Europe, built on the strength of the cultural, economic, and political regional tradition in greater Brandenburg.

The E.U.'s regional focus is perhaps the only solution to Germany's unstable borders. Germany has by far the largest number of neighboring states than other E.U. member states. It is clear from the first attempts at

German nation-building that the country's unusual geopolitical position in the center of Europe was both an invitation to foreign invasions and an opportunity for the country to expand throughout the continent. Many peoples have invaded Germany, including the Vikings, the Danes, the Swedes, Hungarians, and French. On the flip side of the coin, of course Germans have advanced as far as Rome and even Palestine—and under Hitler, against almost all European countries.[16]

From Germany's geographical position a national interest of progressive E.U. expansion develops parallel to Germany's deepening integration in the E.U. By building a E.U. of no internal frontiers and strengthened regions, Germany will potentially gain access and rights to the territories that some still dispute are German. Through peaceful, apparently benevolent, means, Germany will have the opportunity for influence in Central and Eastern Europe, influence which it had previously tried to achieve through military might. And that, in addition to the obvious economic gain for German interests, is why Germany is the leading proponent of an expanded E.U., NATO, and WEU. It is likely the role that Germany will assume from its new seat of government in the heart of Europe, as referred to by U.S. Assistant Secretary of State for Canadian and European Affairs, Richard Holbrooke: "Germany now has the chance to play a different role . . . . That role is for a different Germany, a Germany which exists within boundaries that never existed before. It isn't Weimar. It isn't the Third Reich. It is in the process of defining itself . . . .[Germany at] Year Zero."[17]

Reunified Germany is already the biggest and most powerful E.U. member. There are some 80 million German Europeans, ahead of some 58 million Italian, British, and French Europeans. Germany has by far the greatest Gross Domestic Product (GDP) at market prices too, roughly $1,700 billion for a per capita GDP of $20 billion, compared to France's roughly $1,100 billion for a per capita GDP of $20 billion, and the United Kingdom's roughly $530 billion for a per capita GDP of $9 billion.[18] Germany has the largest export per capita ratio too, some $5 billion, compared to France's $3 billion, and the United Kingdom's roughly $2 billion.[19]

Memories of German hegemony under the Reich's Wilhelm II and the Nazi's Hitler, and concerns for Germany's future power in the E.U., prompted both Francois Mitterrand and Margaret Thatcher's attempts to prevent German reunification.[20] As Thatcher later admitted in her memoir:

The trouble was, in reality there was no force in Europe which could stop German reunification happening. . . . Once Germany was reunified—there was another argument—propagated by the French, but swallowed by the State Department too—that only a 'unified Europe' could keep German power responsibly in check, which was false. . . . Essentially, he [Mitterrand] had a choice between moving ahead further towards a federal Europe in order to tie down the German giant or to abandon and return to that associated with General de Gaulle—the defense of French sovereignty and the striking up of alliances to secure French interests. He made the wrong decision for France.[21]

"Germany is our fatherland, Europe is our future," said Chancellor Kohl.[22] Thatcher and Mitterrand saw this upon German reunification. Margaret Thatcher said: "President Mitterrand went on to say that he shared my worries about a reunified Germany's so-called "mission" in Central Europe."[23]

In the summer of 1994, the European Union approved an expansion program to include Austria, Norway, Finland, and Sweden. In each of these countries, except Norway, public referendums approved joining the E.U. Since January 1, 1995, the European Union has added three more member countries, bringing the total to 15. The three new members raises the E.U.'s population to some 370 million, in addition to increasing its GNP to $7.3 billion.[24] A Norwegian E.U. opposition leader, Anne Enger Lahnstein, said after the Norwegian referendum rejecting Norway's membership to the E.U.: "Our resistance to the E.U. is based on the experiences of generations. We don't want to be ruled from abroad."[25] Thus, the E.U. will move along without Norway, which shouldn't be too much of a hindrance.

It was a top priority of the reunified Germany's Presidency of the Council of European Union to integrate the northern states of Norway, Sweden, and Finland, as well as the German-speaking Austrians. With that goal partially achieved, it is easy to see the weight of the European Union shift in Germany's favor. The Germans share a common culture and language and centuries of close relations with Austria. The Swedes' language is Germanic, and therefore Sweden and Austria have closer cultural ties to Germany than any other E.U. member state. Sweden shares common social institutions with Germany: both have a social welfare economy, rather than the Anglo-Saxon economy of pure capitalism.

The E.U.'s expansion to these countries stabilizes both Germany's power base within the Union and the E.U.'s future because these nations are net European Union economic donors and will only benefit the stability and economic well-being of the E.U. In response, the *Washington Post* carried an editorial: "That shifts the balance in the [European] union between Europe's rich North and its poorer South. It also hints at greater influence for a constellation of countries around Germany, at the expense of those to the South and the West."[26]

In addition, discussions have already begun concerning the next E.U. expansion phase. From Berlin, Germany is building its future center of influence. The capital move shifts the focus of Germany and the European Union interest back to center of Europe. But how can the E.U. survive when its most powerful members' capital is only 80 kilometers away from a non-member country, one with which their is historically bad blood?

Chancellor Kohl made it clear in his support for Berlin as the seat of Germany's government on June 20, 1991, that the metropolis is not off at the margins and that Central and Eastern Europe must be integrated into the E.U.

Thus, it was not surprising that three years after the vote for Berlin Chancellor Kohl would state: "With the expansion [of the E.U.] comes the moment of truth. . . . It is of vital importance for Germany that Poland becomes part of the European Union," said Chancellor Kohl.[27] Hungary, Poland, the Czech and Slovak Republics, Bulgaria and Romania, through the European Council in Copenhagen in June, 1993, were offered a clear prospect of membership.[28] E.U. expansion raises Berlin's profile too. Berlin has, as outlined in previous chapters, deep cultural and economic roots to these countries. And the Berlin government has repeatedly hosted delegations from Poland, Hungary, and the Czech Republic in Berlin for cooperative discussions.

The Union's expansion progress was illustrated as the E.U. leaders gathered in Essen, Germany, on December 9 and 10, 1995, at the end of Germany's chair of the Council of the European Union.[29] It was another step forward for securing Germany's future influence. After the summit, Kohl said that it "was an historical hour for the European Union and Europe." The Union leaders welcomed the prime ministers of Poland, Hungary, the Czech Republic, Slovakia, Romania, and Bulgaria at Kohl's urging. But in addition, the E.U. also allocated $6.6 billion in economic aid for these countries. Taking the form of 14 multi-billion-dollar projects, the aid package had as its main goal the integration of these Eastern states into the E.U.'s road, rail and electricity network.[30] Warnings of Germany's rising clout in the Union arose as the Mediterranean members—France, Italy, Spain, and Greece cautioned that the North-South economic disparity was greater than that between East-West and that immigration and Islamic fundamentalism all posed more of a threat to the stability of the E.U than the reforms in Central Europe. In response to these warnings, the E.U. also approved a $3.3 billion aid package to the southern E.U. states over the next five years, to be used for development projects in the Mediterranean area.[31]

Certainly, one could argue that the successful expansion of Austria, Sweden and Finland supports and encourages the prospect of Central and East European countries for E.U. membership. Nevertheless, one could also argue that broadening European integration does not deepen it, and could pose a danger to the stability of the Union itself. Deepening the Union includes increased cooperation and harmonization of pan-European policies, such as a combined effort to fight crime and a uniform asylum law.

How can a Germany that surrenders much of its national sovereignty to the E.U. be a threat to the U.K. or France? Without question, the threat of Germany solely pursuing its national interest has been reduced by the closer ties to the European and transatlantic institutions, in addition to the degree of institutionalization and interdependence of the industrialized world's economic and security arrangements.

It is likely that Chancellor Kohl wants to reach the same goals through the European Union as German Reich Chancellor Otto von Bismarck sought to achieve for Prussia through German Unification in 1871: namely a state in equilibrium, basically an entity halfway between a supranational state (a federal state for Bismarck) and a confederation of states: a Europe (Germany) united enough to stand together reliably in the event of war, and sufficiently disunited to co-exist in peacetime, among which Germany (Prussia) is the biggest and the most powerful, and the one that calls the tune. In addition, Chancellor Kohl likely envisions a vehicle to facilitate Polish-German reconciliation through an expanded E.U., as was facilitated through the E.C. between Germany and France.

The E.U. is already deeply involved in the New Europe and the expansion Eastward of the E.U. is well under way. One can say with confidence that, in contrast to 1992, the E.U. in 2000 will have been the catalyst of a free and open Europe. There will be no internal frontiers and some countries with a single European currency. Germany's dominating influence from Berlin and its pull back to its Central European tradition will thus have been achieved through the European Union, not war.

Notes

1 The original treaties, still in existence, established three entities: the European Coal and Steel Community (ESSC), the European Atomic Energy Community (Euratom) and the European Economic Community (EEC). The EEC has been formally renamed the European Community by the treaty on European Union. *The European Union: A Guide.* European Delegation of the United States, 1994. pg 3.

2 *Towards European Union* Commission of the European Commission, February 1992.

3 Hans-Hermann Nikolei, "Frankreichs Politiker warnen wieder vor Grossdeutschland", September 3, 1992

4 Ibid.

5 *In Europe's Name* Timonthy Garton Ash, Vintage Books, 1993, pg. 258, 275

6 "Die Kunst der Erinnerung bedeutet auch, sich nicht endlos das alter Unrecht vorzuhalten und Misstrauen zwischen juengen Polen und Deutschen zu saeen . . . aber das gegenseitige kennenlernen ist das beste Mittel, um solche Haltungen zu daempfen . . . ich selbst habe meine Meinung ueber die Deutschen grundlegen geandert. Wir haben im Grunde eine ziemlich aehnliche Mentaliataet." source: Annette Ramelsberger, "Zwei Staedte werder Partner", Die Berliner Zeitung, August 13, 1991

7 "Die Totalamputation eines Viertels von Deutschland, das nach Versailles noch ubrig war, sei nicht durch die 'freie Selbstbestimmung des deutschen Staatvolkes gedeckt." source: Der Tagesspiegel, "Czaja: Vertrag mit Polen 'nicht mittragbar'", September 10, 1991

8 Ibid.

9 Berliner Morgenpost, "Diepgen: Freizuegigkeit in ganz Europa bedeutet auch das Recht auf Rueckkehr in die Heimat", September 10, 1991

10 Julie Kim, "Poland, Czech Republic, Slovakia, and Hungary: Recent Developments", Congressional Research Service Issue Brief, July 19, 1994

11 Michael L. Mueller, "Hoechste EG-Foerderstufe fuer den Ost-Teil Berlins", Berliner Morgenpost, April 28, 1992

12 Berlin Landespressedienst aus dem Senat, April 8, 1993, page 18

13 The European Union refers to a three "pillar" construction encompassing the European Community (EC) and the two new pillars — Common Foreign and Security (including defense) and Justice and Home Affairs (e.g. immigration, crime, and terrorism). Source: "Post-Maastricht: EC Now Named European Union", December 13, 1993, Office of Press and Public Affairs, European Commission Delegation.

14 Dana Milbank, "With European Union as a Safety Net, Many Regional Groups Seek Autonomy", The Wall Street Journal, February 24, 1995

15 *Towards European Union* Commission of European Communities, February, 1992, pg. 5

16 "Vor Grossspurigkeit wird gewarnt", Die Zeit, October 7, 1994
17 John Marks, U.S. News and World Report, May 16, 1994, pg. 52
18 *International Financial Statistics* International Monetary Fund, November, 1994
19 Ibid.
20 "Vor Grossspurigkeit wird gewarnt", Die Zeit, October 7, 1994
21 *The Downing Street Years* Margaret Thatcher, HarperCollins Publishing, 1993, pg. 797,783,798
22 *In Europe's Name* Timonthy Garton Ash, Vintage Books, 1993, pg. 385
23 *The Downing Street Years* Margaret Thatcher, HarperCollins Publishing, 1993, pg. 798.
24 "Austria, Finland and Sweden Join the European Union", The Week in Germany, January 6, 1995
25 Fred Barbash, "Norway Vote Rejects EU Membership", The Washington Post, November 29, 1994
26 "Europe in the Next Century", Washington Post Editorial Page, March 13, 1994
27 "Kohl nennt Debatten ueber die Dauer seiner Amtszeit unsinnig", Frankfurter Allgemeine Zeitung, October 8, 1994
28 *Germany's Presidency of the European Union* Press and Information Office of the Federal Government of Germany, pg. 26 June, 1994
29 The heart of the EU's expansion program is a working paper known as the "White Book", which list the criteria that these countries must meet for membership.
30 William Brozdiak, "Spector of Bosnia Looms as EU Looks Eastward for Expansion", The Washington Post, December 11, 1994, pg. A 35
31 Craig R. Whitney, "West Europeans Cast a Cautious Line Eastward" The New York Times, December 9, 1994

Conclusion

The Berlin-Brandenburg
Academy of Arts

Germans' ability to triumph over their difficult reunification is linked to their ability to unite around their traditions of language and culture, i.e., the arts. Therefore, after having attempted in this book to describe the unique historical point at which Berlin now finds itself, I would like to close by describing a cooperative attempt to develop a united Berlin-Brandenburg Academy of Arts, in the Prussian tradition. Out of the once ideologically centered former West Berlin and East Berlin Academy of Arts, we will look into this example of a divided society and people trying to overcome their past. In a larger picture, Europe's future rides on the ability of such Cold-War-entrenched institutions, to cooperate, unite, and move forward. The future academy is Berlin and Brandenburg's united statement to Europe about the region's identity and goals.

My awareness of the Academy of Arts reunion began at the lunch table with my assistant friend, Melitta, in the Berlin parliament's cafeteria. Melitta had been trying to get me interested in the proposed reunion of Berlin's two arts academies for months before our lunch meeting. The subject had never appealed to me because it seemed to be just another complicated reunification issue where the debates were never ending and the results minimal.

In this regard the spark of curiosity and interest that characterized my initial experience in the Berlin government was waning. At the outset, I was eager to learn about new topics having to do with German reunification. But now, almost two years later, most reunification issues seemed to be leading to the same conclusion: frustration, division, and bitterness. Maybe that is why I had always brushed Melitta's invitations aside. Rather than sticking my nose into another seemingly dead-end impasse of East and West Germans trying to forge a consensus, I found I preferred to shelter myself on the Committee for Federal and European Affairs and talk about the future— speculating about the Maastricht Treaty and what it will mean for the region.

But on that drizzly winter day in the cafeteria, she cornered me at the lunch table. In a excited way, as if she had just seen something spectacular, Melitta told me that the Berlin parliament had, after countless debates, surprisingly postponed the Berlin-Brandenburg Academy of Arts unification treaty.

In response, I nonchalantly asked her why. She was so flustered by this news that she didn't have time to go into the details. I was soon to see why. Days later, as I was returning to my bird perch office atop the parliament on a quiet afternoon, Melitta came storming by me up the staircase, asking me to follow her. I traced her path into the conference room in the southeast corner of the fifth floor (one of my favorite rooms because of its panoramic view over Leipziger Platz and the Spreebogen). I greeted the faces I knew and quietly took one of the few empty seats. From the one minute to the next I found myself sitting in a serious CDU cultural committee meeting to discuss an upcoming special hearing on the Berlin-Brandenburg Academy of Arts federal treaty ratification.

CDU cultural speaker, Dr. LehMann-Brauns pointed out the significance of the distinguished guests from around the world who had come to testify. Despite my lack of awareness of the issue, it became strikingly clear to me how intense the atmosphere in the room was, much more so than usual. As we pushed in our chairs and filed out of the room, like a sports team coming out of the locker room at half-time, energy and motivation filled the air. I happily joined in the procession, naively riding this unusual high of enthusiasm and energy.

Descending the grand stairway, we approached the blocked conference room door. As the security officials made a path for us to move through after checking the representatives badges, Dr. LehMann-Brauns pulled me by the arm as he waved to the security officials that I was okay. Although the official hearing was not to begin for another thirty minutes, the atmosphere was almost bubbling with anticipation, nervousness, and excitement. People were scrambling for places among the spectators. The walls were lined with people in the rectangular West facing East room.

On the easternmost side of the room was a semicircular group of tables set up for the representatives, the Senator, and the special committee chairman, Herr Wohlraube. In the middle of the setup was a single seat and table. My attention was captured by that lonely witness stand. Sitting in the back row with Melitta, I undid a button on my shirt; it was hot, the weather had been in the mid 90s.

In an effort to figure out what was going on, I used the time to ask Melitta a few questions. "Can you tell me what this is exactly about? Why are so many people anxious and nervous?"

"The federal treaty to unite the former East German Academy of Arts and the West Berlin Academy of Arts was supposed to be voted on Thursday," Melitta said. "But many people have expressed opposition to the unification and Dr. LehMann-Brauns and many well-known artists have organized this public hearing before it will be voted on. The speculation is that some members of the former East Berlin Academy worked for the Stasi," she said.

As her last words rang through my consciousness, I found myself dreaming back to a conversation we had just had just weeks before. Curious about her background (we were always curious about each other, maybe it was because we came from such opposite places), I asked her how it was in East Germany and how one was accepted to the Academy. "It was like that in all secondary schools, all schools in general," she said. "The GDR was made for the worker and the farmer, everything else was regarded as bad—intellect was sought out and consequently put down. If your parents were intellectual, had jobs, then the State wouldn't give you a place in the school system. I am so happy for my daughter, she had no schooling outside of what my boyfriend and I used to do for her," she said with a melancholic voice. "That is until reunification," she said with an intent look on her face, "until it was free and we were all given rights." As she began gazing for long minutes on end out of the window, I prepared to get up and let her be alone.

As if she sensed my movement, she thwarted my escape with a soft, passionate voice. "You just cannot imagine what it was like," she began as her watery eyes drew sympathy from my soul, "in 1987 my brother and his wife, they were both doctors, you know only of such cases in the family, nothing like this was talked about, printed or made public . . . their son, 18 years old, perfect grades, had the life-long goal to become a doctor. But he wasn't accepted, the government refused to give him a study place, repeatedly rejected him for no reason. It ruined him. He just couldn't understand. He was ultimately so dejected that he committed suicide." Her voice became compassionate and the nature of her story, her visible emotions drew me toward her. "Gosh," she then said matter-of-factly, "if he had just waited two years, just two more years, then it would have been possible, but it just wasn't meant to be . . . his parents are still having a hard time. You just don't know how many such cases there were like this, no one knows of all of the suffering that went on. Everything was just kept quiet, nobody trusted anyone."

Then as quickly as that was mentioned, she began to change the subject. Her behavior reminded me of Sabina at Humboldt University, when she had told me about her father. There seemed to be no clear order, no priority in her story telling, in her remembrances, it was all looked upon as being one big chunk of time, with stories told without logic or sequence, yet presented as a whole.

"We believed what we saw," she continued, "it probably would have been better for us if we wouldn't have seen any Western TV, it was so gray here, it was all run-down, and then when we'd see these pictures, those smiling faces and happy people, we would dream of the West. If they had let us travel, if they had let us see the propaganda for what it was, then we probably would have worked harder for the country." A nostalgic air surrounded her person. "The good was also there, yes," she said with an upbeat tone, "my brother's son is an example of how unfair and wrong the government was, but it really did have some good parts too. But now everyone is realizing that those advertisements are meaningless, and that money and material goods are nothing in the big picture. Just like we always learned, a throwaway society."

Then regaining my focus, I was acutely aware of a trembling atmosphere in the room, no wonder, I thought to myself, many of these people in this room are probably still living the tossed-up world Melitta had described. The intensity settled as the representatives took their seats. Somehow, just by the faces present, I had the feeling something significant was getting underway. In a flamboyant manner, Herr Wohlraube introduced the reputable president of the West Berlin Academy, Walter Jens, by asking him why he was against dissolving both of the former academies and for a totally new beginning for the Academy of Arts, and finally with emphasis, why he was against a Gauck Authority investigation of the academy members, especially from the Eastern academy. This was an introduction, I thought to myself, with the same provocative arrogance with which Wohlraube had chaired the Committee on Federal and European Affairs.

As the aging, thin, gray-haired man slowly approached the witness stand, I pulled my chair a little closer, curious to hear what explanation he had. For the first time since we had arrived, the conference room was perfectly still. It was so quiet that I could hear the construction hammering going on outside. Jens' appearance and movements held my attention. This was a man everyone was writing about and of whom everyone has an opinion.

And it is no wonder, I thought to myself, as he spoke in an old, scratchy voice more provocative than Wohlraube's: "We are autonomous and have decided not to pursue such a path, and we will not be told from representatives what we should do!" Questions followed, and the debate flared. The air became increasingly thick with smoke.

Guenter Kunert, a well-known East German author, accused Jens of "siding with the culprits" for refusing to investigate academy members for possible association with the Stasi.[1] Jens promptly reacted with a nervous twitch of his right arm, more obvious due to his presence on the witness stand. He began to shudder. Suddenly his right arm rose shaking at Kunert, as he mumbled in a loud, but at the time incomprehensible German that frightened me: "*Unglaublich, Unterstellung der uebelstge Art!*" (Unbelievable, insinuation in the worst way!)

After these words landed, the conference room was searching for air, and the steamed windows seemed to flex a little from the heavy breathing of the overcrowded room. A deep pause fell, after Jens turned off his microphone and retreated to the rows of invited guests. Somewhat in shock, I whispered my thoughts to Melitta: "What now, who wants to speak after that announcement?"

The four-hour-long debate settled down somewhat as various artists took their turn at the witness stand, either in favor of the unity or for a dissolution of the former West Berlin Academy and East Berlin Academy of Arts and for a completely new Berlin-Brandenburg Academy of Arts. That is until the Hungarian-born composer Gyoergy Lygeti was called forward.

"I have lived through the days of terror, my family and I were forced to hide from the Nazis, not allowed to even appear in society, let alone express our art," said Lygeti. "It is just the same as it was in the East," as the place erupted in whispers and movement, as if he had just said the unthinkable. "I will not sit at the table with the same people who have persecuted me and my art for all those years, and until they are cleared out of the academy, I have withdrawn my membership. Don't you see," he continued with a searching voice: "We are making the same mistakes they made after World War II, when everyone was just allowed to keep participating and nobody asked each other about their roles in the past." He went on to call the atmosphere in Germany "poisoned" in this regard.[2]

These passionate words spoken by Gyoergy Lygeti, juxtaposed with Walter Jens' belligerent speech, inspired me to follow the developments more closely and volunteer my efforts to the cause spearheaded by Dr. LehMann-Brauns of pressuring the Academy for a new beginning and subject their members to a Gauck investigation. And the more I learned, the more motivated I became. In short, I was changed from that day forward.

One week after the electrifying special hearing on the Berlin-Brandenburg Academy of Arts, I had been closely following the debate and gathered some more information. Berlin's cultural scene was boiling over in a fervor of anticipation and preparation for the final hearings before the parliamentary vote set for June 17, 1993. German newspapers were filled with the intellectual debate. All of the famous artists and key players had taken sides in the brewing confrontation. In response to the questions still floating in my mind, I organized the sources of information available to me from my work for the Berlin-CDU and wrote the following report:

Walter Jens' biography commands respect. There is no question that he is convinced that the proposed union of West Berlin and East Berlin's respective Academy of Arts will promote growth and build bridges in a country where so many need to be built. He is personally going against the grain in German society to create a new unified institution, not one formed by the West or the East, rather by the institution itself.

But Jens has also associated himself with some bad characters who have hung on after the German Democratic Republic's Arts Academy evaporated, raising many questions and leaving the controversial academy suspended in a cloud of suspicion. On December 9, 1991, 69 of the once 110 East German Academy full members (all citizens of the GDR) re-elected themselves and proclaimed to be "new."[3] During this precarious self re-election, some members withdrew out of protest, including Karl Mickel, Nura Quevedo, and Wieland Foerster. In his protest speech, Herr Foerster stated that: "The academy should have begun immediately with a public, honest, critical incorporation of its history. With this failure they have set a precedent and they find themselves now only in strategic movements."

Less than three months later, in a special meeting of Berlin's two academy members on February 1 and 2, 1992, the unified assembly decided for a unification of the respective academies, in the spirit of the Prussian Academy of Arts established in 1696.[4] Under President Walter Jens, the Academy asked for a legal reunion between two German States, thereby nullifying their autonomy and asking for approval of the governing legal body, from every state parliament.

What was the East Germany Academy of Arts? Let's imagine we were in 1986 and the academy was in operation. The Berlin Wall divides Europe. The Cold War is raging and Berlin's two art academies are going strong, promoting their bipolar ideologies.

Thanks to the distinguished former secretary of the West Berlin Academy of Arts Literature Department and now professor for literature at Berlin's Technical University, Hans-Dieter Zimmermann, and painter Roger David Servais, who is also a member of the Gauck Authority's special investigation team, in conjunction with the SED Research Center at Berlin's Free University (FU), one now has the chance to look into the organization and work of the GDR's Academy of Arts. The West Berlin Academy was always transparent.

To the world, the academy was presented as being under the control of the government and the members (both normal members and corresponding members, i.e., foreign members) were to be elected to the academy from the normal members during their regular assembly meetings. The single-party apparatus, the communist SED, controlled the academy at all levels. Dr. Manfred Wilke and Dr. Joachen Staat from Berlin's Free University SED Research Institute reported the following:

> The Free University Research Center of the SED investigated certain documents pertaining to the German Democratic Republic's Academy of Arts. Of special significance are the decisions of the secretary of the Central Committee of the SED on April 23, 1974.[5] Here the new administration of the Academy was "approved" and the proposed list of new full time members reviewed. The vote of the Academy's President, Vice President, and new members in the assembly meetings can take place only after the approval of the SED leadership. Therein is the dominance of the SED members, especially through the office of the president, guaranteed.

Wilke and Staat concluded that it is a case of "clear threefold party control, first the party group proposals, then the departments, and finally the proposals of the Central Committee of the SED had to be approved by the board of directors."

What did the SED expect from their "approved members"? A document entitled "Qualifications for SED members to the Academy of Arts" states:

> The precondition for the development of such a progressive culture is the ruthless and extensive war against American cultural barbarism and against the remaining ashes of the German-Prussian militarism and imperialism. Each member must in this fight, supported from the basis of the Marx-Lenin aesthetic, stand in the first rows of the Academy.[6]

One of the chief principles behind the Berlin-Brandenburg Academy of Arts initiative is to break from the past, to move out and beyond the clouds of suspicion surrounding the academy's polluted past. The point of joining the academies is the formation of a new entity, away from both the strict SED party-controlled institution and the very liberal West Berlin Academy. Now, the second time around, some Germans are preoccupied with making a break with history and starting anew. Others are opposed—hence the sensitivity.

Three of the ten members of the GDR Academy's board of directors are already members of the West Berlin Academy of Arts: Heiner Carow, Wolfgang Kolhaase, and Siegfried Mathias. Two further members of the board would also become members if it came to a "en bloc" (block) acceptance of the academy members into the "new academy": Manfred Werkwerth, the long time President of the GDR Academy of Arts, and his Vice President and chief ideologist, Robert Weimann. Then one half of the former GDR Academy of Arts board of directors would be members of the new Berlin-Brandenburg Academy of Arts.

From page two of the protocol of the East Berlin Academy of Arts from July and August 1986, with the signatures of the corresponding member from West Berlin Walter Jens:

> In the future [the progressive development of socialist art] must be of special importance and work of the academy, in correspondence with the decisions from the XI Party meeting of the SED government.[7]

And the third page ends with a word promising dedication to the "party hierarchy." In order that we produce "great works of socialism and freedom, we promise the distinguished member of the cooperative, Herr Erich Honecker, and the delegates of the XI SED Party meeting of Germany's unified socialist party to do our best in the name of all of the members of the Academy and the President of the Academy." On the fourth and fifth pages the report continues with Werkwerth proudly reporting to the parliamentary assembly: "Or Marx in Africa, what an achievement, the monument from our member Jo Jastram in Addis Ababa is the first Marx monument on the African continent."[8]

Jo Jastram, who presented the starving Ethiopians with a gigantic statue of Marx's head will be a member of the new academy if there should be the "en bloc" acceptance. And so will Fritz Cremer, a sculptor trained in the Nazi years, who later contributed "Der US Besitzer" ("The U.S. Occupier"—a crude sculpture of a Satan figure with a holster and pistol wrapped around his frail body). According to Roger Servais, Cremer originally intended to place his contribution on Alexanderplatz and let people spit on it.

This one protocol sheet illustrates a lot about the former German Democratic Republic's cultural center. Turning the page, we find a report of the academy's visit to the GDR's National Army headquarters, the NVA (National Volks Army). That must have gotten the attention of the pacifist Walter Jens, who protested against the NATO modernization plans, and who sheltered American Army deserters. What must he have thought as he saw the pictures of academy members standing in the close circle of friends with the NVA commanders, e.g. President Werkwerth with commander Randisch? In Werkwerth's speech to the celebration, he stated: "And we let our like-minded partners know on which position we are also working, we are preserving and protecting freedom. That means hard work for all of us." Does Walter Jens belong to this group of "like minded"? So it appears—he remained a true member of the GDR Academy of Arts until the Berlin Wall came tumbling down.[9]

The Marxist jargon was the West's criticism of Eastern society, in the East it was the opposite, the legitimization of the repressive SED regime. Didn't Jens know that the GDR was a military state, from kindergarten through the Young Pioneers and the Freie Deutsche Jugend into the Academy of Arts and the NVA? Whoever skipped the NVA draft was automatically reprimanded by the state and closed off from society. Did Jens, as a member of the GDR Academy of Arts, provide shelter for any of the NVA dodgers too?

Perhaps that was not all clear to this homme des lettres, but he certainly must have recognized what was at work from the protocol sheets and other documents that he received as a member.

Generations will look back and recognize Berlin to be the center of Germany's unification because Berliners are the only ones forced to work together and reach some type of sustainable compromise. After unifying every public institution, from the post office to their own parliament, Germans have discovered a way to weed out persons who cooperated with the former East German communist regime through the infamous Gauck Authority. Every public official in Berlin was investigated for possible cooperative work with the Stasi.

Therefore, when the Berlin parliament was asked to ratify the federal treaty in succession with every other German state, many Berlin representatives automatically asked for a Gauck investigation.

The liberal parties (including the conservative mayor himself) supported the artist's decision not to have a Gauck Authority investigation. The most baffling question is why? Why wouldn't they want to break with the past and clear out the suspicions surrounding a few members, putting the reputation of the future academy in jeopardy? Why carry bad eggs along in a curious union—a union of one-time arch-rivals, under the auspices of a European Berlin-Brandenburg Academy of Arts? How does Mayor Diepgen expect the postman from Berlin's Marzahn District to understand why he had to be investigated, why he had to go through the rigor of any background investigation, while artists from the former regime who want to participate in the taxpayer-funded Academy do not? The more baffling the questions I stumbled on, the more inspired I became to work with the minority of artists and representatives fighting for justice on the issue. Consequently, I wrote press announcements for Dr. LehMann-Brauns in an intensive campaign to mobilize international media attention to the scandal. Meanwhile Jens was publicly protesting against the parliament's interference into the academy's internal affairs.

Spearheaded by Dr. Lehmann-Brauns, the controversy slowly became exposed to the public and their elected officials' radar screens. The dirty past, the ugly German history and difficult questions that are so easy to shy away from, were glaring again. What began as a normal through-the-doors bill (one that every German state had already ratified) truly hit the rocks in Berlin.

The reformation of the traditional Prussian Academy of Arts in the name of the Berlin-Brandenburg Academy of Arts offers a unique chance to see how Germans create something entirely new out of abused, polarized institutions. The tough days are being had now, to create a new unified institution with common purposes. Everyone was involved in the debate, from international artists, representatives to bus drivers. The debate also cut to the core of Germany's identity crisis; the *Aufarbeitung der Geschichte* (critical incorporation of history).

When the arguments were finally put aside, I was sure at that time, that the new academy would better represent Germany than any other artistic institution. Why? Because it was a perfect example of the transcendence resulting from Germany's social, political, and cultural collision.   The debate was hot, the reproaches were flying, and yet I don't think that the persons nor political parties involved were aware of the common goal they all were striving for: the search for compromise and cooperation.

With the final Academy of Arts public hearing set for June 15,1993, two days before the big decision in parliament, it seemed as if my efforts to mobilize international interest in the issue had been in vain. Like one international reporter said: "Associations with the Stasi are no longer a hot issue— if it had been last year then perhaps, but no more."

Meanwhile rumors were circulating in the press that the liberal parties were going to vote for the academies' fusion, despite growing public protest. The mayor was fighting hard to defend his position. He found himself backed into a corner with strong opposition coming from his own party circle, not to mention from the national party group chairman himself, Chancellor Kohl, who of course had his hand in this Prussian affair too.[10] At that point, Mayor Diepgen was trying to save face after having already approved the treaty. In an effort to consolidate his losses, he did all he could to pass the unification bill through parliament—no matter what the cost.

In the last party group meeting the day before the parliamentary vote, the atmosphere was tense on the issue. Upon asking one representative what his impression was, he coolly said to me, "it's up in the air—fifty-fifty." Then pointing to the head table where the party group chairmen were sitting he said: "Just look at them—they are just as divided as we are. Although this meeting is supposed to decide the party group's official position for Thursday's vote, I doubt they will be able to find any common ground. Anyway, I am against the treaty."

Mayor Diepgen's subsequent explanation for why he supported the treaty was centered on making a symbolic statement of unity during these reunification days. Then he abruptly ended by calling for the representatives to support his position.

When Diepgen's rival, Dr. LehMann-Brauns, took the microphone, I hoped he would be able to take advantage of Diepgen's weak arguments. Speaking of principle, and not forgetting the discriminated members of the past, he successfully captured the full attention of Berlin's CDU representatives. Berliners have a very sensitive ear for discrimination—they just need to be reminded of their past. I was sure that his arguments were sounder, his reasoning more clear. Nevertheless, I was suspicious that in the game of political poker we all were unaware of what was being said amongst the party leaders behind closed doors. Also, the opinion of Berlin CDU parliamentary chairman Klaus Landowsky was critical, and he appeared unsure as he sat back in a uncharacteristically low profile.

Indeed, my friend's prognosis proved correct. As the party group meeting adjourned, I was still as unclear as before—no consensus was in sight. With the tide still changing, my motivation was strengthened to push until the end. And so making my way up to my office, I made another round of follow-up calls to all the international media contacts I had made. After repeated rejection, I finally received a kind invitation from Clive Freeman, the chairman of the International Press Club in Berlin, to take part in their yearly ball that same evening. Making my way to the British Officers' Club in Berlin's Charlottenberg District, I was optimistic that this was the break that I had been waiting for.

I had been so wrapped up in the debate that I had forgotten about the Allied Powers in Berlin, when I walked past the security post, just hearing the soldier's accent as he directed me to the entrance gave me another jolt and reminded me of the transition of the present, of the occupation, and World War II. As I surveyed the country-club setting on this warm sunny day, the Hungarian composer Gyoergy Lygeti's words immediately came to mind: "Don't you all see, we are making the same mistakes again."

Like a salesman, I made my way from group to group giving my sales pitch about the scandal that was still preventable. I invited many people to come back to the public hearing going on now in the new Berlin Parliament. One after the other, I received nothing but cold shoulders, except from Melvin J. Laskey, the distinguished former editor of *Encounter* and *Der Monat*, who accompanied me back to the parliament that evening to meet with the representatives and opposition artists.

But I was very disappointed. If they are the international journalists reporting to the world about Berlin and Germany, why would they not at least take an interest in informing themselves about the Berlin parliament's biggest grass-roots initiative since reunification? On June 16, 1993, I tried once again to call all the people I had just met. But later my bubble burst a little again, as I walked into my boss' office for a breather and to update him on the latest developments. Going through my checkup list, he poignantly interrupted me and said: "It is already too late, even if somebody would take up the issue, it would only be reported about after the decision was made."

Away from my sideline efforts, the day was hectic in preparation for the next day's big vote. Three separate committees were meeting and they were all going to vote on the proposal before it would be brought to the parliamentary floor.

People were scurrying around with their rules of procedure books, trying to determine the possible outcome if it was rejected by one committee. It was a classic legal dual between the parliamentary and executive branches. At this stage, coalition lines were falling left and right, no one knew where the other parties stood in their internal debates. We were hoping that the FDP would come to the CDU side, while the Alliance 90/The Greens party group was experiencing a fierce internal debate. Representatives opinions were apparently changing like the wind. Herr Kramer from Alliance 90/The Greens was coming to the conservatives' side, but having difficulty convincing his colleagues. The CDU still had no official position themselves.

The parliament was alive. Nothing was clear, excitement and tension filled the air at work like I had never experienced before. Rumors were circulating that the CDU executive committee was considering withdrawing its previous support for the mayor, despite the implications this would have for him and Berlin's coalition government. Apparently negotiations were occurring between the SPD and the CDU coalition partners. Who can tell what is going on behind closed doors?

The day was long, full of disappointment as the cultural committee and the Berlin-Brandenburg committee both voted in favor of the treaty. A feeling of defeat filled our hearts as Melitta and I began to reflect back on what had just transpired. Was this the end? We began talking about what we did wrong, what we could have done better.

Sitting in her office, I assumed my typical posture by gazing out of the window toward the Reichstag, hypnotized by the rhythmic blowing of the German flag on its southeast tower. I was overcome with a feeling of disappointment, of how I failed to motivate any foreign journalist to report about the most historic hour of Berlin's legislative branch since reunification. This was the first time since the fall of the Wall, that so many citizens and lobby groups become involved in the legislative process. During this time of increasing public dismay with their elected officials and politics in general, this issue had stimulated democratic participation and involvement from as far away as Bonn, Munich, Jerusalem, and New York.

An unprecedented level of public hearings, exchanges of opinion with representatives, and dialogue were in full-swing. Democracy was in full gear with unprecedented levels of public interest and participation, interest group mobilization; the press (unfortunately only German) was writing scores of reports and analysis of the subject, citizens were coming from afar to voice their opinions, the normal political party lines fell like the Wall, with the normally cool and controlled leaders uncertain of their support and their opinions desperately trying to please everyone, and the executive branch wavering in light of possible defeat and embarrassment. The legislature branch was standing up for itself, using its power, which they always seemed to prefer to subordinate. It was chaos and uncertainty. It was democracy at its best. Could this be the beginning of a new surge of public involvement in Berlin's parliament, building new channels of cooperation and involvement among citizens, lobby groups, representatives, and law making? Would later generations look back on this time as another one of the dramatic changes resulting from reunification, one in which the normally submissive parliament, on the heels of a grass-roots initiative, wielded another degree of influence and power over the once perceived impermeable executive branch?

Suddenly the door came flying open and an assistant from the Main Committee looked at us with a cool smile on his face. "We're going to vote against it," he said, "I cannot say anymore, but when we meet in another hour, they're going to vote it down."

Rising from the last station of defeat, we immediately jumped at the news, full of hope. Melitta and I looked at each other with a look of irony and burst out laughing. "Maybe this is the break we needed," she said. The encouraging news wiped away our fatigue as we rushed to the committee room. It was full of people. Then sure enough, the CDU in conjunction with the SPD voted down the treaty bill. Going home that night, everything was more uncertain to me than ever. What impact does this have? Some were saying that they were just representatives from the SPD who voted against it, but that tomorrow they would all vote in harmony. Others speculated that a deal was struck behind closed doors that we were unaware of. Despite all the uncertainty, one thing was clear. The latest consensus from my party group friends was that there were not enough votes to vote down the treaty. Nevertheless, I knew in the back of my mind that the Committee on Federal and European Affairs still had to vote on the treaty tomorrow morning, and so I still had hope.

Up bright and early the next day, "The Day of the Parliament," I was caught up in the storm of excitement and anticipation. Making my way to the still very lonely Berlin parliament on the former East-West divide, I was overcome with nostalgic feelings of just being able to come here, to witness the dramatic end of what has become a burning national issue. Today, the fiftieth Berlin parliamentary session since Germany's first unified elections in 1990, was a fitting end for my last month of working for the Berlin-CDU. It truly exemplified post-reunification Berlin. There was conflict, East-West rivalry, there was direct historical relevance. There was a time warp too. Forty years ago, Soviet tanks opened fire on crowds in East Berlin protesting for freedom and rights. Today, the first time since I'd arrived, the grand coalition was on the rocks like never before.

After greeting Dr. LehMann-Brauns and the other CDU representatives before the my last committee hearing in the Berlin parliament, I was aware of the fatigue and feelings of dejection Dr. LehMann-Brauns was suffering from. It looked as if he had not seen the light of day in a long while. And as he gave his last public speech on the debate, pleading with the representatives to vote against the treaty, of the precedent it was setting and the symbolism involved, I noticed that the fire in his words, his inspiration were absent, it was clear he was out of steam. Even the news from yesterday's committee didn't seem to pick him up, he told me later he was as unsure as I was of the implications it would have and that he was just going along with the flow. I felt much sympathy for him and I was moved by his dedication to the principle at hand and his steady conviction. And so it didn't appear to have much of an effect on him as the committee voted in favor of the treaty. He slowly got up and left the room.

Thinking that I might follow him, I suddenly overheard the speaker open a debate about the Allies and their future museum. Slowly my attention wandered away from the divisive academy debate as my curiosity was naturally provoked. The mayor wisely asked the question: "How will the Allies be looked upon in 2050? How will all of these historic days be regarded?" I couldn't believe what I was hearing—these are the very questions that I have continually been asking myself since I began writing, always on the fringe of my consciousness, but so hard to capture and answer.

A range of opinions were filled the conference room; the PDS representative spoke of imperialistic Americans, the CDU representatives recalled the critical role the Americans played in the crucial years after the War. The SPD drew in line with the conservative CDU, and formed the majority consensus in 1993.

Although the representatives' views were often divergent, as they were arguing it became clear to me what a unique role America still plays in the minds of these people, what a special and overwhelming favorable role. Then, as if I was floating above myself, I was looking over the committee room and I could see myself sitting in this room. It suddenly became acutely clear that I never would have been so widely accepted (likely as accepted as a foreigner could be in a foreign state parliament) if I had been from another country. Being an American had opened many opportunities for me in Berlin. But change was in the air. Who will be looked upon favorably in 50 years?

After discussion about a city museum to commemorate the Allies, the hearing was cut short in light of the special ceremony taking place in the Reichstag.

As the representatives organized themselves in the main hall for the walk to the Reichstag, I waited for Dr. LehMann-Brauns, but he had vanished somewhere. Leaving the building on this beautiful windy spring day, a remaining piece of the Wall came shining into my focus. As we reached the corner of Leipzigerstrasse, Stressemanstrasse, and Ebertstrasse, i.e., Potsdamer Platz, thoughts of this historical day, about the Academy debate, the discussion about the Allies, filled my heart and mind. History was once again pressing down on me.

Suddenly I lost myself in reflection as I gazed over the barren, windblown square. Looking to my right, I spotted Dr. LehMann-Brauns walking alone at a slow, thoughtful pace. I automatically slowed down to keep pace with him. I thought to myself that it was the appropriate occasion to congratulate him on all of his efforts. A little smile came over his face as he shrugged his shoulders and replied in a kind voice: "We gave it our best shot, but things don't look good." We both stood in a silent pause, in reflection on all the effort spent. Then suddenly Herr Kramer came running up from behind, and with a big happy smile and eyes full of enthusiasm said: "The FDP is going to vote against it, they have just decided."

Dr. LehMann-Brauns face lit up and a bigger, more genuine smile filled his face, as he chuckled to himself and thanked Herr Kramer for the news. I was as unsure as usual of the affect this would have and I asked him for his opinion. He told me that this could mean the support we needed to reject the treaty, but it was of course too early to tell. "We will have to see what Landowsky says at the special party group meeting after the ceremony, I mean before the parliamentary session," he said as the other representatives came swarming to him again.

We approached the sleepy but impressive looking Reichstag for the 40th memorial of the workers rebellion against the Soviet occupation. Suddenly a police barricade hindered our progress as the new SPD Chairman and Chancellor candidate Scharping exited his big black shining Mercedes and entered the Reichstag flanked by security personnel. Seeing all the German governors at the entrance quickly erased the memories I was having of the past and prognoses for the future.

With my new glasses on, I took my seat in the filled Hall. Scenes of the Reichstag, of the walk we had just made, flashed across my eyes as my mind skipped forward and I saw a view into the future; there were construction crews, dust, and detours all around, just like where we came from.

As I was reliving my private thoughts, like a movie preview showing me highlights of the new releases, the lights in the Reichstag were slowly dimmed and now I was literally watching a history film in recognition of the workers rebellion in East Berlin. This short documentary film portrayed the uprising to the critical hours when the Soviet tanks went rolling through the streets and the occupation forces declared Marshal Law. As we saw the tanks appear and the shots fired and the people fleeing, I jumped a little in my seat, in horror of the sight. I was lost somewhere in myself, somewhere between then, now, tomorrow. I tried to recognize the areas that I know today, but I still couldn't orient myself. Is that the Reichstag way off in the background?

Then, as abruptly as the film ended at the climatic moment and the lights came on, a group of twenty or so survivors of the uprising moved onto the stage and were presented national medals of honor from the Chancellor. Mayor Diepgen stated that the victims and protesters of the workers rebellion wanted to bring on reunification. Decades later their goals had been achieved and their efforts were not forgotten.

As the ceremony came to a close, a children's choir came running up to the stage. While I was relaxing in reflection on what I had just experienced, suddenly my attention was once again captivated as the band picked up speed and the first voices were to be heard: the German national anthem was being played. What a fitting way for me to depart the Reichstag, to hear the German national anthem being played in a large public forum for the first time. The reservation of Germans was for me very fitting, typical of the atmosphere to be found in Germany.

The small band drowned out the few singers in the beginning. They played and played their music, but the children's voices weren't strong enough to fill up the large room. No one in my row was even singing— and I must confess that I was embarrassed for them. All of the soldiers in my row had the *Bundeswehr-Ost* (Bundeswehr-East) badges on. Although I was getting ready to reproach them in my mind, it came to me that they probably didn't even know their new national hymn, yet. They were probably still recalling their East German national anthem. I wondered to myself what they must be imagining in their minds. And I think I have been through a time warp. How long will it take before they loudly sing their new national anthem?

As the band struck the final chord, my mind raced back to the forthcoming vote. It is much more than just a union of the academies, it was the principle, in light of the obvious military suppression of freedom, of the downfall of the public protest, in view of the authoritarian rule that the firing tanks brought to East Berlin for decades thereafter. Those that lost their lives on this day, 40 years ago, did so in the allegiance to their democratic principles. Today the Berlin parliament would decide on their principles of openness, else it would be just another victory for letting former Academy members be accepted to Europe's new academy, regardless of their previous activities or associations.

Leaving the Reichstag, I think we were all more empowered and inspired to fight for an investigation of members to the new academy. Landowsky inspired the CDU executive board and representatives to postpone the treaty. And as the postponement was pushed through, I think we all took a deep breath in relief and reflection. It was big success on that day.

Later that evening, the grand coalition partners held their pre-arranged festival in the grand ballroom upstairs to celebrate the last meeting before the summer break. Gaping wounds in the coalition from the academy debate dampened the party atmosphere. The mayor didn't even come. I heartily ate and drank with my friends. As they speculated about the implications of the treaty's postponement for Diepgen and the coalition, I sat back smiling inside—thankful to be spending my last parliamentary session on such a triumphant note.

Regrettably, I must report that in the fall of 1993 the Berlin parliament approved the Berlin-Brandenburg Academy of Arts treaty without any changes. Thus, the new academy operates with both uncensored East and West Germans. In response, international artists have continued to withdraw their membership, including such notable figures as Vaclav Havel.

Notes

1   Christian Muenter, "Akademie Anhoerung wurde Tribunal ueber Walter Jens", Berliner Morgenpost, May 26, 1993
2   Der Tagesspiegel, "Wendungen, Windungen", May 26, 1993
3   Friedrich Dieckermann, "Berliner Kuechenkonfusionen", Frankfurter Allgemeine Zeitung, May 18, 1993, pg. 33
4   Abgeordnetenhaus von Berlin, 12. Wahlperiode, Drucksache 12/1991, pg. 3
5   Frei-Universitaet-Forschungsverbund SED-Staat, "Dokument 2: Umlauf Protokoll des Sekretariats des ZK der SED" Nr. 41/74, April 23, 1974
6   Ibid, pg. 33, 34
7   Hans-Dieter Zimmermann and Roger Servais, "Dokumente zum Streit um die Akademie der Kuenste", Berlin, August 1993, pg. 5
8   Ibid, pg. 6
9   Ibid, pg. 6
10 Hans-Ruediger Karutz, "Brief-Krieg zwischen Kohl und Diepgen, Kanzler prostestierte erneut gegen En-Bloc-Uebernahme belastet Ost-Mitglieder der 'Akademie der Kuenste'", Die Welt, June 11, 1993

Twenty-first century Berlin, "Der Spiegel" 08/95
Luftbild: S. Doblinger — Computer simulation: Dalecki and Partner

Epilogue

A Fantasy

Today is February 23, 2000, and I am in Berlin for the first time since the turn of the millennium. Although I have been far away, I have followed the developments to the best of my ability from across the Atlantic. Years ago there was a lot of debate and speculation in Europe surrounding the future of Germany and its return to its traditional capital in Berlin. Hard choices were being made as to whether the European nation-state could be supplanted by a supranational European Union of regions. Now it has all come full circle. The visionaries of those post-Cold War years, led by Mitterrand, Delors, and Kohl, laid the framework for today's unified continent from Lisbon to Tallinn out of the rubble of the Wall. Germany's longest running chancellor was right that the re-emergence of Brandenburg, with Berlin as its capital, would be the locomotive for Europe to overcome the former political, economic, and social division of the continent.

Contrary to many apprehensions about the future of German-Polish relations, their bilateral relations are characterized in the twenty-first millennium as close regional cooperation. German and Polish reconciliation has been facilitated by the E.U. The border, that highly contested Oder-Neisse line, the whole concept of national borders in Europe back in 1994 was very important. Now they are all but obsolete—permeable to every European to reside and do business along the entire East Sea coast, from Antwerp to Koenigsberg. A single European currency went into effect in 1999, on schedule, and has helped to diffuse the national time-bomb that Europe outran in those critical years in the early 1990s. Much like the disputed territories between France and Germany, Alsace-Lorraine after WWII, Poles and Germans have grown to work and cooperate freely and without inhibition.

Berlin is an exciting and dynamic area in which to live. It is a vibrant multi-ethnic European capital city. Berliners are united and very proud of their capital. The first place I visit on this cold wintry day is the CDU in the European Union's Brandenburg regional parliament. The parliament is in Berlin and the governor resides in Potsdam. The governor, nevertheless, travels the *Koenigsweg* from Potsdam to Berlin regularly to meet the parliament.

Exiting the train at Potsdamer Platz, I am overwhelmed by the impressive nature of the train station within the big glass-roofed building. Pictures on display show where the Berlin Wall literally split the continent. There were also pictures reminding the guests of the traditional 1920s character too. Riding the escalator up from the platform was like riding into Wonderland. There are plants everywhere and the fresh air enhanced by the huge glass rooftop overhead with the sun beams illuminating the shopping area where a big waterfall covers the right side. Walking on the marble floor, my attention is drawn to a huge red line splitting the floor in a sometimes zig-zag, chaotic fashion. It symbolizes where the Wall used to divide Europe. But no one seems to be paying attention, people are flowing from one side to the other in a care-free fashion. Both sides look the same.

Back in 1994, the first American President to visit Berlin after reunification was right: "Nothing will stop us, everything is possible, Berlin is free." This place is a tribute to those words. The contrast to the mid-1990s is strong. Suddenly, I become disoriented as I reflect back on those difficult post-reunification days when everything was so uncertain and everyone so pessimistic. Chuckling to myself, I noticed on my right the same place where I used to visit the outhouse erected next to the train station exit in 1993; it was the only standing structure back when there was nothing here besides the windblown fields of history. Today it is the foot of a towering 100-foot waterfall.

Exiting the grand place, I look overhead to see the Mercedes emblem rotating above a bright Sony sign. Crossing over Leipzigerstrasse, speeding cars are overshadowed by the modern state-of-the-art tram, from which people are exiting and entering at ease. Turning onto Niederkirchnerstrasse, I am taken aback by the European Union's Brandenburg parliament, on top of which there is both the E.U. flag and the black eagle flag of Prussia waving in rhythm. Otherwise, the house looks the same as it did back when I used to cross over from the sandy fields and stumble over the construction site through the door, with pieces of the Wall in the background.

Although traipsing through the parliament is nostalgic for me, none of the faces are the same—new actors are in power. After looking around for a few minutes, I exited the building easily. This once lonely attraction is today neighbored by a modern and bustling vicinity. The Topography of Terror exhibition has matured from its precarious station of old into an international museum and meeting place in memory of the victims of the Third Reich. It is aesthetically pleasurable and very inviting. Berlin is proud of its multi-ethnic international identity—the rising xenophobia of the early 1990s has all but evaporated. Making my way through the entrance, I immediately recognize large crowds of people moving and flowing from the park in and out of one of three buildings. Tourists and visitors are enjoying this place, a real refuge and relief from the big city life. After walking through the museum, I continue to the other side.

Next thing I know I have arrived at the American Business Center at Checkpoint Charlie on Friedrichstrasse. Just turning the corner onto the once barren checkpoint, I am immediately taken aback by the size of the building filling the once empty lot. Remnants of the Wall and the former Allied checkpoint are still to be seen, but the rest is new and modern. Friedrichstrasse is a bustling street like Fifth Avenue, with shops and stores carrying only the best items. So much is foreign to me here now that I do not take much interest. Instead, I move quickly through the crowded sidewalks to Berlin's heart, the Unter den Linden.

Arriving at the corner, I look to my right and am happy to see the Berlin castle facade has been rebuilt and the whole street has come to life around it. Although it is winter, the street is in full bloom. Upon asking passersby what is inside the castle, they smile and tell me that it is an international conference center, including an international library. Walking closer, I see that the whole space has been put together with this key piece of Berlin's architecture.

Unter den Linden is the center of the German capital, we all feel it now, much like we were prevented from in the past. The whole Spreeinsel has been re-modeled, it all looks very new to me. Further, modern high rises on Alexanderplatz dominate the skyline and create a good contrast to the old and new.

Turning back around, I wander the other direction, toward Europe's meeting point, the Brandenburg Gate. Approaching closer, I hardly recognize anything. The gate that formerly stood alone on the former divide has been filled in with neighbors on both sides. I was pulled there like a magnet. I am curious to see what is on the other side, on the Western side. On my left, the Russian Embassy is still alive and well, this is one of the only constants of the whole place since I used to wander here in 1993. However, one major difference is that the monument of Lenin, the huge head, has been removed. The Brandenburg Gate is so interesting looking. It is the center of this otherwise busy and bustling government center, with the embassies of Britain, United States, and France lined on both sides. Many pedestrians are gathered here, there are cafes on both sides of the entrances to the buildings. To my left, the once barren field is part of the federal governments' campus, with very handsome buildings, and a walkway with signs to the monument commemorating European Jews murdered in WWII. Little can one imagine, but underneath us, on this historic walkway, high speed trains are arriving and departing the capital. Power and speed radiate from this dynamic center of Europe.

Walking through the gate shivers ran up my spine, I felt as if I had crossed a new point in history, a new dawn of time for the continent and the people who live here.

Index